EQUAL OPPORTUNITIES IN SCHOOLS

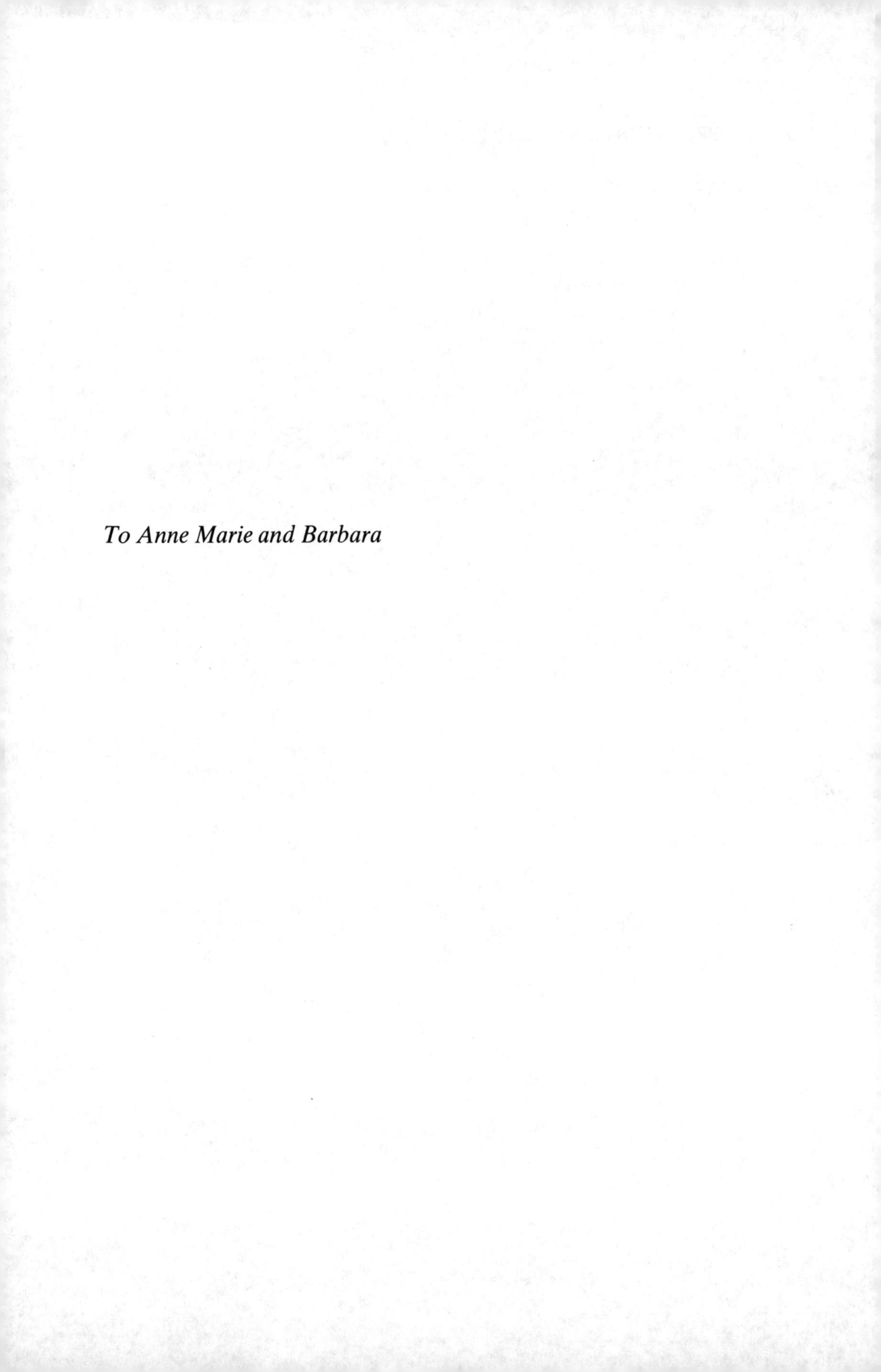

To Anne Marie and Barbara

Equal Opportunities in Schools

New Dimensions in Topic Work

George Antonouris

and *Jack Wilson*

CASSELL

NICHOLS PUBLISHING
NEW YORK

First published 1989 by Cassell Educational Limited
Artillery House, Artillery Row, London SW1P 1RT

Published in the United States of America by Nichols Publishing
P.O. Box 96, New York, New York 10024
Nichols is an imprint of GP Publishing Inc.

British Library Cataloguing in Publication Data

Antonouris, George
Equal opportunities in schools:
new dimensions in topic work.
1. Great Britain. Primary schools. Curriculum
subjects: Social studies. Topics. Teaching
methods
I. Title II. Wilson, Jack, *1929–*
372.8′3044′0941

ISBN: 0–304–32202–4

Library of Congress Cataloging-in-Publication Data

Antonouris, George
Equal opportunities in schools: new dimensions in topic
work / George Antonouris and Jack Wilson, *1929–*.
p. cm.
Bibliography: p. 187
Includes index.
1. Social sciences—Study and teaching (Elementary)—Great
Britain. 2. Project method in teaching. I. Title.
LB1584.5.G7W55 1988
372.8′3′0941—dc19 88–19658

ISBN: 0–89397–329–7 CIP

Phototypesetting by Fakenham Photosetting Limited, Fakenham, Norfolk

Printed and bound in Great Britain by Mackays of Chatham Ltd.

Last digit is print no: 9 8 7 6 5 4 3 2 1

Contents

Acknowledgements

We would like to thank the following who gave permission for the reproduction of copyright material:

Afro-Caribbean Education Resource Centre, which holds the rights to reproduce 'Ndidi's Story', published in *Dragon's Teeth* in February 1979.

Commission For Racial Equality, publishers of *Education Journal*, for the review by Phil Barnett on the Alexander and Dewjee book, *The Wonderful Adventures of Mrs Seacole in Many Lands*.

Equal Opportunities Commission for two checklists analysing reading material found in Hannon (1981, pages 19–20).

National Committee on Racism in Children's Books, the publishers of *Dragon's Teeth*, for the reviews of 'Ndidi's Story' and the Alexander and Dewjee book.

Office of Population Censuses and Surveys, publishers of the international migration figures (1977) reprinted in Table 4.

Scholastic Publications, publishers of *Junior Education*, for the article entitled 'Coming and Going' (December 1980).

The Islamic Cultural Centre for the leaflet *Islam at a Glance*.

We would also like to thank colleagues Ros Richardson, Headteacher of St Edmund C of E Primary School, Mary Hayes and Dr Anne Bloomfield, Senior Lecturers in Education at Trent Polytechnic, for their contributions to the chapter 3 discussion of CDT, Information Technology, and Dance and Drama respectively, Melanie Wilson for initiating the story called 'Everybody knows that!' and Jenny Price for helping to develop it for chapter 8, as well as for use in schools. Barbara Wilson of Radcliffe-on-Trent Infant School, Nottinghamshire, has tried out many of the ideas developed in Part I of this book and we are grateful to her for permission to reproduce examples of children's work and for her valuable evaluations and advice. Mention has also been made of work undertaken by teachers and pupils in schools in Armthorpe near Doncaster, who tried out the book's ideas over the winter of 1988.

We acknowledge our debt to BEd and PGCE students at Trent Polytechnic, who helped the development of ideas and practices over the period 1984–8, especially Geoffrey Lowe, Pauline Poole, Alicya Sekowska and Wendy Skelton. Last but not least, we appreciate the help given to us by Joan Kemp, who typed Part I of the manuscript with professionalism, patience and understanding.

Acknowledgements

[illegible]

Preface

This book presents four new dimensions for teachers preparing topic work in Social Studies. Part I focuses on planning (chapter 2), teaching (chapter 3) and evaluation (chapter 4), and Part II suggests ways of permeating all work with an equal opportunities perspective.

The first new dimension proposes three fundamental ideas to help plan the development of pupil understanding, namely influence and control of the environment, social and power relations in group behaviour, environmental and group change. These ideas represent important social generalisations that topic examples sub-divide into specific subordinate concepts, which are returned to over and over again throughout the pupil's primary school career. In addition, thinking processes are identified which are intended to be the basis for learning activities and tasks that, as pupils respond to them, foster concept formation.

The second new dimension offers teachers the notion of an activities 'ladder', incorporating both the analysis of the ideas being considered and the thinking processes mentioned above. This suggests that concept-related activities should involve identifying and describing, classifying, comparing, seeking causes, predicting effects, making judgements and generalising.

The third new dimension presents criteria to help teachers evaluate pupil task outcomes by considering the extent to which they indicate inclusiveness of thought, elaboration of response, tentativeness, abstractness and decentring.

Part II comprises the fourth new dimension, that of equal opportunities. Chapter 5 summarises racial and gender issues and proposes a foundation charter for teachers wishing to develop the school as an equal opportunities zone. Chapter 6 attempts to show how traditional topics can be permeated with the perspective, while chapter 7 suggests the inclusion in all schools of 'cultural studies', such as Eid and Diwali. Chapter 8 presents more controversial issues, challenging prejudices, exposing myths and combating stereotypes. Chapter 9 encapsulates this new dimension in an equal opportunities school policy stressing organisation, behaviour and curriculum.

Introduction

The problems associated with the teaching of 'topic' in our primary schools seem comprehensive. First, there is the problem of definition. Eggleston and Kerry (1985) refer to topic work as a form of integrated studies. Their research within the Schools Council project, designed to explore the development of pupils thinking through topic work, provides us with various descriptions of what is happening in classrooms when what teachers acknowledge as topic work is going on: '. . . classroom activity . . . concerned with work which draws upon information gleaned from more than one conventional discipline'. There seems to be great variety in this classroom activity as teachers initiate it in their individual classrooms and indeed in individual schools. What is difficult to find is any consensus as to what children will learn and be able to do. What is also provided by Eggleston and Kerry's research (1985) is confirmation that the majority of primary schools allocate very significant amounts of class time to topic work—perhaps averaging out at almost 50 per cent of the time available in any one week.

It seems strange—indeed incredible—in the light of the extent to which topic work must occupy primary schools and teachers, that it continues to be so amorphous a curriculum animal about whose cover, content, learning intentions and evaluation there is such little agreement.

There is considerable disparity of practice in terms of curriculum cover. In some respects this may not particularly matter. If topics, in investigating a theme such as 'Ourselves', involve pupils in a range of different work that might in other situations be labelled separately as History, Language, Science, Mathematics, etc., then such an approach may well have the motivational ingredients claimed by proponents of integrated situations, who find little to support subject divisions as a basis for curriculum design. There is, of course, the problem of curriculum balance, which integrated situations seem frequently to neglect. Notwithstanding that particular issue, it is clear that there are a variety of possible permutations as to which curriculum areas come under the topic umbrella. This book concerns itself with those topics that are an amalgam of Geography, History and Social Studies and will try to provide a rationale for restricting the extent to which subject integration occurs in the planning of topic work. Restriction is advocated because the enjoyment, interest and curiosity which the integrated approach claims to foster cannot be and should not be the totality of intention for what goes on in the primary school. The issues of what will be learned and the balance of that learning must be addressed.

Herein, then, lies the fundamental problem about current topic work in primary schools. In a majority of instances teachers seem to have few, if any, worthwhile learning intentions and such learning as does occur is frequently superficial.

Teachers' aims and intentions for topic work were found by Eggleston and Kerry to be concerned almost entirely with the practice of the basic skills of reading, writing, oracy and, to a lesser extent, numeracy. This tendency for primary schools to concentrate on the so called 'basics' is well known and well documented. As Alexander (1984) points out, there is a myth about progressivism in primary education. The pre-Plowden situation, with the majority of primary schools reasonably competent in the basics but giving cause for concern in the rest of the curriculum, has not changed. Primary rhetoric and primary reality are—on the basis of a wealth of research—for Alexander (1984, page 11) a long way apart. Case studies completed during the Schools Council survey demonstrated a great deal of activity—a topic on Water involved measuring the depth of a stream, listing names of boats on canals, the flora and fauna, and culling information about lighthouses, oases, canals, etc. from library books. A topic on Great Britain involved pupils in the 'major activity' of using the school library to compile a data bank of information, a fair copy of which was written up and displayed. The researchers make it clear that they found few schools that had gone beyond the level of finding and recording information. Only a handful were seen to be concerned with higher-order skills, concepts and key ideas. To many teachers, topic work was seen to be a simple matter of data collection, with a great deal of copying from books or, at best, pupils developing and practising the study skills involved in using catalogues, contents pages and an index. This book will try to show that topic work can be the vehicle for the learning of fundamental ideas from within the Social Studies disciplines and of a range of higher-order thinking skills necessary for our pupils if we wish them to understand the society they are part of and to operate successfully within it.

A further problem relates to progress in learning. Eggleston and Kerry (1985) cite only one example of a school that had thought through the issues of progression in learning through topic work. Most schools seemed to consider progression impossible to detect as the pupils moved through topics on Water and then Clothing through the Ages, beyond an increased efficiency 'in acquiring and translating information from published sources'.

Whatever the quality of the materials that the School Council project intends to publish to make topic work a more effective means of promoting pupils' thinking, it does appear that current practice in this part of the curriculum, with limited exceptions, is distinctly ineffective and unsuccessful. This unsatisfactory state of affairs seems difficult to change—despite the efforts of a few teachers, academics and others interested in curriculum development over, at the very least, the past ten years.

In such areas as cognitive development in children, pedagogical skill in teachers and the identification of key ideas in the teaching of Social Studies, there has been a range of publications that one might have thought would have fostered change. The work of Blyth and his colleagues (1976) is an important milestone in this context, and the Inner London Education Authority's *Social Studies in the Primary School* (1979) and Gunning, Gunning and Wilson (1981) are other examples of those who sought to influence practice in Britain.

Similar thinking has developed in the United States, much pre-dating and influencing British material. The taxonomies of educational objectives by Bloom *et al.* (1956), Bruner's classic *Towards a Theory of Instruction* (1966), Taba *et al.*'s *Social Studies Curriculum* (1969) and publications by several others, such as Hunkins (1972), have all been substantially ignored in British primary education.

All these developments have been concerned to identify the key ideas in Social Studies that a balanced curriculum would offer our children at school. They have all, too, been concerned with progression in understanding from an immature and unsophisticated grasp of an idea to one more mature and more sophisticated. Each one has repeated and reinforced the importance of the processes by which such progression might be brought about, taking into account the ways in which the contentions of Piaget and Dewey might help teachers to be effective. One wonders why the Schools Council project finds so few teachers and so few schools that have incorporated these ideas into their planning. Their suggestion that the pool of people from which school teachers are drawn does not include the appropriate range of knowledge and expertise may well be right. Perhaps teacher education must pay much more attention to the acquisition of such knowledge and to promoting the kind of change in curriculum content and implementation that will provide a different and more widely based curriculum menu at a more intellectually respectable level.

Teachers have always tended to underrate theory and more than one researched set of theories has failed to make any real impact on the way teachers teach. This antipathy towards theorising may be lessening as more and more young teachers, not only members of an all-graduate profession, but also holders of higher degrees, take up the class teacher role. In any case the theory behind what is advocated in the curriculum development proposed by Bruner, Blyth, ILEA and Gunning *et al.* is not particularly new—it follows a pattern teachers have accepted and implemented successfully over a long period in at least one curriculum area, Mathematics.

In the teaching of Mathematics, teachers have accepted that there are a limited number of mathematical ideas their pupils have to come to understand. Ask any teacher which idea is missing from the following list and it will take seconds, a minute or two at the most to identify it:

Numeration
Four rules of number
Fractions and ratio
Money
Mass
Length
Area
Volume/capacity
Two-dimensional shape
Three-dimensional shape
Graphical representation

Teachers will also, no doubt, be aware that the decision as to which are the important mathematical ideas all children need to understand was made by mathematicians rather than by teachers. What teachers know is that society expects them to accept that mathematicians know their business and that they, the teachers, should get on with the business of teaching these ideas. This is a social and professional obligation teachers seem to acknowledge and agree with.

What is even more interesting is that no teacher would suggest that length is fully explored in the infant school and need not be included in what happens in the junior school. They accept that each mathematical idea is returned to over and over again. As a child moves from year group to year group and from teacher to teacher she or he will encounter each idea in such a way that her or his understanding of it becomes a little more sophisticated and more complex at each encounter. The process is fairly slow, so that activity, experience and practice can ensure progression in understanding, a progression that every teacher will be able to articulate in terms of its order and sequence. If the development of the concept of length shown in Figure 1 is not appropriately sequential the error will soon be spotted.

8. Can consistently select appropriate unit and instruments to measure using kilometres, metres, centimetres, millimetres

7. Is able to use standard units (kilometres, millimetres)

6. Can record standardised measures using decimal notation (3 m 62 cm = 3.62 m)

5. Is able to use standard units (metres and centimetres), estimating and measuring

4. Can compare lengths presented in different positions and shapes

3. Can compare length accurately against arbitrary and personal units

2. Can order objects by length using vocabulary (longest, tallest)

1. Can compare length of objects and use vocabulary correctly, e.g., longer, taller

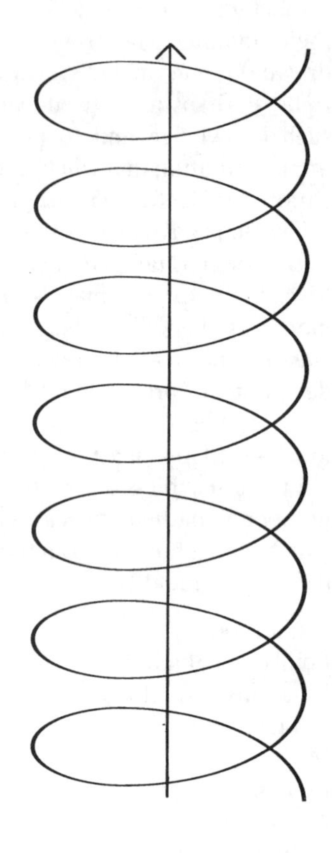

Figure 1. Length spiral.

The notion that there are a limited number of key ideas within the realm of Social Studies which children need to come to understand if they are to be regarded as educated, and that these ideas need to be introduced and reintroduced into their learning activities over and over again throughout the period of their school career in an increasingly more abstract and generalised way, is central to the purpose of this book. If by using this book teachers become as familiar with these ideas and how they might be successfully and progressively understood by their pupils as they are with the ideas within mathematical education, its purpose will have been achieved.

The aims of topic work must related to the aims of the primary school and we shall address the question of aims as a first priority; in particular, in answering two critical questions:

What knowledge is worthwhile in the context of topic work?
How can children be helped to think in an analytical and critical way in topic activities?

There will be other aims teachers should want topic work to achieve—a whole range of learning and development within the affective domain as well as the cognitive—development concerned with attitudes and social skills which are an essential part of the educative process and to which topic work can make a contribution. These matters are also addressed.

In addition it is our intention to permeate the book with an 'equal opportunities' perspective. This means that there is a deliberate intention to ensure the omission of gender and racial stereotypes and the equal representation of female and ethnic minorities in the approach to topic work we wish to promote. These dimensions of the book are regarded as central to its philosophy, both in terms of the teacher's approach to the work that the pupils will be engaged in during topic lessons and in terms of the knowledge, skills and attitudes that work will foster. The detail of the integration of these matters into the process of planning, teaching and evaluating topics will, as we have already said, permeate the book throughout, but it may be useful to outline here these two dimensions and our views about them.

THE RACIAL DIMENSION TO TOPIC WORK

Cultural diversity in Britain

We live in a multi-racial, multi-ethnic society and teaching materials should reflect that fact. Topics should include white British, black British and brown British as a normal part of everyday life. Both majority white groups and minority white, black and brown groups should be seen living and working in this country.

Cultural pluralism in a world context

The world is perceived as comprising a plurality of cultural systems, each one having recognised strengths and weaknesses. The indigenous British culture is *not* seen as the measuring rod for all other cultures; it is *not* considered to be more complex, comprehensive, developed and superior to all others, but takes its place as one of many cultures around the world containing certain strengths and weaknesses.

Stress is placed on *similarities between cultures* rather than differences. *Common experiences* are emphasised first and foremost and different adaptations come second. For example, focus is placed on the basic needs for food, shelter, clothing, living in groups, security, spiritual comfort, etc. All over the world, people have things in common, such as they live in families, wear clothes, eat meat, fish, vegetables, fruit, live

Table 1 *Ethnocentric and multicultural topic work*

Ethnocentric topic work stresses	Multicultural topic work stresses
Britain as a totally white society	Variety of black and brown people as a natural feature of British life
Anglo-Saxon focus	Variety of white groups in UK
European focus	African, Asian and European focus
White standards as the norm	Standards as relative
Unfavourable standards of black and brown groups	Different groups have different standards which are not inferior
White culture as superior	Black and brown cultures as different but not inferior
One British culture seen as the measuring rod for all others	Britain seen as culturally diverse with different cultures having similar and also different measuring rods of their own
Black culture seen as a problem	Understanding the multiplicity of cultures seen as a problem
Negative images of black or brown peoples, e.g., natives, backward, coloured, immigrants	Positive images of black and brown peoples, e.g., Black British, Asian British, Afro-Caribbean British
Scientific knowledge and technical skills based on inventions and developments in the western world alone	Knowledge and skills based on inventions and developments in all parts of the world

in dwellings, protect themselves, pray, etc., but different physical, material and social conditions have created diversity of experiences, and therefore different adaptations have developed.

Inter-cultural understanding

One of the functions of the school is to encourage understanding of cultural diversity in Britain and cultural pluralism in a world context.

This book, therefore, rejects the ethnocentric model focusing on white, Anglo-Saxon, European standards, knowledge and lifestyles and prefers what has been called a multicultural model, which stresses cultural diversity in Britain, cultural pluralism in a world context and school-based cultural understanding and appreciation (see Table 1).

It is evident that the multicultural perspective presented earlier has been strongly influenced by the Swann Report (1985). This reminded teachers that they lived in a 'democratic pluralist society' which prided itself on its diversity and freedom of cultural expression and conscience. It pointed to a society unified in its diversity through the holding of shared values by all (e.g., equality, freedom, democracy), but within those commonly accepted values it noted distinctive cultures and lifestyles. It stressed this plurality of regional, ethnic and religious variations comprising part of a dynamic and ever-changing British culture which was always adapting and absorbing new ideas and influences and amalgamating these to the variety of cultures that already formed part of its 'pluralist conspectus'. Teachers were therefore urged to prepare pupils for this kind of world, whatever the make-up of their particular locality or school. A new approach—Education for All—was proposed, which involved educating all children

Table 2 *Traditional and equal opportunities topic work*

Traditional topic work stresses	Equal opportunities topic work stresses
Britain as a male-dominated society	Men and women as a natural feature of British life
Male focus	Male *and* female focus
Male standards as the norm	Standards as relative
Male culture as superior	Male and female cultures as different but not inferior
Male culture seen as the measuring rod for all others	Britain seen as culturally diverse with different cultures having similar and also different measuring rods of their own
Negative images of women, e.g., followers, passive	Positive images of men and women

towards an understanding of the shared values of society and appreciation of the diversity of cultural, religious and linguistic backgrounds that made up British society. This 'multicultural understanding' would permeate all aspects of the school, rather than be a new topic or discipline welded on to existing practices.

Throughout all topic work the stress should be on identifying common concepts, attributes and characteristics held by all Britons, whether Anglo-Saxon, Cypriot or from one of the Asian or Afro-Caribbean groups. All peoples within Britain hold certain things in common and these should be stressed, with differences coming a poor second.

The aim must be to help children describe, explain and evaluate the cultural diversity around them, and the hope is that they will learn to step outside their own culture in order to place themselves within a multicultural perspective. This will result in the valuing of other cultures and those individuals within them, regardless of race, colour, religion, gender or age. Encouraging growth of respect and understanding for people who practise different cultures is the first step to undermining stereotyping and bias, which condones and sustains discriminatory behaviour.

THE GENDER DIMENSION

This book is actively concerned to promote sexual equality, so it is careful not to reflect traditional sex-typed roles and images. In this kind of topic work girls and boys, men and women are seen as leaders and followers, active and passive, caring and aggressive, physical and emotional, expressive and instrumental. We wish to promote topic work showing males and females fulfilling anti-stereotypical jobs and participating in non-traditional forms of activities, for example, child-rearing, home-making and decision-making roles.

In preparing example topics we have used checklists published by the Equal Opportunities Commission (Hannon, 1981, pages 18–19) and this has led to the adaptation of Table 2 in the form of a gender-based checklist for what has been called traditional and equal opportunity topic work.

The equal opportunities perspective proposed in this book has been widely discussed and developed in North America. A number of educators in the USA and Canada have defended the recognition and celebration of cultural differences in schools and the combating of racism. For example, Appleton (1983) offers a theoretical treatise on cultural pluralism, while Garcia (1982) proposes teaching models and strategies for living in a pluralist society. Banks (1981, 1984) has worked for many years to extend theoretical analysis and offers practical guidelines. Cross *et al.* (1977) suggest teacher professional strategies and Katz (1978) has a worldwide following for her anti-racist training programmes. In Canada, Kehoe (1984), Moodley (1985) and Samuda *et al.* (1984) evaluate educational perspectives and present practical activities while Werner *et al.* (1980) focus on key ethnic issues within the Social Studies curriculum.

American educators have also fought for gender equality and British writers have been influenced by work on sex role stereotyping (e.g., Guttentag and Bray, 1976; Levy *et al.* 1973), sex bias in schools (Fishell and Pottker, 1971; Stacey *et al.*, 1974), and 'sex equity handbooks' that counteract sexism, while extending non-sexist or anti-sexist teacher strategies and curricular materials (Frazier and Sadker, 1973; Sadker and Sadker, 1978). References to all this valuable material can be found in the special American bibliography at the end of the book.

FURTHER READING

Alexander, R. (1984) *Primary Education*. London: Holt, Rinehart & Winston.
Bloom, B. *et al.* (1956) *Taxonomy of Educational Objectives*. New York: David McKay.
Blyth, A. *et al.* (1976) *Place, Time and Society 8–13: Curriculum Planning in History, Geography and Social Science*. London: Collins–ESL for the School Council.
Bruner, J. (1962) *The Process of Education*. Cambridge, MA: Harvard University Press.
Bruner, J. (1966) *Towards a Theory of Instruction*. Cambridge, MA: Harvard University Press.
Durkin, M. C. (1969) *Communities Around Us* (Taba Social Studies Curriculum). Menlo Park, CA: Addison-Wesley.
Durkin, M. C. (1969) *Four Communities Around the World* (Taba Social Studies Curriculum). Menlo Park, CA: Addison-Wesley.
Durkin, M. C. (1969) *The Family* (Taba Social Studies Curriculum). Menlo Park, CA: Addison-Wesley.
Eggleston, S. J. and Kerry, T. (1985) Integrated studies. In Bennett, N. and Desforges, C. (eds), *Recent Advances in Classroom Research*. Edinburgh: Scottish Academic Press.
Gunning, S., Gunning, D. and Wilson, J. (1981) *Topic Teaching in the Primary School*. London: Croom Helm.
Hannon, V. (1981) *Ending Sex Stereotyping in School: a Sourcebook for School-based Teacher Workshops*. Manchester: Equal Opportunities Commission.
Hunkins, F. (1972) *Questioning Strategies and Techniques*. London: Allyn & Bacon.
ILEA (1979) *Social Studies in the Primary School*. London: ILEA.
Swann, Lord (1985) *Education for All*. London: HMSO.
Taba, H. *et al.* (1969) *Social Studies Curriculum. Teachers' Guides*. Menlo Park, CA: Addison-Wesley.
Taba, H. *et al.* (1971) *A Teacher's Handbook to Elementary Social Studies*. Menlo Park, CA: Addison-Wesley.

Part I

Teaching Topics

Jack Wilson

Chapter 1

Making Topic Work Worthwhile

If primary schools are to provide both greater breadth and greater depth to the curriculum, then topic work, and the extensive time allocated to it, must concern itself with much more than providing opportunities to practise language activities (Eggleston and Kerry, 1985). Inevitably topic work will remain a vehicle for language development but in ways that provide for pupils to use a range of those language functions that are an essential element in their progressively more sophisticated understanding of the world they live in. To do this topic work must be regarded as being a curriculum area in its own right, with its own body of knowledge to be learned, rather than simply as an organisational label given to a method of working (Eggleston and Kerry, 1985, page 75).

There is a move today, both in schools and in teacher training institutions, to abandon the name 'topic' and refer instead to 'enquiry', which at the very least suggests a move towards activity and a search for answers. In this book we wish to go even further and suggest that the primary curriculum should include two major areas of enquiry—scientific enquiry, which will encompass the crucially important aspects of primary science, and social enquiry. Social enquiry lies within the area of the humanities and includes what in the past has been referred to as History and Geography but in addition has as part of its portfolio those areas of knowledge that are seldom if ever part of the primary teacher's curriculum vocabulary—Social Studies, Anthropology and Psychology. There are in these studies important, indeed crucial, ideas that all children need to develop if they are to understand the world they live in now and in the future.

These ideas are unlikely to be addressed at sufficient depth and with sufficient rigour unless they are allocated sufficient and specific curriculum time. With topic work taking up anything up to 70 per cent of the curriculum time available (Eggleston and Kerry, 1985, page 82), it would seem reasonable that the kind of enquiry we are advocating should be allocated some portion of it. It is appropriate, too, since topics undertaken in primary schools frequently have titles that suggest a geographical, historical or social studies emphasis. Topics on farms; people in historical time (The Victorians); contemporary groups of people (The Family); and titles which suggest an integration of content (Transport, Communication, Our Town) can all form a basis for achieving those two major aims of the whole primary curriculum that we have already suggested, viz. that pupils will

(a) learn worthwhile knowledge,
(b) develop their ability to think in an analytical and critical way.

These aims immediately raise two questions which every teacher must be able to answer.

> What knowledge is worthwhile?
>
> How shall I get the children to think in an analytical and critical way?

These questions and the answers to them are the basis for the planning, teaching and evaluation of good topic work.

For most teachers the first thing they do, when they have decided upon or been given a particular topic to teach, is to gather as many sources of information as possible about it—pictures for pupils to look at, artefacts to handle, a collection of information books from the library to read. They arrange for pupils to collect and observe data and evidence, negotiate a visit to somewhere that will illustrate and exemplify the particular notions that the topic will encompass, and so on. The success of any topic depends to a considerable extent upon the pupils' having access to a variety of resource materials that will interest them, arouse their curiosity and provide the stimulus and starting points for the range of different activities the teacher anticipates the topic will employ—reading, writing, observing, collecting, drawing, painting, making, acting and talking.

Let us look at an example of a fairly frequently rehearsed topic, Fire. Part of such a topic might very well be devoted to a consideration of fire officers and the job they do. Now this part of the topic is likely to arouse the interest of primary school pupils and there are many sources of information that can be made available to them. Such a sequence was indeed undertaken in a Nottinghamshire primary school early one summer term. A classroom display was mounted. Pictures were part of the display, as were some model fire engines the children had brought in and some borrowed artefacts—helmets, an axe, a smoke mask and a bright reflective jacket. In addition the county library had provided a collection of books dealing with many aspects of fire and fire officers, and these were carefully mounted in front of the display so that they were accessible and so that the pupils could use both the text and the illustrations as additional information sources. This was all a valuable stimulus from which a lot of work would develop but the climax of the first week was when a fire tender came on to the school field. The fire officers provided opportunities for the pupils to handle much of their equipment and to watch how it was used.

It is not difficult to appreciate that the pupils could discover for themselves or have pointed out to them a whole range of interesting facts and information from such a wealth of material.

- Fire officers attend many different kinds of fires and also go to traffic accidents and to situations where people are trapped.
- Fires quite frequently give out lots of smoke and this is very dangerous.
- Fire officers wear uniforms.

- They also have protective clothing, such as waterproof trousers, helmets, breathing apparatus.
- Fire officers use a range of equipment, such as ladders, hoses, fire engines, axes, two-way radios, etc.
- Fire engines are usually painted red and have a siren and a flashing light.
- Modern fire engines are different from old-fashioned fire engines.
- Some fire officers have white helmets, others have yellow helmets.
- Some fire officers can tell other fire officers what to do.
- Fire officers have to learn to be fire officers and to practise fighting fires.

The first aim for topic work that this book has established is that pupils should learn worthwhile knowledge. Certainly these facts and items of information are knowledge or at least one form of knowledge. The question is, is this worthwhile knowledge that is worth spending time—valuable and expensive time—getting children to learn and remember? The answer is '*no*', it is not a worthwhile activity getting children to remember, recall and record this kind of information if that is as far as the learning is intended to go.

Setting the children the task of drawing the fire officer in uniform or writing a description of a fire engine and its equipment is a recall and record exercise and is very low down on any list of worthwhile activities. Of course, such exercises are not absolutely useless, but in terms of the choices teachers have available to them they are not really significant in relation to those kind of activities that will promote understanding and skill. Unfortunately a great many primary school topics are concerned with children finding out facts, researching facts, looking up facts in books and then, in some form or other, recalling and recording those facts in writing, drawing or some other form that can, it is hoped, be put on display. Of course, it is difficult to conceive how one might undertake a topic on Fires and Fire Officers without collecting and using facts; it is when things stop there that the problem arises, since the facts and information listed above can be used to introduce and develop important concepts and generalisations. In the context of our fire officers the concepts that can be introduced would certainly include interdependence, technology, specialisation, efficiency and authority. These are concepts that can be understood at a high level of generality and abstraction but which nevertheless can, equally appropriately, be understood by young children within the context of the experiences the topic is providing.

Concepts and generalisations are the kinds of knowledge that we acquire as we become educated. They are worthwhile learning because the understanding we develop in one context helps us to understand other situations in different contexts—information by itself does not. Learning that a fire officer has an axe cannot be transferred to a new situation in any meaningful way; it only tells us about fire officers. Coming to understand the concept of efficiency by thinking about the way an axe helps a fire officer to do a job better will help us to analyse the idea of efficiency and to understand it. We come to see the relationship between the fire officer, the axe, the fire fighter's role, the speed of work and the obstacles that have to be overcome. Once we begin to understand these relationships we can transfer the idea of efficiency to any job or situation where we are considering what can be done better.

If concepts are so important it would seem reasonable to contend that there should be a structure to topic work similar to that which we have for school Mathematics (see page

3) with a limited number of important ideas being introduced over and over again, providing opportunities to think about these ideas in a variety of contexts and fostering a gradually developing understanding of them over an extended period. As suggested earlier (page 2) teachers are not without help in identifying what these ideas might be. The fundamental ideas or key concepts that have been suggested as the ones that all pupils should be introduced to if they are to understand the society in which they live and to take an increasing effective part in it might be listed as follows:

1. IDEAS ABOUT THE ENVIRONMENT

(a) Influence of environment

How physical conditions affect people.

(b) Control of environment

How people have tried to control and improve the physical conditions in their neighbourhood, region, nation, etc.

2. IDEAS ABOUT GROUP BEHAVIOUR

How people organise themselves together in order to live, work, pray, have leisure, etc.

(a) Social relations

How people relate to each other; co-operate with, compete with, conflict with and depend on each other.

(b) Power relations

Who holds power, authority, leadership between social classes, genders, ethnic and racial groups.

3. IDEAS ABOUT CHANGE

(a) Environmental change

In relation to how the environment influences behaviour and how the environment is controlled.

(b) Group behaviour change

Changes in social and power relationships.

If teachers in our schools can devise ways in which topic work—whether it be about

Fires and Fire Officers, My Family, Homes, The Victorians, Transport or anything else in the realm of the humanities—allows their pupils to think about these three basic ideas concerning society then the notion of worthwhileness will be established and the quality of what pupils do in topic lessons will be significantly improved.

Each of these ideas, as it is developed in the different topics undertaken and as the pupils' understanding of it increases, slowly and over a long period of time, will, of course, introduce and develop understanding of a range of subordinate concepts. For example, it is inevitable that in coming to understand the idea that people's lives—the jobs they do, clothes they wear, food they eat, etc.—are influenced by the environment they live in, pupils will have to consider such other ideas as climate and weather, land forms, hills, valleys, islands, rivers, estuaries, harbours, fishing grounds, seasonal changes, enemies, and so on.

How can we use the information about fire officers listed earlier to develop some or all of these ideas? Let us look at a few examples.

1. The information about old-fashioned and modern fire engines provides the possibility to get children to consider the idea of social and technological change, particularly the cause and effect of such change.
2. The information about certain kinds of special equipment can be related to how discoveries, knowledge and training enable fire officers to control their environment better and make it safer, more efficient, etc.
3. The fire officer's training and special knowledge bring in the notion of dependence and interdependence, particularly the value of specialisation in terms of how society is organised—each member of society being relied upon and relying on others.
4. The information made available to the pupils would include examples of men and women from ethnic minority cultures working in the fire service and having positions of responsibility. Their customs and traditions will be seen to be part of the day-to-day activities found in a fire station. Similarly, women could be included in situations where they were shown to have skill and responsibility on an equal basis to men, so that as the ideas were developed the notion of the validity of equal opportunity and equal ability could be established.

However, worthwhile ideas do not develop on their own. Children need help in the development of understanding. They need to be given the opportunity to think about an idea in as many different ways and from as many different points of view as possible. The thinking they do, however, must rise above the level of simple description or of simple paraphrasing of what they have already been told or can easily acquire from reading books, looking at pictures, going on visits and so on. Pupils will show their understanding of an idea and will increase their understanding of it as they are increasingly made to reorganise and re-present the information they have about it.

This means that teachers, in the questions they ask of their pupils and the tasks they set them, must deliberately foster different kinds of thinking, that require the pupil to analyse the information she or he has before an answer is possible. Such questions and tasks are likely to include the following demands on the pupils.

1. To classify information—the 'which, what and how' question, e.g.,
   - Are the people in the picture nomads?

- Are the people in the picture *rich* or *poor*?
- What sort of *climate* does the country in the picture have?
- What do we call people like those in the picture? (This seeks answers involving use of new concepts, e.g., colonists, convicts, nomads, warriors, etc.)
- How many different kinds of transport methods can you see in the picture?
- Which of the people are farmers, which are traders?

2. To interpret information—these 'why' questions and tasks require a further development in thinking in that they expect more elucidation and inference from the pupil, e.g.,
   - Why does the miner in the picture wear a helmet?
   - Why are the castle walls in the picture so thick?
   - Why does a police officer have a helmet?
   - Why do we need police officers?
   - Why do you have to come to school?
   - Why do people wear uniforms?

3. To extrapolate from the information—these questions/tasks invite pupls to extend what they identify in the information available by asking 'What will/would/might happen if . . .?', e.g.,
   - What do you think will happen next in the picture?
   - How would the lives of the people in the picture be changed if the weather got colder?
   - What will happen if the flood-water in the picture gets any higher?
   - What happens if someone breaks the rule?
   - What happens when the police officer catches the robber?
   - What might happen if a car drives fast in a city?
   - What happens to people when their houses are pulled down?

4. To evaluate the information—these tasks ask pupils to determine the value of what they have seen, heard, read or experienced. They have to decide between good and bad, right and wrong, fair and unfair, etc. Some examples would be:
   - Look at the map and say which is the best place to cross the road.
   - Which warriors in the picture have the best weapons?
   - Would you like to live in a house like the one in the picture?
   - Does our graph show which was the best place to plant the seeds?
   - Is it cruel to catch fish the way they are doing in the picture?
   - Is X a good rule?
   - Which of these has most authority? (a police officer, a teacher, a bus-conductor)
   - Is that a fair punishment?
   - What game do you prefer to play?
   - Do you like living in Clifton?
   - Is Clifton a good place for shopping?
   - What is the best way to spend a holiday?

Of course these tasks could be set in the full range of primary school activity. The questions as they are listed above might suggest an oral or written answer but it would be equally valid and appropriate to structure the question so that its answer is through drawing and painting, making something, having a discussion, playing a role or, indeed, the whole gamut of good primary school activity. The important variable is not the nature of the activity but the kind of thinking that it provokes.

So the teacher's job is to make the link between the idea to be explored and the thinking processes the pupils will use to explore it. A popular primary school topic, Norman Castles, can be used to illustrate these links. A topic on Castles might provide information about where the castle had been built—its site—and how it was built—the thickness and height of the walls, the towers, the moat, drawbridge and other relevant facts.

This presents an opportunity to explore ideas about environment, both its influence and its control. The building of the castle would be influenced by the nature of the site—the presence or otherwise of a river, of cliffs, hills, visibility, etc. At the same time the people were controlling their environment—making it safer, more difficult for enemies to attack and conquer them. Exploring these ideas would inevitably introduce to the pupils such subordinate ideas as defence, attack, site, resources, communication, architecture and design, among others.

A sequence of topic work could then usefully require them to:

1. Describe or draw a picture of the particular castle.
2. List all the ways in which the Normans made it difficult to attack their castle.
3. Draw examples from the list above and display them under two headings:
   things to do with the way the castle was designed and built,
   things to do with where it was built.
4. Explain a particular feature of the castle, saying why the Normans included it in their design or site, e.g., the narrow slit-like openings in the wall.
5. Write a story about a day when the castle was attacked and the bridge across the moat could not be drawn up.
6. Examine a map of the locality and decide which would be the best place to build a castle.
7. Examine pictures of different castles and decide which would be the easiest to defend/most difficult to attack.

Pupils are made to think about the information they have, to analyse and reorganise it in order to give their answer. They start with simple description (1), but quickly move on to giving examples of the idea they intend to analyse (2). They then move on to classification (3) interpretation (4) extrapolation (5) and evaluation (6 and 7).

Of course this is a straightforward example but it illustrates the links between the idea and the thinking processes that are necessary if understanding is to develop. Teachers will quickly see additional and alternative ways of developing and exploiting those strategies. This initial way of considering the thinking process is developed on page 25 into a 'ladder' of tasks that link the selected idea and thinking processes together.

FURTHER READING

Eggleston, S. J. and Kerry, T. (1985) Integrated studies. In Bennett, N. and Desforges, C. (eds), *Recent Advances in Classroom Research*. Edinburgh: Scottish Academic Press.

Chapter 2

Planning

The proposals put forward by the Government in 1987 for a National Curriculum (DES, 1987) indicated an intention to raise standards of attainment in schools throughout England and Wales by setting clear targets for what children, over the full range of ability, should be able to achieve. These targets are to be pursued within the context of a broad and balanced range of 'core' and 'foundation' subjects that all pupils will study.

Such proposals seem to have considerable merit, as does the Government's aim to secure wide agreement about what those objectives might be within the context of particular subjects. This is especially so in the area of primary school topic work where, as we indicated in the introduction to this book, research shows little in the way of clear objectives or agreement about content, or indeed process.

Implicit in the methods we are proposing is the need for a rigorous approach to the planning and development of a systematic curriculum. This will involve identifying and developing with all pupils that knowledge and those skills and attitudes that lie within the broad framework of subjects which form the main body of the curriculum.

This book hopes to help clarify the objectives and assist in securing agreement about what might be taught and learned in the area of social enquiry as we have defined it by proposing:

- a clear recognition of the important ideas that all pupils should be helped to understand in the area of History, Geography and Social Studies (see page 14).
- ways of setting tasks for pupils to undertake which will encourage the development of those intellectual skills so essential to problem-solving in this and other areas of the curriculum (see page 17).
- some indication of the ways in which topic work can foster appropriate attitudes and other aspects of affective development which are an essential element of the curriculum in its widest sense.

These are the three basic premises on which planning should be based if consensus is to be achieved and the balance in terms of content and progression, through an increasing ability to think about and demonstrate a more sophisticated understanding of agreed ideas, is to be an attainable national curriculum objective.

Schools, then, must consider these questions at three levels: at the level of the school policy for topic work in History, Geography and Social Studies; at the level of individual classroom topics intended to last perhaps several weeks, with several hours per week allocated to them; and at the level of the individual lesson which makes up a unit of learning within a topic sequence. For each of these, teachers will need to indicate clear aims and objectives for both content—what is to be learned—and process—how that learning will be achieved.

THE SCHOOL POLICY

We have already claimed that topic work in this area will only foster worthwhile learning if it helps pupils to develop their understanding of those fundamental ideas that form the essential conceptual structure of the integrated disciplines that make up social enquiry. The school policy should make these ideas explicit. What might be the fundamental ideas the school wishes to pursue and how are they to be expressed? There is considerable advice and suggestion about what they might be. For the purposes of this book we have proposed three:

1. Ideas about environment
   - the influence of environment
   - the control of environment

2. Ideas about group behaviour
   - social relations
   - power relations

3. Ideas about change
   - environmental change
   - group behaviour change

However, as we indicated earlier these are not the only possibilities. Other curriculum thinkers have proposed similar lists, organised and expressed in somewhat different terms, which could be used as a basis for planning. Schools may wish to consider these as alternatives, since choosing them, if they feel more comfortable to handle, will not alter the general principles we are advocating.

Alternative lists include:

1. Schools Council (Blyth *et al.*, 1976)
   Communication
   Power
   Values and beliefs
   Conflict/consensus
   Similarity/difference
   Continuity/change
   Causes/consequences

2. ILEA (1979)
   The division of labour
   The distribution of power and authority
   Conflict
   Social control
   Interdependence
   Co-operation
   Social change
   Tradition

3. Wilson (1983)
   People's lives are influenced by the environment they live in
   People are gradually increasing their ability to control their environment
   People depend upon each other
   People organise themselves in social groups and control the behaviour of group members
   People are constantly affected by social and technological change
   People benefit from contact and communication between individuals and groups

It will be seen that the main differences between these lists are in presentation. If any of the lists is taken it will be possible to see its content included explicitly or implicitly in each of the others. They are all, for example, concerned that pupils consider the idea of change and how that has affected society. This is an important generalisation since as people interact with their environment, both physical and social, they and their environment are changed, sometimes for the better, sometimes to their own or their environment's detriment. Understanding this and developing the ability to predict the outcomes of change is crucial to the welfare of the individual and of society as a whole. Similarly all the lists advocate that pupils develop an understanding of authority or power in the social context. This understanding is not only concerned with the rules and laws that all societies have had to devise to control and mould the behaviour of their members, but also with the notion that individuals and groups exerting authority and power can significantly affect other people's lives. It is also concerned with such other things as the impartiality of treatment irrespective of such matters as race, colour, gender, social class and religion. Power in this sense might also take in the extent to which individuals see themselves and others as having duties, responsibilities and rights within the social groups of which they are members.

Some schools, which have already written policy documents and have included one of these lists of fundamental or key ideas (sometimes referred to as key concepts), have gone a stage further and listed examples of subordinate or second-level ideas (concepts) derived from each fundamental or key idea (see page 15). This is useful both in the initial policy-writing stage and when new members of staff, and especially probationer teachers, are using the policy document as a basis for their planning. The subordinate ideas give a clearer indication of the kind of content that must be included in topic lessons if the intended learning is to be achieved. They indicate too the kind of things pupils will have to reason about to understand and be able to apply the generalisations we want them to learn. The notion that people are influenced by the environment they live in is a generalisation that can be applied over and over again to a wide variety of different situations, as a process of reasoning about and coming to understand them. It

Main idea	Subordinate ideas
1(a) Influence of environment	weather, climate, rainfall, temperature, winds, latitude, longitude, seasons, tropical equator, rivers, soil, rock, desert, forest, island, continent, natural harbour, hills, valleys, etc.
1(b) control of environment	communication, transport, irrigation, man-made harbours, defences, settlements, ways of distributing land (strip system), machinery, devices to cultivate land, harvest crops, keeping things fresh, etc.

helps us to understand why people behave in different ways—why farmers in East Anglia produce different products from farmers in Kenya. The important word here, of course, is 'understand'. Children can be told the differences between farms in East Anglia and Kenya and they can probably remember some of the differences. However, if they have an understanding of the generalisations they can work out the differences themselves. This is the kind of discovery learning that has been advocated for so long in the English primary school system but has seldom been successfully operated.

The policy document might list both the main ideas (or key concepts or generalisations) and examples of the subordinate ideas (or concepts) that are likely to be encountered along the way. Above is an example on ideas about the environment.

The list of subordinate ideas need not be exhaustive and teachers will soon begin to make up their own lists, but the policy ought to make it clear that what we want pupils to understand is that people wear certain kinds of clothes, grow certain kinds of crops, work in fishing rather than in farming, are coalminers rather than nomadic herders, etc., for reasons which can be worked out, in many cases, by finding out about the environment they live in. Similarly, we want pupils to be knowledgeable about the ways in which people have controlled their environment to make it safer from their enemies or from the elements, more productive, more comfortable, etc. The reasoning here concerns the cause(s) of the problem(s) and the effect(s) of the remedy(ies). If the people of a coastal village build a harbour wall with a lighthouse, then there are important reasons for doing so which our pupils could work out for themselves by predicting the benefits that will accrue. Initially, however, the teacher's function is to provide opportunities for the pupils to seek evidence and gather information from which they will recognise the many ways in which people have improved or controlled their environment. They also need to recognise that this is an ongoing, dynamic aspect of society. When people picked up flint to help them skin animals they took a step towards controlling the environment. Teachers will recognise that there is overlap here with the idea of change. Indeed many subordinate ideas may be appropriately developed in relation to more than one of the main ideas. This does not matter and is perhaps worth encouraging.

Once the key ideas have been made explicit, together with examples of subordinate ideas, then the policy document needs to make it quite clear that every social enquiry topic undertaken in the school must have, as a central aim, the intention to develop the understanding, by pupils, of all or some of these ideas. Whether the staff decide at the start of each school year what particular topic themes will be undertaken by each year group (with a similar list devised for scientific enquiry) or whether individual teachers can decide independently what themes they choose is a matter of internal school policy. However, what the headteacher, or teacher with responsibility for this curriculum area, must ensure is that the themes chosen will provide suitable contexts for the ideas to be explored and that none of the ideas, over the long term, will be neglected (Figure 2).

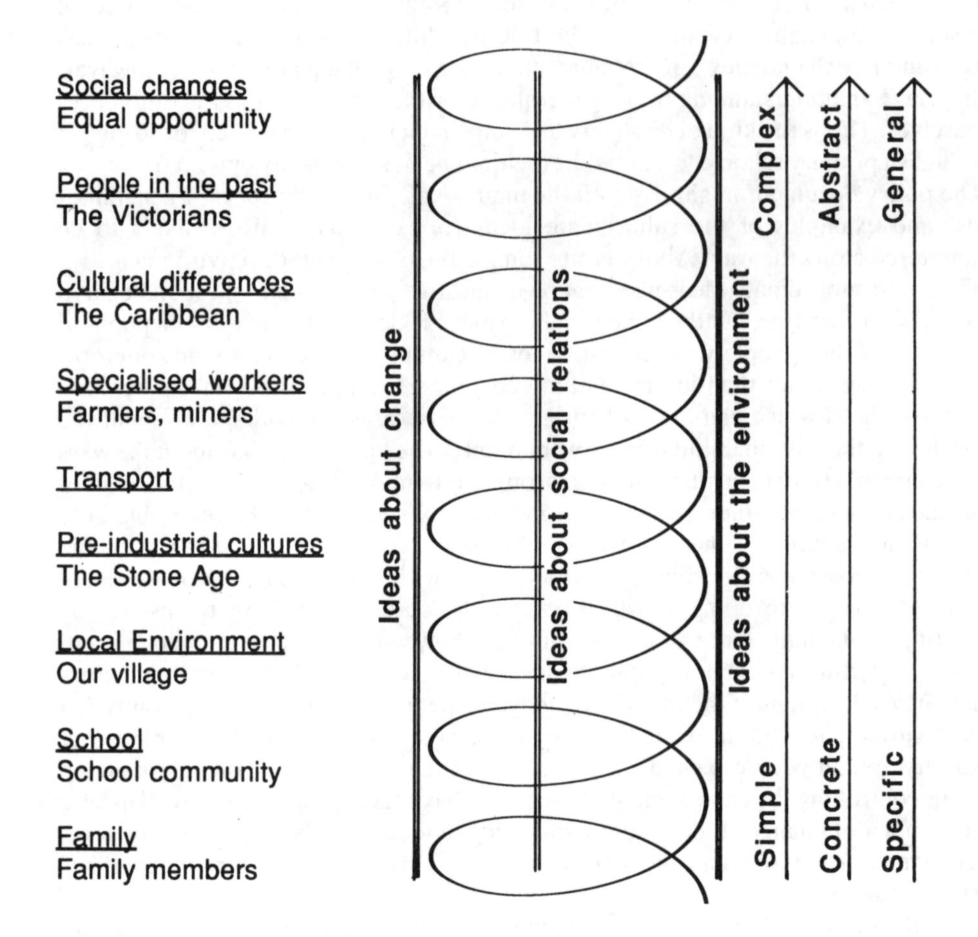

Figure 2. The spiral of development of fundamental ideas.

Table 3 shows three possible topic themes undertaken in one year group. It suggests that the teacher has decided that, for example, the topic on Egypt will concentrate on only a limited number of ideas but the topic on the Building Site will consider many more. Over the year, each idea has been considered in one or more contexts so that over the child's primary school career each will have been pursued several times. In addition, the Egypt topic is mainly geographical, and the Building Site topic is partially a study of a specialised group in society and may therefore be considered as Social Studies based. The American Indian topic will, developed in the way suggested, have significant historical content. In this way the balance within the social enquiry area between History, Geography and Social Studies can be monitored. However, such themes do not provide a rigid subject-based framework or pose a threat to the integrated approach since, for example, the American Indian topic considers the idea of environmental influence in some detail—an idea that is more geographical in its nature than it is historical. In the same way a study of the Building Site will probably include consideration of the way the building of houses has changed over time in relation to such things as the equipment used, the knowledge available, the materials used, the role of women, etc. These are all aspects of the history of architecture and building.

It is also crucial, at school policy level, to spell out the ways in which the more rigorous and analytical thinking processes we wish to advocate will be secured. While it is important that the best of present-day primary school practice is maintained in the extent to which there is first-hand experience, vicarious concrete experience where first-hand involvement is not available, variety of activity, etc., to support a child's thinking processes it is equally important to lift that thinking up and beyond the level of describing and recalling their experiences.

We have already stated that the kind of thinking we ought to promote through topic work will require pupils to reorganise the information they gain and re-present it in a form which shows that it has been used to solve a problem—a problem of classification, of having to explain and interpret, of having to evaluate and give an opinion, of having to go beyond the immediately available information and predict a future situation. To achieve this, teachers must develop the ability to ask open rather than closed questions and to ask a range of open-ended questions or set a range of open-ended tasks so that the information the pupil has researched or been given is reasoned about rather than regurgitated. Closed questions have predetermined answers, usually already known to the teacher. 'Which river does the city of London stand on?' is a closed question. There is only one answer and a pupil's answer will be either right or wrong. What is more, the pupil cannot reason out the answer, he or she can remember it, or may have forgotten it or may never have known it. He or she could, of course, have a guess and 50 per cent of the time is likely to guess correctly. Closed questions are often useful, especially as a means of leading to more open questions. They are useful, for example, when we want to help the pupil to recall some information which is then to be used in a more rigorous and analytical way, e.g.,

Closed 'Which river does the city of London stand on?'
'The River Thames.'

Closed 'Can sea-going ships reach London via the Thames?'
'Yes.'

Open 'What might happen if the Thames became silted up and ships could no longer reach London?'

Table 3 *Topic themes*

Year group: fourth year	Term 1	Term 2	Term 3
	The Building Site	Egypt	The American Indians
1. Influence of environment	Traditional emphasis on house built of local materials and designed to suit local climatic and other environmental conditions	Physical features, climate, etc., in relation to: farming, communications, strategic position, tourism (also archaeological prominence)	Differences between Plains and Forest Indians—shelter, source of food, etc.
2. Control of environment	Counteracting environmental conditions, e.g., designs to provide shade, cavity walls, double glazing, damp proofing	Water supplies, e.g., Aswan Dam Communications, e.g., Suez Canal Farming methods, e.g., irrigation	Tools, weapons, beliefs, hunting systems
3. Social relations	Interdependence—specialised roles, knowledge and skills		Role of men and women, interdependence in tribe, initiation ceremonies, choosing leaders, values, beliefs
4. Power relations	Planning permission, building standards, safety, health regulations		Conflict with white settlers, tribal customs
5. Change—environment	New knowledge, materials, technology	Farming methods and products, new knowledge, technology	Settlement of America, Indian reservations
6. Change—group behaviour	Role of women in architecture, surveying, etc.	Tourism, effect of new communication systems, etc.	Effect of contact with white people, treatment of Indians today

The final question is open-ended. There are lots of possible consequences of the Thames silting up which would make a difference to London in terms of its commercial, industrial and other activities. Every pupil in a class may give a different answer and each one could be correct. What is important is that pupils can work answers out for themselves, they can predict possible consequences, from the known situation they can extrapolate to a changed situation. In doing so they are being analytical and practising important problem-solving techniques.

The school policy may usefully give examples of closed and open questions and how they might be used. What might also be worthwhile is to suggest a questioning or task setting pattern which could be used as a basis for the planning of the thinking processes. Such a pattern might be useful until teachers have become accustomed to setting a greater number of tasks demanding reasoning and fewer tasks demanding recall.

A workable pattern could be devised on the basis of what has been described as a ladder for thinking about an idea or a concept. This suggests that when an idea has been selected tasks are set that require pupils to, as appropriate:

1. identify and describe the idea,
2. undertake appropriate classifications,
3. compare, seek similarities and differences,
4. suggest causes, look for reasons,
5. predict and explain consequences and effects,
6. make judgements about and give opinions on,
7. apply the knowledge gained to new situations and make generalisations.

Using such a pattern will help to ensure: that a range of different thinking processes are used; continuity of activity; and coherence between the content and the process.

It may not always be appropriate to set tasks in each of categories 1 to 7—some are perhaps alternatives. The tasks can vary. Describing something can be a talking activity but it could involve writing, drawing or painting, or making something. In most cases pursuing an idea from 1 to 7 may take quite a long time, several hours of pupil time, and in the process there is a clear progression from the point of identification and description to the point where the pupil can transfer his or her understanding of that idea in one context to new contexts. This ability to move from specific known situations to new, unknown and more general situations, in other words to generalise, is a fundamental aspect of intellectual development and of problem-solving ability.

Tasks can be set in this way, according to a pattern, in the majority of topic contexts and children who have performed tasks reasonably well at each stage on the 'ladder' will have an understanding of the idea involved, which, by the very nature of the stages they have gone through, they will have discovered and worked out for themselves. It will also allow, as we shall see later, pupils of different abilities to work on the same tasks and so avoid the situation where the less able child is given a less demanding task to do or where the more able finishes quickly. Let us look at some examples—it might be useful to include similar examples in the policy document.

A topic on Nottingham, Our Village, The Romans, The Caribbean or India might very well provide opportunities to study the subordinate idea of 'settlement' or 'site' under the main notion that the decision by an individual or a group of people to live in a certain place is partially at least a function of environmental conditions. If the teacher wishes to pursue such an opportunity then the pupil must be afforded access to appropriate sources of information so that the site or settlement can be *described*. It might be possible to go and look, examine documents and maps, look in books or talk to people. The work the pupil produces could take several different forms but, as an example, could be a plan or map together with a written commentary showing and telling the main characteristics of the settlement.

This description might include or could certainly lead on to the pupils beginning to *classify* or *categorise* settlements according to their main characteristics—close to river for trade and communication, on a natural harbour to provide easy access to fishing grounds but also protection from the sea, in a good defensive position at a time when fear of attack prevailed. Certainly a useful group discussion could be developed around the descriptions with, in some cases, differences of opinion arising as to what was the main priority for those people who originally settled on the site, which is now part of Nottingham or Our Village, etc.

While it is not mandatory to go through each stage in order—some may be missed out altogether or some taken in a different order—in our example it might be useful to consider the *similarities/differences* between the settlement being looked at and others we have looked at before or others we know of but haven't studied. How does the site of Nottingham differ from that of Lincoln? This is a useful analysis to make and can be done by comparing one housing estate with another as well as village with village, town with town, castle with castle, etc.

The characteristics of the settlement need then to be *reasoned* about in more detail. What caused the early settlers to choose this site with these characteristics? It may be decided that they chose a good defensive position above all else, but why—what *caused* that priority? Here there may be a need to read about the period and research the political climate of the time. There will be many occasions when the historical facts and chronology will have to be quite extensively researched. The differences will be that the seeking of information will be part of the process of solving problems, of finding out the truth, rather than information *per se*. It may be possible to have some role play activity, with a group of original settlers debating the best place for a site with each case being argued from a basis of researched information.

Pupils can then be asked to consider the consequences, the effects of people settling where they did. Once settlements are established their presence affects other people and other things. The hinterland may change in a variety of ways, other people may be affected, their way of life might be disrupted, and so on. The effects and consequences will not only be fairly numerous in any such situation but would be different if a different site had been chosen. So the teacher may wish to pose such a 'What might have happened if . . .?' question, asking for a reasoned answer spoken, drawn, written, made or acted.

What is also likely is that the effects, both short and long term, may have been good in some instances and bad in others or good for some people and bad for others. This gives opportunities for *opinions to be expressed*, for *judgements to be made* and for pupils to see that things are seldom clear-cut and that there are always two sides to a question. This in turn provides for the development of empathy and of trying to see both points of view whenever there is a minority/majority situation or conflict of interests. You have a different point of view according to whether you are an English colonial settler or an Australian Aborigine, a Roman soldier or an Anglo-Saxon villager, an owner occupier on a private housing estate or a council house tenant.

The final stage can give rise to tasks to be undertaken but is more importantly a matter of a gradually developing ability to generalise about the whole business of the choosing of a site and settling there. An understanding of 'settlement' developed in the context of the growth of Nottingham will have many aspects, if the suggested stages have been followed, which will usefully transfer to the same idea in the context of, say, a new town or a new housing estate. Similarly, topics on The Stone Age or The Norman Conquest, even Our School, can develop the idea of site or settlement from within differing contexts but towards a common contribution to the understanding of the variables involved and the ability to generalise across the various themes chosen.

The sequence described on page 17 suggests how the pattern of tasks might be applied to work in a topic on Castles. Here the main idea being developed is also concerned with environment—influence and control—and two subordinate ideas are being pursued simultaneously—site and defence. This is a useful and natural combination since the two ideas are closely related in this content.

Let us look, briefly, at a further example of how the pattern of thinking through a sequence of tasks model could be applied in other situations: a topic on Homes or My Family.

Main idea: environmental change.
Subordinate ideas: technology, inventions, efficiency, labour saving, economic, cleanliness, health.

(It has to be remembered that the vocabulary used here is at the teacher's level. Some of it may be appropriate to introduce to pupils. Sometimes, however, the teacher must substitute more appropriate language. There is no reason at all why infants should not consider the notion of efficiency, but they are likely to be better able to pursue the idea if the teacher breaks it down into parts that infants can relate to their experience. These parts will be expressed in terms of doing something faster, with less hard work, with only one person instead of several, etc.)

Information to be gathered and described, e.g., how people do their washing now and how it used to be done 100 years ago—automatic washing machines, hand washing, boilers, dolly tubs, mangles.

Listing the main differences in operation and classifying these differences in terms of the time spent, whether the work is hard or easy, etc.

Seeking causes for these changes. Finding out about appropriate discoveries (electricity) and inventions (electric motors, washing powders, new materials for clothes), changes in women's attitudes, etc.

Reasoning about the effects. The notion of labour saving and release of time for people to use for other purposes; making work easier, changing patterns of behaviour (why was Monday always washing day?); doing the job better; clean clothes more frequently available; effects on health, and so on.

Seeking and giving opinions. Questions such as: Do your parents like their washing machine and why? Which way would you prefer to do the washing and why? Some testing and evaluation of different ways of washing clothes, of different washing soaps, etc.

Generalisations can be made across to similar situations, such as central heating, cleaning the house, cooking and preserving food, the layout of kitchens and the materials used.

All of these activities can be pursued at various levels suited to the age, ability and experience of the pupils involved. The main factor is that the pupils can think these things out, at an appropriate level, for themselves.

This 'ladder' approach is open to considerable flexibility and, indeed, is not intended to impose a rigid structure on classroom tasks and activities. However, the policy document should encourage teachers, initially at least, to devise tasks at each stage and follow the order suggested as probably the most logical.

Of course, finding the information that is required and presenting findings after that information has been worked on are important skills and not to be neglected. In recent years many teachers have provided their pupils with research-type activities to undertake but frequently the information was still presented by the children in the same form in which it had been discovered. If this happens the point of the exercise is, at best, diminished to a fairly mechanical exercise.

These two important skills have been described very succinctly by the Schools Council publication referred to earlier:

- The ability to find information from a variety of sources in a variety of ways.
- The ability to communicate findings through an appropriate medium.

These descriptions give teachers valuable clues to some of the tasks they should set. The first clue is that pupils should not be told the information in a purely didactic way nor told how to present their findings and conclusions.

Pupils can learn how to find information from a wide range of sources. Educational visits are one valuable means of seeking and collecting evidence but need careful planning (see page 47). Books are an obvious source but pupils will need, if they are to use books effectively, to learn how to use the contents page, the index and the kind of library classification the school has set up. Pictures, plans, maps, charts and graphs must also be used. This means learning how to read and interpret such sources, and the symbols and representations they use. The skill of interpretation here is particularly important since it should become an important aspect of the pupils' method of presenting findings appropriately.

As the pupil progresses and becomes more sophisticated in researching information and evidence then newspapers, documents, artefacts, interviews and simulations can be added to the strategies used with the pupil, perhaps increasingly using sources outside the school as well as inside. Researchers with any skill and sophistication nearly always seek information from more than one source and check one source against another. It would be exciting if schools could develop such an approach in their pupils, so that they were not satisfied simply to copy something down from a book or always accept their first impressions as being the definitive evidence.

Communicating findings and outcomes can also be a very skilful activity. Certainly we want pupils to be able to tell each other, their teachers and their parents what they have discovered, worked out and concluded, and tasks must provide for this. Similarly we want them to write a clear and legible account. The full range of communication methods needs to be used—plans, maps, diagrams, charts, drawings, graphs and even poetry and music. What is important here is that one method of communication will be more appropriate, more effective, more efficient than another in a certain context. The skill of the communicator is in selecting the most appropriate method for the particular information that is to be communicated. With initial guidance children can develop this skill to a high degree of sophistication.

The whole business of selecting the ideas to be understood and developing the thinking strategies that will aid understanding are the most important considerations for the school topic policy. However, there are two further matters it might address. These concern the development of appropriate attitudes by pupils to the things they do in school and the need for children to become skilful socially within the context of the school community. These, of course, are matters that are not peculiar to the topic work curriculum but pervade the whole school. However, the social enquiry curriculum is particularly significant in this context since it can help the child's social and attitudinal development not only through the processes it employs but also through its content.

In terms of their social development it is important that children progress from their initial state of egocentricism to one where they autonomously modify and control their own behaviour on the basis of the inner ideals of conduct they personally hold to be good. In moving towards this latter state they will come to understand the need for rules and guidelines for behaviour in certain situations and the need for each individual to recognise and accept that behaviour which in some way interferes with the rights of others to equal and fair treatment is unacceptable. It is unlikely that children will develop these social skills and understandings unless they are made an explicit aspect of topic work, that is, that they become clear, stated objectives which are later evaluated to see whether they have been achieved.

Achievement of such objectives is more likely to be gained if the content of social enquiry topic work considers, whenever it is appropriate, such matters as:

1. The need for rules and laws. These should be considered in contexts that stress the way rules could provide for greater efficiency, safety, fairness, etc., i.e. the cause and effect need to be a paramount consideration.
2. The need in social contexts for some people to have authority over others. Again it is the reasoning that is important: why a football team needs a captain; why parents can do things children cannot; why fire officers can make the headteacher provide special equipment or notices while the school play is on; why captains of big ships have to obey the harbour pilot.
3. The way in which groups of people are interdependent, at local, national and international level. Society is made up of groups of specialists—police officers, doctors, postal workers, teachers—each depending on the others for certain important and necessary services; countries are also interdependent in many ways, which children need to tease out.
4. The reasons for conflict in the contemporary world—men and women, black and white people, working class and middle class—and the development of equal opportunities.

This content is, of course, related to the fundamental ideas concerning group behaviour. In this context they are concurrent concerns. The point is to emphasise that social enquiry is concerned to get pupils to enquire into the social groups that they presently belong to or will belong to in the near future. The aim is that children study social groups not from the outside but as members of those groups, modifying their behaviour so that it is acceptable to other group members.

The way topic lessons are planned, and the activities and roles pupils undertake, are also important to this process of social development. Children will best learn how to behave within a group situation if they work in group situations participating in ways that:

1. Require them to decide upon the way the group will behave, deciding on the rules to be applied, who will do what, etc.
2. Allow them to take the responsibility of leading the group; deciding on the qualities needed in a leader at particular times; helping to choose a leader; being willing to follow the leader.
3. Provide contexts in which it can be seen that different groups achieve similar results and outcomes in different ways.
4. Provide contexts in which different points of view are tolerated, and where the feelings of individuals are respected.

Most topics can be organised so that pupils work together in large or small groups, but simply putting children into groups of whatever size will not guarantee that they will develop their ability to operate within that group effectively, unless tasks they underake and the outcomes that are demanded of them are designed to promote effective group behaviour.

Finally, the policy document may wish to suggest that the methods the teacher employs in topic lessons will contribute to the feelings the children have about the work they have to do. Will they, for example:

- be curious, want to explore, ask questions, see how things work;
- persevere, continue to work even when difficulties arise, try different ways of solving a problem;
- develop some independence, begin to use their own initiative and not rely on being told, defend their ideas even when not in line with the ideas of others if the evidence convinces them they are right;
- be open minded, take account of all the evidence, being willing to consider new ideas and other points of view;
- be responsible, understand that their actions have implications for others, increasingly consider alternative courses of action, envisage the possible outcomes and take into account others as well as themselves?

These are not insignificant qualities and no topic work policy should ignore the ways in which both content and process can foster them. Later sections of this book will show these aspects of affective development reflected in the aims and objectives of topic lessons. Harlen *et al.*, in the Schools Council publication *Match and Mismatch* (1977), paid considerable attention to what we have described above as attitudinal qualities. Their checklists are invaluable guides for the kind of behaviour to look for and encourage. Several of the chapters in the 'Finding answers' section indicate how these qualities can be encouraged in practice. Although they use primary Science as a context, the classroom activities and ethos they propose are readily applicable to other curriculum areas.

SCHEMES OF WORK

Each individual topic will need to be planned as a coherent and progressive sequence of work with clear aims and objectives devised at the outset. This does not preclude the teacher, especially the more experienced teacher, from modifying the plan to include interesting and worthwhile work opportunities that arise at a later stage. However, if the child is to progress up the spiral of competence in understanding, skill and attitude then each sequence of work has to be seen to be as part of the whole, deliberately planned to make its particular contribution. More and more teachers are now planning topic sequences, lasting for several weeks, very carefully and in considerable detail. The ideas that can be developed from the information and evidence that they plan to make available to the children need clarifying and analysing so that appropriate tasks at appropriate levels can be devised. The days when teachers claimed to provide, with no pre-planning, a whole day's work or more on the basis of the dead hedgehog a child brought into school are gone. Either such teachers were very remarkable in their ability to see worthwhile learning opportunities or the work they set was, for the most part, superficial.

There is no one definitive way in which teachers are expected to plan an extended topic sequence, although perhaps there are still a few headteachers who demand a descriptive weekly forecast or weekly record of the work undertaken. What is probably essential is an indication of what work will be undertaken over the full term of the topic in relation to:

- the aims to be achieved
- the main ideas to be developed
- the subordinate ideas that will be involved
- the main content that will be introduced
- the major visible outcomes it is hoped will transpire.

The following are examples of various schemes of work that incorporate the majority of the characteristics shown above. The first is by a student preparing for teaching practice and has a fairly full set of aims. In terms of presentation the sequence has been split up into units of work, each with its own clearly stated 'main learning' and content. The main learning is, of course, an aspect of one of the fundamental ideas. The subordinate ideas are within the body of the content and are not made explicit. However, it is apparent that the content as it is presented to and worked on by the pupils will require them to consider ideas to do with environment and climate, lifestyle and culture, latitude, environment and communication, physical adaptation to environmental conditions, technology as a factor in changing lifestyles, social roles, interdependence within social groups, and the effect on culture of the movement and integration of groups. These concepts and ideas illustrate the idea that the main reason for tackling Eskimos as a theme is that the theme contains important and difficult ideas within the general study of group behaviour which are central to any study of society.

TOPIC ON ESKIMOS (THE INUIT PEOPLE)

Plan

Aims

Children will develop an understanding of other ways of life, dissimilar to their own, and of the reasons for cultural differences. They will also develop the ability to empathise with people who face problems outside their range of personal experience.

They will develop powers of discrimination and evaluation in the context of contact and assimilation with another culture. They will also develop the ability to retrieve, collate and analyse information collected from various sources.

They will develop co-operation and a sense of worthwhile interdependence by assigning to various groups of children different parts of the topic, on which they will have to report to the others.

Unit 1

Main learning—influence of environment

People are affected by their environment and this plays a major part in establishing their lifestyle.

Content

Study of traditional Eskimo life—housing, hunting, clothing and transport. Show how their general lifestyle is influenced by the climate. Local animal life influences the Eskimos' choice of food. Arctic nights and days. Entertainment and folklore are related to their lifestyle. The Eskimo has evolved physically to combat the cold.

Unit 2

Main learning—social and power relations

People depend on each other (particularly in adverse conditions).

Content

Social structure of Eskimos. Everyone has a clearly defined role—women, hunters, etc. Everyone must fulfil some need in order to survive.

Unit 3

Main learning—change

Society is never static. Technological change can alter the environment (or, at least, its effects).

Content

Contact with other cultures. Eskimo culture is gradually disappearing as it is being assimilated into the North American continent. Those who live further north are less affected by change. This contact is not all good—introduction of new diseases, etc.

The effects of technology make Eskimo life less harsh—clothing, rifles, skidoos, sophisticated hunting apparatus, supermarkets provide ample food, permanent housing and settlements, hospitals. Less time spent simply surviving, more time for education, leisure, etc.

A similar scheme of work, also devised by a student, plans for activities which are very specific and are described in terms of the subordinate ideas, although it is not difficult to relate them to the three key ideas we have suggested:

	Idea developed	Related key idea
Unit 1	Relationship of builders' materials to climate, etc.	Environmental influence
Unit 2	Authority, rules, etc. Leadership	Group behaviour, power relations
Unit 3	Technological change	Changes in environmental control

TOPIC ON BUILDING

This is based on visits to a local building site, together with schools television broadcasts.

Plan

Aims

That pupils will develop their understanding of a range of Social Studies concepts within the context of a study of a building site, e.g. change, interdependence, authority, environmental influence and control.

To develop a range of thinking strategies by providing pupils with opportunities to classify, evaluate, interpret, extrapolate from and analyse information from pictures, books, television, day to day experience, an organised visit, etc.

Unit 1

Main learning

That traditional houses and shelters were built of local materials and designed to suit local climatic and other conditions.

Content

Comparison of shelters built by people living in different environmental conditions—hot, cold, dry, wet, nomadic, settled, wood, stone, clay, animal skin, etc.

Unit 2

Main learning

Buildings today are subject to a range of regulations to do with safety, health, use of land, etc.

Content

Identifying, describing and reasoning about the various regulations and why they are necessary. Looking at plans and materials. Role play through a planning committee sequence.

Unit 3

Main learning

Building methods have changed in relation to new knowledge, new materials and new technology.

Content

Keeping houses warm in winter, preventing houses getting damp, use of plastics and rot-proof materials, use of machinery for excavating, transporting, mixing, etc.

The following three schemes of work were devised by practising teachers. They show slightly different approaches in the way the plans are presented and similar variety in the way the main ideas are expressed. These differences are not significant and indeed show an interesting mixture of the use of key ideas and subordinate ideas as the organising tool. What is significant, however, is that they all identify ideas that are readily recognised as being related to those concepts which are the keys to the understanding of society and how it operates.

TOPIC ON SCARBOROUGH AND WHITBY ENVIRONS

Possible information sources	Main generalisation	Subordinate concepts
Specialised groups: coastguards, lifeboat service, fishermen	Interdependence	Specialisation, efficiency, training, knowledge, skill, technology
Harbours, lighthouses, sea defences, navigation aids	Control of environment	Currents, tides, forces/friction, signals, codes, technology, man-made features
Sea, sandbanks, coastline, fish, position in relation to other countries, beaches, shops/hotels, pleasure boats	Influence of environment	Work, settlement, industry, tourism, defence, castle, services, entertainment, seasonal, harbour, natural feature
Changes in: function of buildings; methods of working; occupation and employment; equipment and apparatus; number of tourists	Social and technological change	Technology, efficiency, values, power/energy, preservation, industry, supply and demand, competition
Rules about: entering harbour; radio channels; ships' lights; life boats; quarantine	Authority and control	Safety, survival, rule, law

TOPIC ON BULWELL WITH UPPER JUNIORS

Information	Main idea	Concepts
Growth of Bulwell, jobs in Bulwell	Environmental influence	Site, work, mining, geology, transport
Road changes in Bulwell, by-pass, motorway	Control of environment	Convenience, efficiency, safety, trade, communication
Changes in coal industry	Social and technological change	Technology, safety, efficiency, standard of living, trade union
Police, fire officers, rescue teams, coal miners	Social and power relations	Interdependence, specialisation, knowledge, skill, training, efficiency, authority
Local council	Social and power relations	Authority, vote, taxation
Aspects appropriate to infants		
Road changes in Bulwell, one-way system	Control of environment	Shopping, safety, efficiency
Coal miners: protective clothing, machines, grandpa/daddy as a miner, pit head baths, etc.	Change	Safety, technology, efficiency, health
Fire officers: special clothing, special equipment, special knowledge, special skills	Control of environment	Protection, recognition, specialisation, training, skill, efficiency, authority

TOPIC ON THE SCHOOL

Possible information sources	Main generalisation	Subordinate concepts
School building: design, other schools, older/younger, classrooms, arrangement of desks, use of space, kinds of equipment	Change	Values/attitudes, experience, co-operation, technology, discovery learning, independence
People in school: teachers, ancillary workers, professional/ commercial visitors, parents	Interdependence	Specialisation, efficiency, technology, training, co-operation
Rules and regulations: uniform, special clothing, moving about the school, dinner, wet playtimes, safety from fire, lollipop lady	Authority	Rules/law, responsibility, interdependence, safety, survival, management, discipline

THE LESSON

Probably one of the first things that happens when students become qualified teachers is that they stop writing detailed lesson plans. This may be inevitable in view of the demands made upon the individual teacher to cater for the full curriculum cover expected in the normal primary school classroom. Student teachers, with fewer demands made upon them, can develop their lesson plans in some detail, but whatever the level of detail the objectives of the lesson should be carefully considered, since they provide the basis for the things that will actually happen in the classroom. These things include the procedures followed by the teacher, the activities undertaken by the pupils and the learning that results.

It might be useful here to make a clear distinction between aims and objectives as they are used in this book, although it is recognised that these two words are often used as if they are synonymous and therefore inter-changeable.

Aims refer to what is intended to be achieved in the long term. 'Pupils will develop the ability to use a range of intellectual skills' is an example of a long-term aim since to reach the point where pupils bring a range of intellectual thinking strategies consistently, effectively and with a high degree of sophistication to the work they are doing, will take a long time with most children and will never be achieved with some. However, an aim should still be as clear as possible and refer explicitly to what pupils will learn to understand or do.

The aim 'that children will develop into fully rounded individuals', so frequently seen in documents emanating from quite high places in the educational world, has little value. Such an aim is unclear and is open to a range of interpretations. It is difficult to imagine what the teacher should do or indeed what the child might do, in terms of learning, to achieve it.

Aims for topic work that claim pupils will:

'develop their understanding of a range of fundamental and transferable ideas about society'
'develop their ability to think in an analytical and critical way'
'develop their ability to co-operate and empathise with others'
'develop a range of attitudinal behaviour such as curiosity, open mindedness, etc.'

are, however, valuable. They are clear, can quickly be translated into classroom procedures and activities and indicate that the important kinds of learning/development are in the areas of knowledge, skills and attitudes. A good scheme of work will always have aims in each of these categories:

1. Knowledge aims concerned with the researching and collection of information from a wide variety of sources which is reorganised through concepts and generalisations.
2. Intellectual skill aims, which are the thinking strategies used to reorganise information, so helping conceptual understanding and transfer to develop.
3. Affective aims concerned with fostering a willingness to work co-operatively with others and developing those attitudes and values that will aid the learning process.

Objectives are even more specific than aims and are derived from aims. They are about the specific learning or development intended in the short term—a lesson or even part of a lesson. As with aims, this relationship to learning and development is critical if objectives are to be useful planning devices. Objectives like 'the children will make a frieze of Eskimo life' or 'the children will be introduced to the concept of pollution' are poor objectives. They are about pupils and teachers doing things. They do not identify the learning or development that is intended. If this learning and development is not clear in the teacher's mind as it is planned then planning becomes vague, *ad hoc* and, at best, speculative. Evaluation becomes difficult and progression will become a matter of chance rather than professional and expert pedagogy.

If we turn back to the scheme of work for the topic on Fire on page 12, there might be there an aim which claims that the sequence of work will develop the pupil's understanding of a range of Social Studies concepts, including as an example the concept of change. However, the concept of change is a complex one and it is unlikely that any pupil will acquire it, even in the context of a study of fire, other than very slowly over a period of time. This means that a lesson objective could not, reasonably, claim the same learning as the scheme for the whole topic over the six-week period. The lesson objective derived from the aim must be a function of analysing the concept of change—breaking it into its component parts to ensure progression in understanding.

One lesson (see page 15) may be concerned with:

- identifying examples of changes
- collecting evidence of change
- comparing old and new for similarities and differences.

Another lesson, or part of a lesson, may be devoted to:

- seeking/researching causes of change
- collecting evidence or predicting effects and consequences of change
- making judgements and giving opinions about these effects.

So an objective derived from the aim might be 'the children will collect evidence of the ways in which fire engines have changed since 1900' or 'the children will list the advantages to the fire officer of having personal radio communication in terms of such things as safety, efficiency, etc.' Both of these objectives suggest quite small increments of learning in the progression towards understanding this important idea. These increments revolve around the notion that:

- the fact that changes take place can be confirmed by evidence
- changes do not just happen—there are causes which can be discovered
- changes have effects which can be observed or predicted
- changes affect different people in different ways—some good, some less good depending on the context in which the changes occur.

Lessons should also have other objectives concerned with reasoning processes and with aspects of affective development. Understanding is not simply a matter of knowing 'what'. It is also a matter of reasoning or knowing 'how', and few lessons and no topic sequence should omit a variety of opportunities to develop thinking strategies or intellectual skills. We have already identified these skills in terms of such processes as classifying, interpreting, extrapolating, evaluating. Some lessons may involve pupils in all of these, some may be primarily concerned with one. The objective that pupils list the advantages to fire officers of having personal radio communication will involve pupils in seeking consequences, predicting effects, extrapolating from one situation to a new and changed situation. The lesson in which this takes place can then have a second objective which specifies the thinking strategies that will be practised and developed: 'children will develop the skills of prediction and extrapolation'.

A student planning a lesson within a topic sequence on clothing wanted her pupils to learn that the clothing people wear is a function of the effect of the environment in which they live and work. Climate is a factor here but so is the nature of work—soldiers wear uniforms, police officers wear reflective jackets, coal miners wear helmets. It can be seen that the student was pursuing key ideas about environmental influence and control. However, in the lesson being planned she had quite specific objectives concerned with getting her pupils to identify and describe the different kinds of clothing people wear and putting each kind into a category (e.g., clothing for hot climates, clothing for cold climates, clothing for recognition, clothing for protection, etc.) which they have reasoned out for themselves. Her objectives included both the search for information and the reasoning about that information.

> The pupils will develop their ability to:
>
> - research and process information by identifying and describing different types of clothing
> - reason by classifying types of clothing according to their main purpose.

There is, as with aims, a third category of objective—that referring to affective development. Affective development is a crucial process since it is concerned with the way children feel about school. Any such feeling or emotion, stimulated often enough, will become a habitual method of adjusting and reacting to future similar situations and, in the long term, to life in general. If children find school a pleasant place to be in then they are likely to approach the activities school provides with willingness and enthusiasm. Such children will want to participate, to be co-operative, are more likely to be curious, to persevere, to be confident about their own ability and therefore become more independent, responsible, open-minded and self-critical. Children who associate school with unpleasant feelings and with failure will seek to avoid real involvement in classroom and school activities. Some may become alienated to the point of being difficult to control and manage. They will all underachieve.

Lessons must be concerned, in parallel with developing knowledge and intellectual skill, with providing, through the methods employed, for positive attitudes to develop together with the abilities they foster. Methods should provide for learning situations which offer the children a framework in which to co-operate, persevere, be curious, open-minded, self-critical, etc.

We have already mentioned (page 30) the valuable work done in this area by Harlen *et al.* (1977) and the practical examples they provide. We shall return to their work later when we deal with progression and evaluation. It is sufficient here to suggest that no lesson plan can be regarded as having been fully thought through if it does not have affective objectives.

The lesson on Clothes referred to above involved a variety of activity, including:

- discussion
- children working in groups classifying pictures
- reworking classification to see whether any type of clothing fits into more than one category.

Discussion involves co-operation and respect for other points of view, group work similarly means sharing tasks and undertaking roles, reworking classifications means persevering. These are deliberate intentions framed within a stated objective, which in terms of a written lesson plan would be expressed as an intention to 'develop the pupils' ability to co-operate and persevere in problem-solving situations'.

The student now has the basis for a lesson plan which will develop the idea that clothes serve specific purposes—that there are causes/reasons why people wear certain kinds of clothing in particular contexts. This will develop not only the notion that certain types of clothing are the most appropriate for a specific activity but also the fact that people who wear clothing quite different from our own do so not because they are strange or peculiar or in some way inferior to us, but because those are the most suitable clothes in the context in which they live. This sensitivity to and acceptance of personal differences is an important aspect of any curriculum which claims it has a multicultural and equal opportunities perspective and which aims to minimise the less acceptable aspects of ethnocentrism. At the same time the pupils have co-operated together to solve the classification problem posed. It is a problem because it requires the pupils to give reasons for the clothing categories they have proposed and for placing a clothing type in a particular category.

Such problems, like most human problems, are more easily solved by the combined effort of a group. The harder the problem the more co-operation is beneficial. The pupils become aware of these benefits and develop a positive attitude towards working with others, and are likely to want to repeat such behaviour. They will also learn that co-operation involves compromises and sometimes having to accept the views of others as being more valuable than their own.

All these valuable aspects of the educational process will be developing simultaneously in the good lesson—gaining knowledge, reasoning, developing social skills and positive attitudes. In the student's note book it will be presented as:

Lesson: Class 1G *Date: 13 November*
Topic: Clothes *1.30–2.45 p.m.*

Objectives

The pupils will develop their ability to:

(a) research and process information by identifying and describing different types of clothing
(b) reason by classifying types of clothing according to its main purpose
(c) co-operate and persevere in problem-solving situations.

Materials

Six pieces of paper
Six pencils
Pictures cut from magazines covering the following groups of clothing:
- clothes from hot countries
- clothes from cold countries
- protective clothes
- sportswear
- uniforms
- rich clothes
- poor clothes

Scissors
Card to mount the pictures on
Cardboard labels for each group
Pens
Glue
Wooden hoops

Method

I shall start the session by saying that for three lessons we shall be doing some work on clothing. I shall then say, 'I have brought with me a lot of pictures of people wearing different clothes,' and place the pictures in the centre of each group table.

1. Allow a few minutes' free play with the pictures allowing the children to become familiar with them. Encourage discussion between themselves and with me.
2. Ask the children to put the pictures into groups. Say, 'Can you now put the pictures into groups?' Encourage discussion and co-operation. The children will group the pictures in front of them on the table. Watch the children as they

group the pictures. Listen to their discussion as they group the pictures. Continue until the children feel that they have successfully grouped the pictures. Visit each group.

3. Question the children: 'What name would you give to this group?' Pick out a picture and ask, 'Why have you put this picture with these in this group?' Ask whether the children agree that the pictures are correctly grouped. Discard any pictures which are agreed through discussion to be in the wrong groups. Continue to replace pictures until the groups are agreed and place the name of each group beside them. Stress all possibilities and alternatives. Encourage divergent thinking with reasoning to support the thinking. Give praise where it is due and encouragement.
4. Show the children that some of the pictures can fit into more than one group by using hoops on the table which overlap showing an intersection. Encourage the children to place pictures appropriately within the sections formed by the hoops, e.g., an overlap between uniform clothes and protective clothes in the picture of the nurses.
5. Having completed the classification successfully discuss the group of pictures showing uniforms with the children. Ask, 'Why do police officers wear uniforms? Why don't they wear their normal clothes?' Encourage discussion among the group and with me. Give each child a pencil and paper. Say, 'Write down a few reasons to say why police officers wear uniforms.'
6. Working together and sharing tasks—get each group to mount on paper, for display, the clothing they put in any *one* category.
   Ask them to (a) label the display, (b) in writing describe each item of clothing in their display and give reasons why it has been placed in that category.
7. *Closure.* Give praise to the whole class for the way they have worked. Revise and reinforce the main idea within objective 2 by getting one or two individual pupils to rehearse the reasoning behind their classifications.

Planning in this way from the level of the school's overall policy to the individual lesson is intended to ensure that pupils will acquire a broad range of content in the areas of Social Studies, involving fundamental and powerful ideas that are inherent in any study of society and especially in the traditional History and Geography curriculum. The content must be progressively better understood if pupils are to understand the world they live in and their part in it. Traditional content is not excluded. Studies of the Vikings, the Norman Conquest, the 1914–18 War, Farmers of East Anglia or the Equatorial Forests are only unacceptable if the content involved cannot be matched to the pupils' own experience and stage of development.

There will be lessons when a lot of information is researched and collected, when little reasoning takes place. This is not a sign of bad teaching unless over a sequence of lessons the information gathered is not used as a basis for posing and solving problems. The ability to obtain information from first-hand and second-hand sources is a useful skill and is the basis for reasoning about and understanding the core generalisations in the Social Enquiry curriculum. Good teaching will develop the ability to use information, to see the relationships that exist within it, to deduce new relationships, to explain those relationships, to make evaluations and to formulate generalisations that help in the understanding of new information and situations.

FURTHER READING

Blyth, A. *et al.* (1976) *Place, Time and Society 8–13: Curriculum Planning in History, Geography and Social Science*. London: Collins-ESL for the Schools Council.
DES (1987) *The National Curriculum: Consultative Document*. London: HMSO.
Harlen, W. *et al.* (1977) *Schools Council Science 5–13: Match and Mismatch*. Edinburgh: Oliver & Boyd.
ILEA (1979) *Social Studies in the Primary School*. London: ILEA.
Wilson, J. (1983) An approach to topic work. *Primary Contact*, **2**, no. 1, Spring, 60–6.

Chapter 3

Teaching

Devising a curriculum which has as its central aim the acquisition of that kind of knowledge that will allow schools to focus on ideas, principles and generalisations is no easy task. It flies in the face of the assumptions on which many schools operate their current curriculum, despite the exhortations of inspectors, advisers and other curriculum thinkers. Those assumptions stress acquisition of knowledge at a very low level—of description, information and fact. The previous chapter attempts to show that there are much more worthwhile elements of knowledge that even very young pupils can learn and understand and which can in their turn create new knowledge. They can do this because ideas transfer and can be applied to new situations to help explain them. However, such transfer is through a process of thinking, and thinking is a matter of enquiring, analysing, synthesising and concluding. Thinking is a learned process—it is not a matter of accepting the conclusions of someone else's thinking, it is a process of active transactions within a wide range of experience. The purpose of such transactions is to invest the experience and the ideas it exemplifies with meaning. Only then will ideas be truly understood by the learner. Such methods as are implied here—active learning, discovery approaches, enquiry methods—have been heralded by the British primary school and many will claim they use them. However, while it is true that the routinised behaviour of the 'traditional' classroom has virtually disappeared, there is little evidence that the true meaning of active learning is clearly understood and that the promotion of thinking processes in primary school activity is achieved as fully as it might be. We said earlier that devising this new kind of curriculum is not easy. Teaching children to think effectively is equally hard. Nevertheless that is what society wants from its schools, not graduating pupils who can name all the world's deserts and mountain ranges or recite the dates when wars were fought, but individuals capable of intelligent and independent thought.

There are a range of different approaches to what critical thinking involves. We have expressed the view that children will begin this process if they are involved in experiences that require them to identify, describe, classify, compare, seek causes of, reasons for, predict effects, make judgements and express opinions. What teachers will realise is that these processes cannot be learned in anything other than a considerable period of time. The efficient development of each of these thinking processes requires consistent and frequent practice in a wide variety of contexts. Initially children's attempts may be very disappointing. Inevitably, young children's attempts will be unsophisticated. Progression will only occur, quality will only improve if teachers provide those kind of classroom situations and activities that will allow their pupils the frequent practice they need.

This chapter concerns itself with a limited number of activities that are most likely, if used appropriately, to secure the objective we aim to achieve—understanding through thinking. The activities considered do not include the full range of ways of learning that good teachers will employ. Rather, the choice has fallen on methods that can be particularly useful and which are most likely to serve our objective to help pupils acquire thinking competence. Some of these are strategies which have always been available to teachers, although not necessarily well used; some are more recent additions to the teachers' portfolio which seem to us to be significant in helping to achieve the outcomes we wish to promote.

QUESTIONING

The importance of skilful questioning as a means of promoting effective thinking processes and as a part of the process of aiding concept formation has been well rehearsed in educational literature over the past few years and it is not our intention to repeat the full range of advice here. The DES Teacher Education Project (Kerry, 1982) produced an excellent teaching skills workbook which all student teachers and, indeed, all teachers would do well to read and work through. The section on resources in *Topic Teaching in the Primary School* (Gunning *et al.*, 1981) looks at questioning in the context of pictures and books, clearly identifying the intellectual skills that can be readily promoted based on the Bloom model of cognitive objectives (see Bloom *et al.*, 1956).

What might usefully be stressed here, in addition to what has already been outlined on pages 23–5, is that student teachers and teachers with limited experience need to plan the periods of questioning that they intend to initiate in the classroom very carefully indeed. Planning in this context means thinking out the key questions to be asked, the sequence in which they will be introduced and the purpose of each question in terms of the intended outcomes. The outcomes we would wish teachers to aim for have already been outlined in some detail on pages 27–8, where they are referred to as processes of critical thinking. The ladder model that is used in that context (see page 25) reinforces the notion that any attempt to explore an idea through questions and tasks has to establish a knowledge base from which higher-order thinking processes will be launched. Teachers must not feel that every question they ask has to be probing the pupils' ability to think in a sophisticated way. There will always be an initial stage of researching, identifying, describing and fact-finding. Remembering information previously learned is not an activity to be shunned, and there will be many occasions when it will be useful to employ such a strategy. However, these are only useful activities if they prepare pupils for the subsequent rungs on the ladder—involving pupils in seeing patterns and relationships, giving explanations, seeking reasons, making judgements and forming transferable generalisations. Questioning, therefore, using the ways of categorising questions and the strategies for presenting them suggested here, is an essential teacher competence. In addition, the use of redirecting, prompting and other tactics, which the Teacher Education Project workbook deals with so clearly, will help to ensure that all pupils in the classroom benefit equally from that competence.

DISCUSSION

It is very common to hear teachers, and especially student teachers, making the statement that the class or group will have a discussion about a particular issue. What usually then happens is a straightforward question and answer session. As such it is something the teacher has set up, and she or he decides what will be talked about. In addition, the teacher frequently decides on the direction in which the talk will go, asks specific questions so as to manipulate that direction, decides who will take part and by virtue of that has a flow of dialogue that is fundamentally only two-way—teacher to child and child to teacher. In such a situation the children are likely to regard the teacher as the focus of attention and may indeed compete with each other to receive questions and provide answers as a means of gaining approval. It is also possible for pupils to operate successfully in such a situation without having to take account of, or even listen to, the contributions their fellow pupils have made.

Question and answer sessions, as they are outlined above, can be very effective teaching strategies if they include the range of question types discussed in the previous chapter and if the teacher uses the tactics of redirection, probing, prompting, etc., previously described. However, discussion is a quite different teaching strategy and one which primary teachers find difficult to adopt. It may be that teachers have tried to get primary pupils to hold discussions and have been disappointed, but this is likely to be more a function of the way the techniques of discussion are taught in the primary classroom than of any inability on the part of young children to learn those techniques.

Discussion is an activity in which all the participants can be regarded as equals, who address each other and not some central figure or third party. In addition a central factor in a discussion is that the participants listen to each other and then, as they feel appropriate, respond to what others have said. Most of all, discussion is not a competitive situation or eristic battle but rather a search for the truth or an answer to a problem the participants are anxious to solve.

All this may seem too much to demand of young children. Can they reasonably be expected to clarify the issues they wish to discuss, listen carefully to what others say, perhaps modify their own point of view in the light of what someone else has said, maintaining this kind of activity for perhaps fifteen or twenty minutes? The answer is that if, initially, discussions involving young pupils are less than satisfactory it is probably simply because they are used to teacher-dominated situations and being involved in teacher-directed activities. Opportunities must be provided, even with very young pupils, for oral work in which they are not responding to adult questions, no matter how well designed, and where they are put in situations which require them truly to think for themselves.

Once established as part of the normal classroom process, discussions will, by definition, involve pupils in giving opinions and expressing a point of view, justifying their ideas with supporting evidence, giving and seeking reasons, predicting consequences and effects, using concept words in new situations, trying out ideas and setting up and testing hypotheses against the opinions of others. In addition a range of affective learning and development will take place. This affective learning and attitude formation is concerned with an increased ability and willingness to listen to others and to see another person's point of view, to empathise with their situation and to accept that opinions may differ. All these are aspects of the intellectual and affective development we wish to stimulate.

Primary teachers need to proceed carefully and introduce discussion in a structured way which will, initially, support their pupils' efforts. The first kinds of discussions might, for example, be concerned with pupils organising themselves in group situations. This is using discussion to make decisions. If the outcome of part of a class topic on Farming is to be a frieze depicting the way farm machinery has changed over a period of time, then a small group of pupils could be asked to decide how big/long the frieze needs to be, what materials will be used, what medium will be best, what items to include, what order to mount the chosen items, how they will be arranged and presented and what headings and captions will be required.

There will be many instances when such a technique could be employed. It is likely to be increasingly successful if the pupils' decisions are accepted and acted upon, with teacher interference only if their decisions turn out to be impractical—even then the interference must be accompanied by a reasoned explanation.

There is no reason why pupils cannot move very quickly to the discussion of intellectual tasks requiring practice of higher-order thinking strategies. Initially these should be in small groups—four pupils rather than eight—and be concerned with tasks that will take five minutes rather than fifteen. The tasks themselves need to be concrete and specific, supported by information or evidence—pictures, maps, artefacts, etc. At first the number of variables the pupils need to take into account should be limited. For example, pupils who have done some work on castles and know something of the reasoning behind the siting of castles by their designers and builders could be given a suitable map and asked to find a suitable place to build a castle. At first the map may provide clues that will suggest a fairly obvious site, but still promote some discussion within the group. More able, older or practised pupils could be given a map which includes several possible sites, some with certain advantages, some with other advantages, so that difference of opinion and reasoned discussion becomes almost inevitable. Similarly, a group involved in a Desert Island topic could discuss the best way to choose a leader or how jobs may be allocated. What is important is to realise that for a long time discussions in the primary classroom will need a clear focus and that the preparation for this will contribute significantly to the activities' success. The focus will be most effective if, in addition to having the characteristics described above, it poses a problem which can be solved in the limited time that is to be allocated—with initial expectations maintained at reasonable levels.

It is also important to remember that primary pupils see the teacher as an authority figure. If the teacher forms a permanent member of the discussion group she is likely to inhibit the pupils' participation or, at best, the pupils will tend to direct their contributions to her. So, as far as possible, the group should be left to get on by themselves. Of course, since children have to learn to be successful participants in discussions, there is a part for the teacher to play but this must be done as unobtrusively as possible. The effective teacher will join the group from time to time but not as either an active participant or a chairperson. If things are going well then a smile or nod of encouragement may be all that is required before the group is left again. However, occasionally it is wise for the teacher to make an intervention. If, for example, they are really losing track of the purpose of the activity a question may get them back on course, or it may be useful to ask one pupil to summarise how far they have got and what they intend to do next. If one pupil seems to be dominating the discussion too much then a quiet 'What do you think, Anna?' or 'What do the rest of you think?' will help bring others in—especially those who may have contributed little—although it is by no means necessary that everyone makes an equal number of contributions.

Two further matters are important in developing good discussion and teachers should not neglect them. The first is to ensure that discussions do not just fade away. Some member of the group should always be asked to indicate the result—what did they decide, do they have good reasons for what they decided, was anything unresolved? Only if discussion is seen as purposeful and important in the general work of the class will it be taken seriously and given the effort it requires.

Finally, teachers can help their pupils by, from time to time, indicating the kind of things they wish to see happening when a discussion takes place. In addition there will be many opportunities to praise such things when they occur:

> 'Malik asked some interesting questions.'
> 'Fiona gave some very good reasons for . . .'
> 'It was good to see how carefully you listened to each other'
> 'It was good that you looked at the problem from both points of view'.

Such comments will encourage the kind of exploratory thinking, reasoning, justifying, tentativeness, empathising and accommodation of new ideas that the concepts and skills approach is based on.

EDUCATIONAL VISITS

Educational visits are a high-prestige activity—they are frequently expensive and involve parents in one way or another—if only in seeing that their child is appropriately dressed and provided with a packed lunch. Unlike most other classroom activities visits receive a lot of advance publicity and generate a great deal of excitement and curiosity. However, they are frequently unproductive in terms of the learning outcomes, and as Ros Richardson (*Education 3–13*, December 1983) points out, it is often 'a disturbing and salutary experience [for teachers] that a significant number of children, having given every appearance of being well motivated and interested in the visit, gave evidence, in follow-up work, that they had been pre-occupied with what might be described as trivial or even irrelevant details.'

A well prepared educational visit can be a most effective learning experience for a number of very good reasons:

1. Pupils are generally motivated, curious about where they are going, what they will see and do.

2. They provide opportunities for pupils to collect information which can be used later to develop conceptual understanding and intellectual skills.
3. They provide referents of the strongest 'concrete' kind on which to hang concepts.
4. They help the development in children of ideas that:
   (a) evidence exists and can be seen, touched and generally experienced
   (b) collecting evidence is an important part of solving problems, drawing conclusions and making enquiries
   (c) opinions and conclusions can only be developed on the basis of evidence
   (d) evidence is not always complete, is often ambiguous and conclusions may frequently be, at best, tentative.
5. Visits are a valuable context for the development of social skills—co-operation, self-discipline, responsibility, seeing the need for and obeying rules, showing empathy with others.

The most important features of the planning of any visit is that the children's activities on the visit should be *directed.* This direction will largely be through a process of asking questions of them. These questions are likely to ask the children to do four main things: to list; to describe; to measure, count, quantify; to sketch, draw. This is the evidence and will be the basis for a range of activities back in school which will be of a higher order, involving reasoning pocesses such as classifying, interpreting and evaluating.

This direction means, of course, that children must go on a visit with the questions they need to answer written down. A booklet is a good idea, and may also include a number of other things:

1. General information, where the visit is to be, the route for getting there, any special needs, clothing.
2. Rules to be obeyed with reasons, special instructions if a child gets separated, safety factors.
3. General information about the purpose of the visit and what is likely to be seen, without giving too much detail, except in relation to background.
4. A list of questions that children will be expected to find answers to during the visit or tasks they have to complete.
5. Examples of the work to be done in the follow-up sessions. This is particularly important. The more the child knows about the purpose of the visit the better, i.e., the purpose of the visit is not just to find things out at the time but to understand about them as well. So the tasks to be set in follow-up work, or some of them, ought to be included in the booklet.

A visit, of course, ought quite clearly to be closely related to the aims and objectives of the sequence of work of which the visit is a part. These aims and objectives will include the intention that the pupils will develop their understanding of concepts and their thinking abilities. The concepts must be identified before the visit takes place so that it can be used as a source for strengthening that concept learning.

Take, for example, a topic on Homes in which the teacher intends to develop the pupils' ideas about change, i.e., things are as they are for reasons and things change for reasons. These are important understandings and are concerned with concepts such as development and technology, as well as change. A visit is arranged to a museum which has a number of exhibits to do with Homes, one of which is a display of household artefacts dating from Victorian times to the early 1960s—washing materials and implements. The teacher may want the pupils to look at these to strengthen their grasp of the selected concepts and the general notion that washing procedures have changed for reasons to do with new discoveries, new inventions, new knowledge, new materials, new needs and changed values. In addition the teacher will want pupils to understand that things were the way they were for reasons and not because people in the past were in some way quaint or stupid.

What is to be done on the visit? Before the pupils can reason about the changes in washing procedures they need to be able to list the differences between how washing was done and how it is done now and the differences between the implements and machinery that were and are used. They may need help here, so questions can be asked that direct their attention to such things as materials, inventions and energy forms and away from ideas of quaintness. This work will form a springboard for the follow-up activities to be undertaken back at school. Follow-up tasks will be higher up the 'ladder' and involve classifying, interpreting, evaluating and generalising. Such tasks should not be attempted on the visit itself if any quality of thought and outcome is expected. The visit is for finding evidence and recording it in writing, drawings and sketches, taking photographs and so on. The tasks at school can then be quite searching, e.g., from further but more elaborate describing (List the jobs a washing machine does during a 'programme'. How did people do these jobs fifty years ago?), to evaluating (Do you think the washing machine makes a better job of doing the washing than using a dolly tub and scrub board?), to application and generalising (Why might a shop that sells washing machines describe them as 'labour saving'?).

Let us take another example—the visit to a castle (see page 17). The visit will again act as a source of strong concrete referents for strengthening concept learning. So what concepts might such a visit help to develop? We have already suggested the concepts of site and design—the idea that the site and design of a castle is not accidental but determined by rational principles. Concepts like defence, attack, siege and change can also be developed further by a visit to a castle if the pupils are asked the right guiding questions. These questions must guide the pupils towards evidence, evidence which in this case will be gained from buildings and ground formation. Getting the evidence might involve measuring and drawing plans. Lists can be made and notes taken about the hills, cliffs, walls, towers and moats in terms of such qualities as thickness, height, strength and materials used. Visibility can be gauged from various positions and the availability of resources such as water investigated. Again, the reasoning tasks are best left to the follow-up sessions in school, when the evidence can be used to reason about why the castle was built where it was, in what ways it was difficult to attack, why the original wooden palisade was changed to stone walls, etc.

In these ways visits cease to be the ends in themselves they so often are and become a means to an end, based on four straightforward questions:

- What ideas will the visit help pupils to understand?
- What evidence can be collected to foster that understanding?
- How can the evidence best be collected and brought back to school?
- What follow-up tasks can use that evidence so that the pupils think about it in a variety of ways and increase their grasp of the ideas involved?

SETTING WRITING TASKS

From a very early stage in the primary school topic work provides the context for writing activities. The research undertaken by Eggleston and Kerry (1985) suggests that a great many teachers see topic work as the area of the curriculum where the basic skills of literacy, together with numeracy, are practised. We have gone to some considerable lengths in this book to urge teachers to identify the content topic work has to offer so that the breadth and balance the National Curriculum demands can be achieved. Nevertheless, within the framework of understanding identified knowledge and practising recognised thinking abilities, literacy skills inevitably must be used and can be practised and developed. Teachers must therefore present their pupils with frequent opportunities to undertake tasks involving a written answer, varying from fairly short answers to a question to much longer pieces requiring, perhaps, the expression of a range of ideas. If these tasks are to be done effectively then it is necessary to bear in mind that good writing fulfils the intentions the author has, in terms of the subject of the writing and the audience who will receive it. This is the fundamental criterion for effective written communication—a clear relationship between the author, the subject and the audience. Children must come to see their writing in such a framework and topic work can present many situations where such writing development can take place.

Four different kinds of writing are dealt with here that are particularly relevant to topic work in the Social Studies area. There are many interesting and longer treatments of this obviously important variable in the topic curriculum and teachers who may not be familiar with the notions of 'subject' and 'audience' would do well to study them. (See, for example, Halliday, 1969, for an initial introduction to the subject). What is important is that each of the different models of language that a child may use is likely to involve different kinds of thinking processes and be addressed to a different kind of audience. This provides variety and allows the child to escape from the monotony of writing that is always descriptive—so frequently referred to, in error most often, as creative writing. Primary schools are unlikely to produce the 'compleat writer' very often but if they want their pupils to be more creative in written work and to be willing and enthusiastic about it then the opportunity to practise a variety of different models of writing is essential. The first of the models of writing useful in topic lessons is *informational writing*. This is writing that deals with information, reorganising it as well as simply recording it.

The first and perhaps simplest form of informational writing is that which does record the here and now. It may vary in nature from the writing of lists or data to fairly complex and long descriptions. Pupils looking at a number of flint artefacts in a museum may simply list the different purposes for which flint was used—the tools, weapons, jewellery, etc. Lists can also be used in the brain-storming activities that topic work often gives rise to, such as making a list of all the different kinds of work a family has to do in the home or all the different kinds of transport one can think of. Here the audience is the child him or herself. Writing is being used to provide a record of thinking and a reference for later use. No one but the child may see the list but it may be a crucial factor in the quality of later work. Making such lists as a record of what is seen, heard or brought to mind is a form of writing encouraged all too infrequently.

The second kind of informational writing is the careful and detailed description of what has been observed. It lies, like the lists mentioned above, on the first rung of the ladder of activities outlined on page 25. It may be a development of the lists themselves, an expansion from words into sentences. This kind of language allows the child to represent what has been observed, to pass it on to some audience so that the original experience can be shared. The child may be conveying a message about what the castle that was visited was like, what the steam engine at the railway museum looked like—any experience can be conveyed through language in this way. As long as it is not the sole form of writing that pupils are encouraged to practise and develop, it serves a very useful purpose. There is merit, too, in terms of progression in this kind of writing, as indeed with other forms of writing, in applying evaluating criteria, like inclusiveness and elaboration, to it, as suggested elsewhere in this book. (See chapter 4.)

Informational writing does not and must not stay at the level of identifying, listing and describing. Information is an essential ingredient of any attempt to report the past. Such reporting is likely to be at least once removed from personal and first-hand experience so that there is an element of abstractness in any such writing. Writing tasks in the historical area of topic work may start off by reporting the here and now, as detailed above, perhaps listing evidence that can be observed. This provides a basis for moving up the ladder to indicate the extent to which such evidence may be only tentative, possibly ambiguous or limited and incomplete. In addition the historian will wish to put forward possible inferences that can be made from evidence about the way people behaved or the purposes artefacts may have served. This kind of writing task requires the information to be reorganised and presented so that it shows that it has been used to draw conclusions, however tentative. In the same way, information can be used through writing tasks to help pupils put forward hypotheses to suggest what might happen if certain conditions apply or to generalise from what has happened in a specific situation to what might happen in a range of similar situations. Topic work that requires pupils to look at the cause and effect of events, that requires a search for evidence and the drawing of inferences or that involves extrapolating from the known position to some hypothetical or changed situation will involve pupils in this kind of writing and its inherent thinking processes. What is important is that the pupils are helped to move along the continuum from 'concrete' description and here and now reporting to the more abstract levels of inference and hypothesising.

Interactional writing is a crucial element of the writing good topic work should engender. This kind of writing concentrates on influencing the thinking, beliefs and conduct of the reader. Expressing opinions, defending and supporting a given social situation, exposing unfairness or inequality of treatment, explaining and reasoning about why things are as they are, were as they were or why they might be changed are well within the scope of interactional writing—a form of writing that seems sadly neglected in current primary school practice. It involves the writer in getting others to understand, if not to agree with, a point of view. Its underlying intent is to be persuasive and to promote a shift of position. Social Studies type topics provide a wide variety of opportunities for such writing, which can be very easily combined with role play and similar activities. For example, the Place, Time and Society materials mentioned earlier (in chapter 2) refer to a role play activity concerning the changes that took place when the railways were first developed. Some people at the time were for the changes, others were not, as is always the case. This role play situation might usefully be accompanied by the writing of letters, speeches or newspaper articles, all putting a point of view justified through evidence and reasoned argument.

Expressive writing is frequently referred to in any discussion on models of writing that children might develop and practise. It is usually defined as writing that concentrates on revealing the author's self and in particular how the writer reacts emotionally to the social and physical world. Once again Social Studies topics provide for this kind of writing in all its variety—prose, poetry, dramatic dialogue and so on. Learning about society is enhanced if some attempt is made, whenever appropriate, to see a situation as it might affect ourselves and how we would feel or react. Writing about being a Saxon when the Normans invaded, an Eskimo as winter sets in or a fire officer climbing above a blazing building, in terms of the feelings, reactions, hopes and fears such situations might provoke, involves expressive writing.

Imaginative writing is frequently employed in primary schools where, often under the title of creative writing, it is employed to perform all the language functions we have outlined above. However, imaginative writing is, as are all the others, a quite discrete form of communication which is addressed to a different audience. The purpose of such writing is for the child to create a new, perhaps unique, environment linguistically. It will be imaginative or creative to the extent to which it manifests the variables emphasised in the assessment of creativity by, say, such people as J. P. Guilford (1971). These variables are similar to the ones Hilda Taba and her colleagues (Durkin *et al.*, 1969) used as the basis for evaluation strategies, which are discussed in detail elsewhere in this book (page 73). Certainly imaginative writing is neither simply descriptive nor similar to the more superficial forms of informational writing referred to earlier in this chapter.

Imaginative writing is used to present a possible world in words—to synthesise ideas into larger, inclusive patterns that are consistent with each other. The more imaginative the writing the more complex the possible world is likely to be, with a greater number of interrelated ideas being manipulated by the writer simultaneously. Although such writing is imaginative and will not therefore deal directly with the real world, it will, in socially based topics, have implications for it or the pupils' understanding of it. Setting up an imagined world—a desert island, a space station or a hypothetical situation in historical times—might precede activities which then deal with the imagined world fairly literally so that understandings and skills are developed. The scope for this kind of writing is immense and it can form the basis for simulations, games and role play.

Topic work can promote a full range of writing competencies, allowing expression of one's own thoughts and feelings, interaction with others in debate and argument, exchange and communication of information and, perhaps most sophisticated of all, the creation of imaginative and complex social environments. Each involves different kinds of audience, different forms of expression, different vocabularies and different combinations of thinking processes. Children will only develop these abilities if they are allowed to practise them.

PUPILS OF LIMITED LITERACY

Almost every class will include some pupils with limited literary ability—pupils who have difficulty reading and expressing their ideas in writing. This may, in its turn, mean that the conceptual level is also lower than in other children, so that tasks have to be devised to enable them to explore the same idea and skill but at a lower level of difficulty. What is important is that the task is not abandoned and replaced with some alternative task intended primarily to occupy the lower ability pupil while the others get on with the original task.

One useful strategy is to ensure that the task is not too big in terms of the number of variables involved and the conceptual understanding required. This means making an analysis of the task and breaking it down into its component parts. An apparently simple question, like 'Why are fire engines red?', requires, for a satisfactory answer, the pupil to see the relationship between the first fact, that red is a highly visible colour, and the second fact, that it is important that fire engines are easily and quickly seen so that people can give them priority. So even this question might prove difficult if the variables are not identified and the relationship between them is not appreciated. Breaking the task down into two questions can make the task easier, providing for the same kinds of reasoning to be employed but in simpler sequential stages: How do they make fire engines easy to see? Why is it a good thing for people to be able to see fire engines clearly?

Children of limited literacy are not always of lower intellectual ability so they may be able to take part more successfully in topic work tasks if they work as part of a group. The danger here is that the less able pupil may not feel confident enough initially to participate actively. The teacher needs to supervise the division of labour within the group so that all profit. If the task is to answer a range of questions based on a picture or artefact, then one child may have the job of reading out the questions and another of writing down the answers. The less literate child could be the one who summarises the agreed answer and dictates it to the scribe.

It is very important that pupils of limited literacy are helped to increase their fluency and vocabulary and working in a group situation will provide for this. So will involvement in discussion in both group and class situations, and frequent contact with the teacher. The literate child's written work can be seen and greater fluency and elaboration encouraged intermittently. Less literate pupils will profit from teacher's questions that are designed to provide prompts and clues for quite small increments in output.

What is important is that topic lessons do not become sessions for simply practising language—neglecting the specific objectives of reasoning and solving problems. Reports, accounts and attempts to convice and persuade which involve considerable writing can be made less daunting if some of the information and conclusions can be conveyed by drawings, diagrams, graphs, etc. Above all ensure that the pupil secures success and is given appropriate praise for effort.

INFORMATION TECHNOLOGY

Eighty years ago, children were fascinated by the 'magic lantern'. There is nothing magic about computers, but children are irresistibly drawn to the visual images computers provide, and it is important that they do not become the 'magic lantern show' of the 1980s. In the context of topic work there are three roles to consider—that of the computer, that of the teacher, and that of the pupil.

The role of the computer

A computer is only one of many resources in the classroom. Resources need to support, rather than direct, the learning that is taking place. Use of a computer is a derived experience, which is a response to a first-hand experience gained in the concrete world through the pupils' senses. Teachers need to consider which particular aspects of computer use are special, and differentiate it from other more traditional resources available to them. What can it be made to do to assist the learning process?

First, the computer has speed and a large memory. It can be made to control other equipment and to assist in professional presentation of many documents, as in the industrial and commercial world. Most importantly, it enables us to be in control, and to be aware of our responsibility as a result of that control. It allows us to experiment with our own ideas, to make changes before we have to act, to make mistakes that are not seen as permanent, and to see what might happen if . . . without any *real* disasters occurring. The computer no longer needs to be thought of in terms of a machine with the ability to do things quickly, but as a powerful tool with which pupils can manipulate their creative ideas and consider the possible consequences.

The role of the teacher

Part of the teacher's role is to provide resources that are versatile, motivating and appropriate to the topic. Almost all software for computers, in a given situation, may be described as appropriate and motivating for most pupils. To add versatility, some software needs to be 'content free'. This is the type that allows the user to provide his or her own information or content, and to choose how it can be manipulated. The teacher, as a partner in learning, is able to work alongside the pupils—questioning, debating and experimenting. They are able to create and solve problems together as a team. A consideration of some of the types of content-free software will show how they may be integrated into the whole topic.

Databases

Topic work frequently begins with research, and the collection of information or evidence. A database is a collection of pieces of information, which is refined and put into the computer. It can then be processed, or used, in a variety of ways. It is possible to create many 'files' to use with one database program. There are basically two types of database: hierarchical and relational. *The hierarchical type* is concerned with classification. It can be classification of anything—found objects, museum pieces, plants, animals, people, buildings, clothes, even ideas. If, in creating a file for the database, pupils are asked to suggest a question that will define the difference between two items, the question must be able to have a yes/no binary answer. So the pupils need to be very clear about the language they use, and precise about attributes of the item. While creating questions, much of the work can be done away from the computer. By answering the questions created an item is 'found' in the database. The teacher can learn a great deal about the pupils' learning from the kind of questions they create.

A relational database is more complicated to compile and to use, but the time and effort involved in compiling it is very worthwhile in terms of pupils' learning. A relational database is concerned with relationships between the items of information, rather than focusing on the items themselves. Information needs to be prepared in a tabular form, and sometimes needs to be coded. Once the new file has been created, questions may be asked by the pupils, and the answers found quickly by sorting processes in the program. If, for instance, the pupils had created a file containing information from a census about their own area, questions could be asked to discover how many girls of a certain age were in the households at the time. Depending on the census date, the pupils might discover that many girls were housemaids, but that some of the same age were simply living at home. Looking at the address, name, size of household, etc., would help to explain why. It is possible to ask questions referring to numbers rather than words and, instead of lists, pictorial representations may be produced quickly by the machine. Print-outs allow pupils to continue their investigations away from the computer.

Files can be made using information from a wide variety of sources, including census details and information about people, plants, buildings, birds, animals, the weather, places, in fact anything of interest in the environment. The database allows consideration of social structures and the exploration of cause and effect in certain situations. Sometimes its use inspires in pupils questions about previously unthought of directions, perhaps wider investigations not suitable for the classroom.

Simulations and adventure games

A simulation is a program that allows the user to create a situation that would be impossible in reality, perhaps because of safety difficulties, or just expense. An adventure game, in very broad terms, is a journey with choices, alternative events and problems to solve or overcome. A content-free adventure may be one where the user is able to write his or her own situation, with its own alternative events and choices. Both these computer activities may be applicable to topic work, since creating a 'game' to be played by others can be as just challenging as a program with a serious intent, and fun as well. Both types are available for alteration, or for the addition of the user's own information. Sometimes it is appropriate for the teacher to create the new situation, at other times the pupils may be involved.

The programs allow pupils to consider issues common to many situations and times, which help to prepare them for real-life living. In using such programs, pupils learn things about themselves and their own values, as well as about causes and consequences. For instance, if the group topic was about survival, and they were considering an area of land to settle in, a number of questions can be asked. How does the team split up to explore it, and in what order do they explore areas? Where do they choose to live? What does the place offer them? They can consider differing lifestyles and social structures, and explore the results of their joint decisions without in reality starving to death! They can decide who has to work how hard for how long, how food is rationed and what to do about random events (put in by the teachers?). They can be engaged in heated discussion and experience a range of feelings which may later be expressed through many different activities. Alternatively, current events may prompt a consideration of another scenario—the continuity and change elements in studying the similarities in the sinking of a Ro-Ro ferry and the sinking of the *Mary Rose*, or the conflicts and consensus about the coming of the railways or the Channel Tunnel. Their interest might be closer to home: perhaps the pupils are engaged in helping to plan for the Christmas Fayre at their own school—how to control the flow of people around the building, keeping fire exits clear, what to do with Santa's queue.

A computer allows the pupils to work together, discuss and experiment with a range of possibilities that could become a real situation. A practical element of using programs like these is that they provide situations where individuals and groups can present their ideas and strategies to a larger group, and argue for the solutions they suggest. The next type of program would assist them in their presentations.

Word processing and desk-top publishing

A word processing program is one that allows pupils to write something, edit, refine, reorganise and then print it out in an exciting professional form with many copies. Mistakes can be changed before the work is printed, and for many children this makes writing less threatening, and their handwriting skills of less concern. It is also possible to assist the less-skilled or handicapped pupil by using a Concept keyboard to produce words or phrases at the press of a button. The teacher is able to work alongside the pupil, assisting in the re-drafting process. As well as producing group information and news-sheets relating to the topic, pupils may have interviewed members of the community about their lives, and might wish to give them a copy of their 'modern history' books. They might write a play and hand out parts to the actors, or create a class or school magazine or newspaper using such desk-top publication software as Front Page. They might even wish to advertise their topic exhibition with computer-controlled models.

Logo and 'control' programs

With extra hardware it is possible to control electrical items, such as switches and motors, from the computer. Children write procedures that will make things happen in a particular sequence, such as creating a flashing light for a new lighthouse, with the flashes timed to be different from all existing lighthouses. With the basic turtle 'extra' they could still create sequences, for instance, to guide robot emergency vehicles through mining tunnels. Other programs allow the pupils to create music or pictures, but the teacher needs to decide how they are adding to the pupils' first-hand experiences, which are still of prime importance. In the type of program outlined above, the computer is a *tool*, provided by the teacher. It is being used to:

- interrogate the pupils' own information and assist them in forming hypotheses in collaboration with others
- explore the hypotheses in a 'safe' way, but one that is fun and relates to the problems of the real world
- disseminate the findings of the exploration to others in a meaningful way.

In working alongside the pupils, the teacher is better able to evaluate the pupils' understanding of concepts and values, since appropriate feedback becomes more openly available to the teacher because of the processes in which the pupils are engaged.

Using a computer is not without problems. Like all other resources it requires monitoring. The teacher needs to ensure that information is saved regularly. There is nothing worse than working for an hour just before a power cut. It must be ensured that pupils take turns on the equipment to allow fairness of access time, from a concern to avoid pupils' eye strain and for health needs. The teacher also needs to ensure that the pupils develop strategies to enable independent handling of the equipment, just as there are strategies for finding books in libraries.

The role of the child

Some pupils don't like any machines. Not all pupils will automatically be motivated by the computer, but many small successes over time build up to a big one. If pupils feel that they are in control, and have power over the machine, it is more likely that they will have confidence in using it. If pupils are asked to provide problems to solve, they are likely to suggest ideas that are meaningful in their lives. They can, through comparisons and contrasts, see how other people's existences relate to their own. By working in a group, discussing and experimenting, they are helped in their own understanding, study is more meaningful and they learn to cope with other people's views, as well as learning from other people's strategies.

Using a computer, pupils can challenge rules, make their own rules and mistakes, think freely and respond to the consequences. Some pupils are able to make use of a huge database created by their own society, and which is already history—the Domesday Disc. Other pupils have access to network systems in their schools, where a computer in any room can tell them if a particular book is in the school library, or whether it has been borrowed. They may be able to switch on and find a message from their own teacher about the weekly plan, or a message from a helpful member of the community. Very soon pupils will be comparing ideas and information, via computer, with other schools up and down the country. A study of the Vikings, for instance, could become much more personally meaningful if pupils are communicating with others whose local history had been strongly influenced by invasion, and sharing the results of their own evironmental investigations. When lap-top portable computers become as readily affordable as pocket calculators, pupils might be acting as 'reporters in the field' and relaying information not only to the classroom, but to pupils in other countries.

What is important is that having access to a computer can help the pupils to make sense of a whole range of real and simulated experiences which they can analyse and control. The computer should be used by the pupils to support their thinking and provide feedback in the full range of problem-solving processes and the presentation of solutions.

The computer should be used by the pupil, not the pupil by the machine.

DANCE AND DRAMA

The pursuit of knowledge, understanding and skill within the context of a topic is not exclusive to the academic mode. The most discerning and vibrant teachers not only utilise, but positively exploit, an active and creative approach, epitomised in dance and drama. Socially based topic work can provide a resource base from which artistic expression can fruitfully arise, thereby enabling the child's growing awareness and development to emerge from a harmonious and balanced foundation that embraces a wide range of contrasting and complementary expressive forms. The key to this assertion is the teacher's ability to analyse the subject or contextual framework of the topic in the ways developed in earlier pages and the ability to link it to the artistic language or means of expression. This means that the teacher, in drama, will provide the child with opportunities to use speech, movement characterisation and simple narrative to create small projects or dramatic happenings that relate to a specific topic, and, in dance, will provide opportunities for stylised, rhythmical expression as the means of crystallizing, in symbolic form, the essence of ideas that relate to the topic.

The justification for this approach is not to devalue the practice and appreciation of dance and drama in their own right, but to promote the thesis that different forms of learning enhance the child's understanding and perception of knowledge and skills to be gained, and act as reinforcing agencies to this end. In dance and drama, for example, artistic experience is derived through voice and action that in itself obeys the rules and codifications of the artistic language. It is obvious that the topic can become the stimulus, so that learning that has taken place in the classroom relates directly to the artistic process and the emergent artefact that the class, or groups within the class, may produce. In this way one mode of learning is complementary to the other forms and will act as a motivating factor, since success in one area can help overcome difficulties in another.

In a topic on Victorian England, dramatic improvisation and role play will benefit from information gained through rich classroom resources and activities where children will have had recourse to photography, texts, assorted artefacts and objects, and visits to museums or industrial sites. The absorption and expression of what they have derived through reading, writing, discussion and visual display will be evident in the quality of the dramatic experiences they create and perform, whether specific historical events or scenes from social history. Plan 1 (page 60) is an example of a drama session with a group of junior school children in which the teacher assumes the role of the inspector of mines. Approaches of this nature permit the child to interpret information and link it to the dramatic mode of expression through characterisation, verbal interaction and the development of a particular narrative or event. In this manner new creative forms arise that reflect the child's own personal viewpoint or perception of a situation in terms which will include their developing understanding of ideas such as rich and poor.

In dance the content will necessarily focus on aspects of a topic that are best expressed through movement. The notion of Victorian England being the workshop of the world, with emphasis on change and consequent growing industrial power and wealth and the development of communications, is sufficient to generate an exciting movement response that will incorporate partner and group activities. Specific conceptual images of this era—the power and rhythmical actions of machines, the network of road, railways and canals, and the industrial landscapes of factories, viaducts, chimneys and clusters of dwelling houses—allow dynamic, spatial and rhythmical expression to be synthesised into meaningful sequential movements. Plan 2 shows how these ideas were conveyed and experienced in a session with a top junior class who were considering the changes from manual to mechanical power. (See Storer, 1985.)

In both these examples the teacher was concerned to teach specific skills, so that the child acquired the means of expression, but then assumed a role as catalyst so that the child could find his or her own way of linking mental imagery to ideas and ways of thinking through the techniques of dance and drama. The ensuing process is one of exploration and discovery, selection and problem solving, practice and performance of an identifiable artefact—the child's statement of what is understood through dance and drama. The artistic process and the performance to the rest of the group of either the dance or the drama are important and necessary elements of this strategy and will reflect the level of attainment of the children in their ability to absorb and express ideas through creative thought and action. The appraisal and evaluation of the artistic statement will invariably relate to the child's grasp and use of the artistic language and the manner in which it has been applied to other conceptual issues.

In drama this is largely dependent on readily accessible skills—the ability to speak and move. Conversation and action will inevitably arise through improvisation, and the child will need to acquire fluency of verbal language. Communicative skills will develop and social interaction will take place, stimulated by the power of the imagination to transform oneself into another being living in situations and surroundings different from one's own.

The child's creative powers will develop through work within the peer group, when a simple narrative or dramatic structure will arise. Critical powers of selection will be exercised and only the best material will be retained as the emergent artefact assumes dramatic form.

In dance the performance of skilfully executed, meaningful movements is essential. The codification for dance in education is based on the movement themes devised by Rudolf Laban (1879–1958), where the child builds on a conceptual understanding and experiencing of the elements of dance—time, weight, space and flow factors—arising from awareness of self. This involves the ability to create sequential movement through body co-ordination, travelling, elevation and landing, balance, articulation of specific limbs, whole body actions and the experience of dynamic action. Visual perception and analysis provide the on-looker with means of appreciating and assessing what the child is both simultaneously expressing and attaining, but the lived experience of performing and the kinaesthetic appreciation of dance are exclusive to the child as agent of its own performance. Participation is therefore of paramount importance, and learning through the arts, whether dance or drama, can be valued by peer groups and teachers who receive the work through observation and listening, arising out of the unique and exclusively individual experience of participation.

Active involvement—the assimilation of knowledge through dance and drama—is a powerful and dynamic method of learning that is both appropriate and effective for the teaching of topic. Not only is it beneficial for the child who is articulate and literate, but it is especially significant for the child who is restricted in these means, since it is providing a powerful outlet for ideas that are otherwise dormant or have no means of expression.

PLAN 1

Aim: To develop understanding of important social ideas and empathise with people of Victorian times
Class: top junior

Introduction

General warming-up sessions and relaxation to set the tone and mood. *Stare into the lamp and go back in time.*

- People moving—shapes and statuesque.
- Types of people—division of society, overseers and overlords, wealthy, powerful and rich.
- Subservient classes.
- Emphasis on movement, shape, direction, level—significance and meaning of the movement. *Effort analysis.*
- Bringing in conversation. Mingling and stopping, making conversation.
- *Teacher in role.* I will become the inspector of the mines. I will call on witnesses to present their information to me.

[20 minutes]

Main strategy

Divide into small groups. Read the information concerning child labour in the coal mines. Select characters you wish to be.

Josh Gibson, aged 52.
James Knighton, aged 70.
William Hawkins, aged 13.
George Hodgkinson, aged 11.
Robert Blount, aged 10.
The Rev. H. W. Plumptre, Rector of Eastwood.
William Scott Smith Esq., Surgeon of Eastwood.
William Wardle, aged 40.
Joseph Skelton, aged 10.
John Attenborough, Schoolmaster, Greasley.
Ann Wilson, Mother, Underwood.

Work out a scene in which the character is seen in action, based on information provided and as a result of your own knowledge and researches of social hsitory.

[20 minutes]

Conclusion

The character of the factory inspector links together the separate scenes of domestic, social and industrial life of the Nottinghamshire coalfield. Will there be a conclusion? Is there a way of drawing the whole class together?

[20 minutes]

This session could be linked with the dance session 'Britain as the workshop of the world'.

PLAN 2

Aim: To portray Britain as the Victorian workshop of the world through movement expression
Class: top junior

Introduction

Warming-up activities that incorporate the following:

- Imaginative use of directions and levels.
- General space awareness—forwards, backwards, sideways, diagonals.
- Action and stillness.
- Time concept (sudden, sustained).
- Making shapes that will relate to main theme.

Pin, wall, ball, screw, i.e., straight, wide, rounded and twisted.

Whole-body actions that involve shape. Run, jump, roll.

[15 minutes, percussion and voice]

Main strategy

Introduce dynamic concepts. Assume shape and move in a firm, strong manner. Contrast, time element. Listen to a machine. *Effort, action, press.* What actions did the early machines perform? What type of parts did they have? *Rods, wheels, pistons.* Develop rotary and reciprocal movements.

Combine *shape and action.* Partners, working in opposition. *Up/down. Backwards/ forwards. Side/side.*

Rotational movements—cogs, wheels, pulleys, conveyors.

Locomotion—pathways and patterns, *bridge shapes.*

Form a huge railway viaduct.

[30 minutes]

Conclusion

Discuss the pictorial and dynamic aspects of the theme. Draw out visual imagery from the children—discuss in terms of kinaestheic imagery.

Develop a *tableau vivant* through the use of individual, partner and small group activities. Include scenes from factories, mines, machines, chimneys, railways, roads, bridges and viaducts.

CRAFT, DESIGN AND TECHNOLOGY

Craft, Design and Technology or Designing and Making is a fairly recent development in primary schools. It involves children in active learning and, at its best, relates to their direct experiences. Primary CDT bears little resemblance to the old subject-based secondary school image at one time exemplified by the production of wrought-iron tea-pot stands and wooden letter racks. The main aim for the development of CDT in the primary school is that children should be encouraged to think for themselves. CDT is an excellent vehicle for encouraging children to develop the ability to solve problems which often, though not always, have a technological outcome. It involves children in developing the wide range of intellectual skills and concepts we have advocated, together with those social and physical skills likely to aid the transfer of learning.

Because CDT is not a discrete subject but more a process of learning, it follows that its development may take place across the curriculum. While this may help to dispel the myth that CDT is yet another subject in an already overloaded curriculum, it also raises the problem of how it may be structured if haphazard learning is to be avoided. One way that many schools have tackled this problem is to plan for the development of CDT as part of topic work.

The development of CDT topic work

Figure 3 shows the CDT process that is common to problem-solving models generally.

It may be seen that many of the skills/activities indicated in the diagram are common to those we have suggested and an integral part of good topic work.

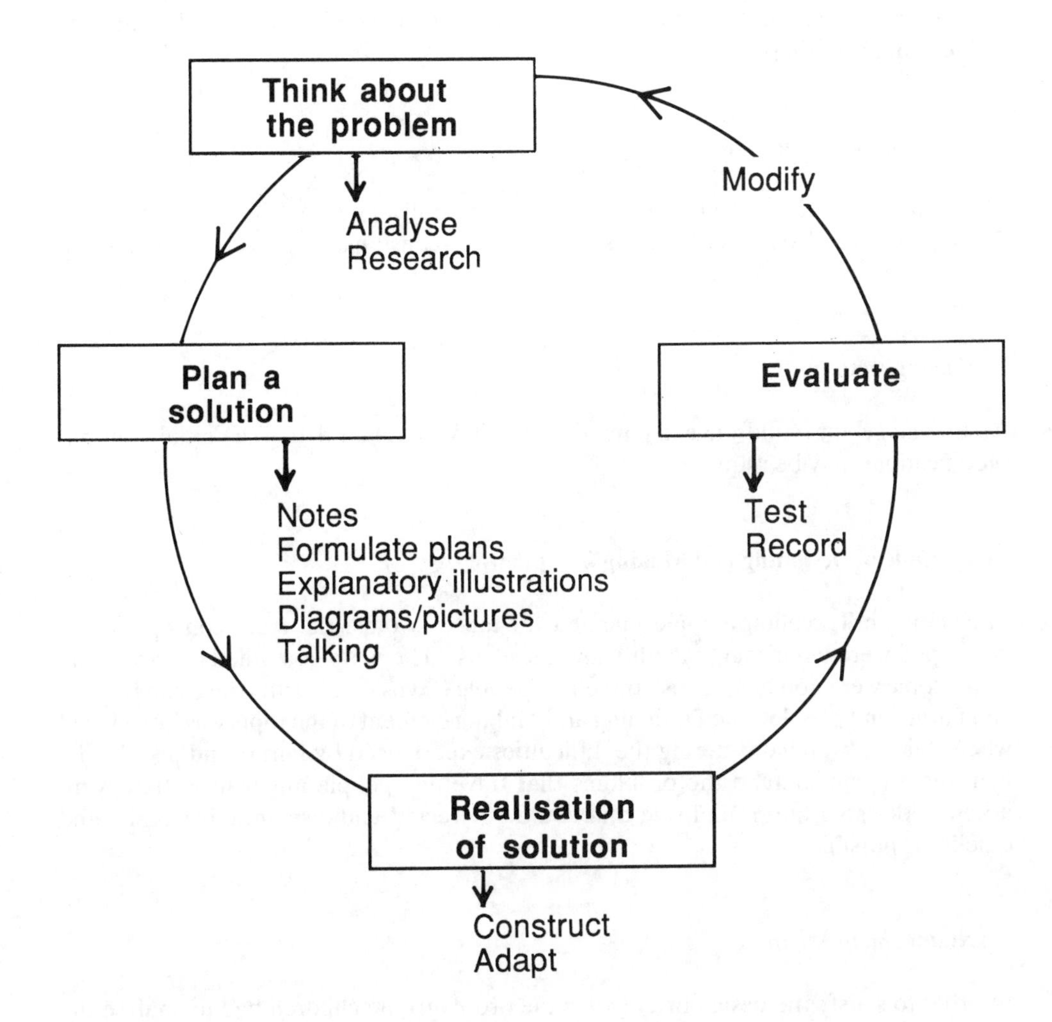

Figure 3. The CDT process.

Analysing the problem and synthesising

This first part of the CDT process involves the children in such activities as: questioning, research, discussion, categorising, collecting and interpreting data, evaluating, making judgements and inferences.

Planning a solution (designing)

In addition to the use of graphic techniques, drawings, plans, models and explanatory diagrams, this aspect of the CDT process involves the children in devising a range of solutions and communicating these to others. It may involve children in collecting data and forming hypotheses.

Realising the solution (making)

While this part of the CDT process model naturally engages the children in the development of physical skills, it also necessitates constant reference to the first two aspects of the process model.

Evaluating (testing)

At this stage the children examine the solution in relation to the initial criteria. Modifications may be required.

An example of Designing and Making in topic work

In a topic on Travelling People planned for ten-year-olds, the main concepts to be developed were 'efficiency, mobility and lifestyles'. The peoples studied as part of the whole topic were nomads, British travelling people (Gypsies), North American Indians and fairground people. The Designing and Making element of the topic was introduced when children were considering the difficulties experienced by fairground people. To help them to understand the problems that travelling people might have they were asked to design a fairground ride that could be erected and dismantled as easily and quickly as possible.

Analysing the problem

In order to satisfy the design brief (solve the problem) the children had to analyse the problem. They were involved, at this stage, in collecting data about old-fashioned and existing fairground rides and in finding the reasons for the need for efficiency in erecting and dismantling rides. Both aspects of the research were planned around visits to the local fair where data was collected by observation and by questioning fairground people. This data was then used as a basis for finding a solution to the problem. At this stage they had to make decisions about what they would make, the most appropriate materials to use (light but strong) and what structures would be safe.

Planning a solution (designing)

The topic was organised so that children were working in groups of three or four. Most of the groups came up with different ideas for a solution to the initial problem, but the two most interesting solutions were based upon well-established fairground rides, that is, the big wheel and a roundabout with horses. The group working on the big wheel worked together to predict the outcome by making a drawing of the finished model. They made detailed drawings of the wheel and cars for people to sit in—the latter were collapsible so that they could be packed efficiently for moving from one fairground to another. An important aspect of the design was the motive power. The children used a motor mounted in a Lego tower to make the Big Wheel work (see Figure 4).

Realising the solution and testing

The construction element of the CDT process is often what the children most enjoy. In this case quite a few of their plans went wrong and they had to return to the design stage to make the necessary amendments. For instance, they had great difficulty in keeping the wheel vertical, the fixings for the cars undid too easily, thus causing a safety hazard, and the motor mounting was not sufficiently sturdy (see Figure 5).

It can be seen from this example that children are encouraged to collect information and use it in an active way. This real involvement helps them to develop further their understanding of the difficulties of being a travelling person and the work can be developed to enhance the topic as a whole. The principle of including Designing and Making to enhance the development of concepts in topic work can be applied just as effectively with younger primary children. For instance, in a topic on transport, to develop the concept 'efficiency' some 5–6-year-olds were asked to design a vehicle that would carry as many big boxes as possible. They went through exactly the same problem-solving process as the older children. They tackled the problem by first collecting data on the sort of transport facilities already existing within a several-mile radius of the site. They listed the types of load usually carried by different forms of transport. They used their information to help them decide what they would like to make. One group decided that they would make a truck out of large construction materials. They drew their solutions first and some made a tape-recording of what they intended to make. Having made the truck and tested it in the school yard, they found two major design faults: when loaded the truck had collapsed in the middle, and the carrying platform was too small to carry a sufficient load. In this example, as in the previous one, children were engaged in first-hand experiences planned to further their understanding of the concepts being developed in the topic.

Setting the problems

The setting of problems is, perhaps, the most difficult aspect of Designing and Making. Much depends upon the teacher's ability to match the problem (design brief) to the ability of the child. If the solving of a problem is to help concept development then the teacher must plan not only the topic but also the Designing and Making element very carefully. There are many different ways of stating a design brief (problem) but there are certain criteria which may be helpful. For instance, consideration should be given to the number of variables, what physical skills are likely to be needed to solve the problem and the level of difficulty of the language used to state the problems. Developed in this way, Designing and Making becomes a significant extension and enhancement of the concepts and skills approach to topic work.

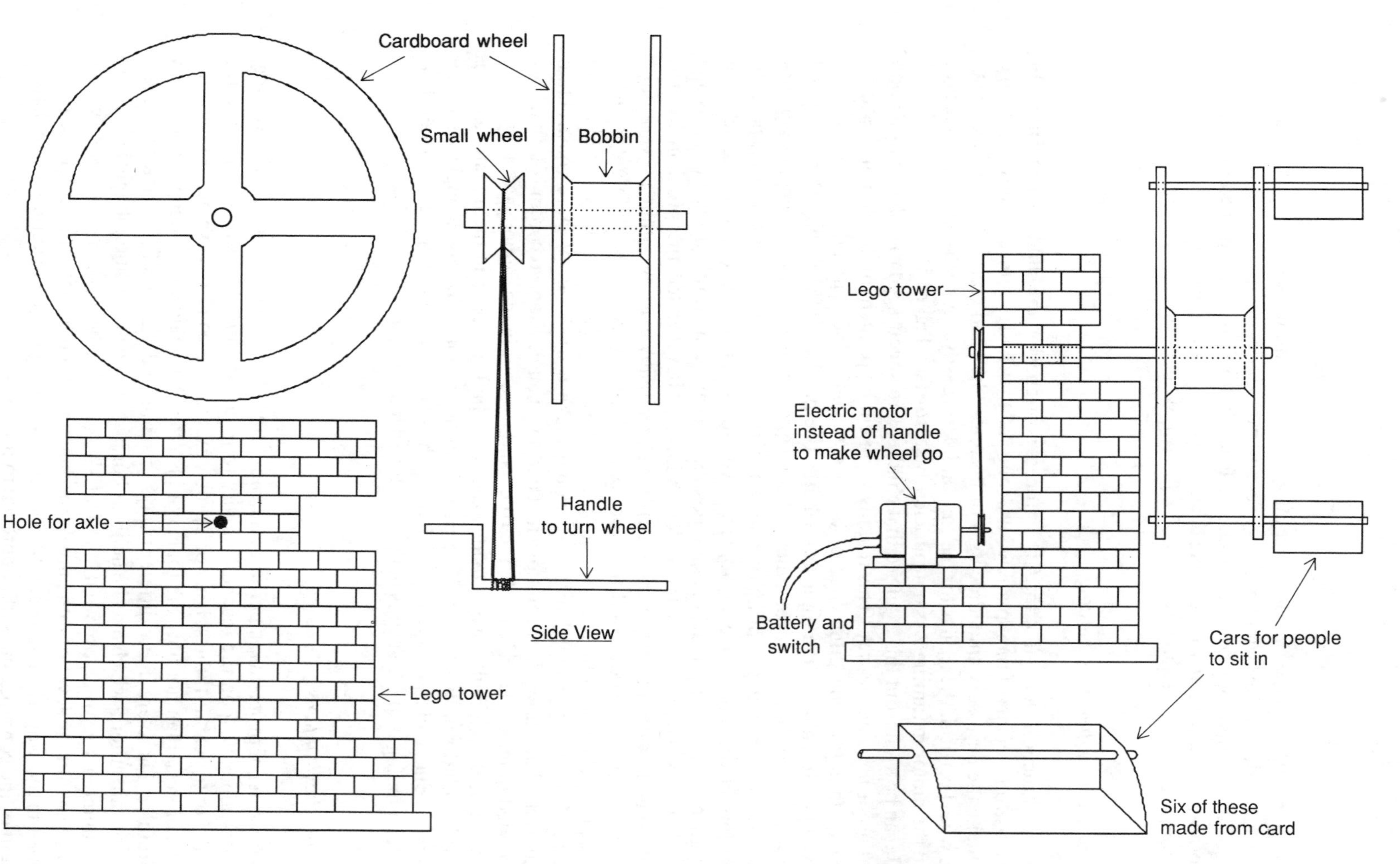

Figure 4. Pupils' design in CDT.

Improved design for keeping motor still

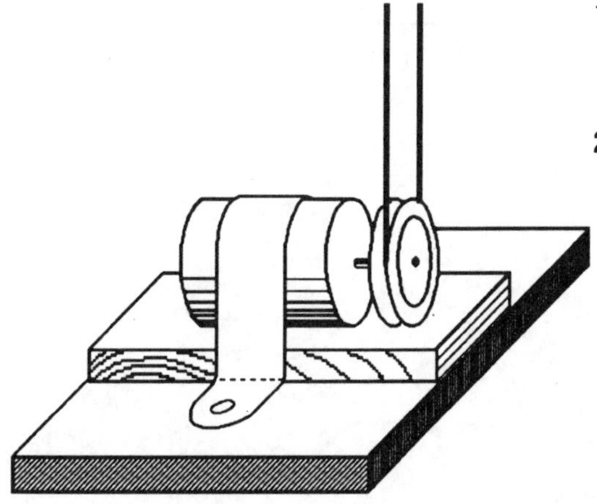

1. Fasten electric motor to wooden base with metal strip.
2. Build Lego tower around it.

Figure 5. The improved design.

FURTHER READING

Bloom, B. S. (ed.) (1956) *Taxonomy of Educational Objectives*, Book 1. Harlow: Longman.

Durkin, M. C. *et al.* (1969) *The Social Studies Curriculum.* Menlo Park, CA: Addison-Wesley.

Guilford, J. P. (1971) Creativity. In Williams, P. *et al.* (eds) *Personalities, Growth and Learning.* Harlow: Longman.

Gunning, S., Gunning, D. and Wilson, J. (1981) *Topic Teaching in the Primary School.* London: Croom Helm.

Halliday, M. A. K. (1969) Relevant models of language. *Educational Review*, **22**, no. 1, November.

Kerry, T. (ed.) (1982) *Teacher Education Project.* London: Macmillan.

Richardson, R. (1983) A new look at the educational visit. *Education 3–13*, December, 18–21.

Storer, R. (1985) Some aspects of Brinsley Colliery and the Lawrence connection. Privately published. Selston, Notts.

Chapter 4

Evaluation

The evaluation of topic work is something about which, at present, few schools and few teachers seem to have clear ideas that can be put into practice with reasonable ease. Evaluation ought to serve a number of purposes, of which the most important is to supplement and refine—if not replace—the impressionistic judgements teachers are prone to make about pupil achievement. Secondly, it must serve to provide evidence of progress in a wide range of knowledge, skill and attitudes. That this has proved difficult for teachers is confirmed by Eggleston and Kerry (1985), who report teachers as contending that progression in topic work was difficult to detect and that it was impossible to articulate the expectations of outcomes from a topic on Water followed by one on Dinosaurs (or Clothing through the Ages or whatever) except perhaps in terms of research and library skills. So, while progress relating to the skills of finding information, using books, contents pages, index pages and so on can perhaps be measured, as can the children's ability to put things 'into their own words' and generally show greater facility to use language appropriately, the central concern of good topic work—intellectual and affective growth—is ignored. Although research skills are important and should not be ignored, teachers need to know, for example, to what extent their pupils' understanding of important ideas is developing. This understanding is one of the central objectives of the work in each individual topic sequence and a central aim of the topic policy. If this progress in understanding is not or cannot be evaluated in a systematic way on the basis of evidence that teachers can observe and collect from the work their pupils do, then evaluation of progress can only be through superficial and fairly *ad hoc* impressions, with all the possibilities of misinterpretation and bias that they suffer from.

In addition to measuring the understanding of ideas, evaluations need to measure the pupils' increasing facility to call upon and use a range of thinking processes and the extent to which pupils' behaviour is a reflection of developing attitudes towards themselves as learners and towards other people as fellow members of the world society.

This kind of evaluation has, of course, a number of important spin-offs. Since development in understanding, skill and attitude are the aims refined into specific objectives in each topic work lesson plan, evaluation provides a measure of the extent to which aims and objectives are being met with each individual pupil and with groups of pupils. There can therefore be measurement of whether teachers have interpreted the objective correctly, matched the content appropriately to the pupils involved and, indeed, whether they need to modify their approach to improve the quality of outcome with this group of pupils next time, or with the next group of pupils when they tackle the same area of work.

It is important to remember that evaluation of topic work has to be continuous, providing sharply focused measures of performance based on evidence gleaned in quite specific situations in relation to a specific and limited objective. It is unlikely that effective evaluations will result if an attempt is made to measure the quality of performance in relation to a range of understanding and skill at the same time, even though, at times, it may seem that similar criteria have to be applied. This means that at reasonably frequent intervals, as the topic progresses, particular pieces of work or particular activities must be selected for evaluation, as they are completed or performed, against criteria that are clearly appropriate to the specific objective on which the work is based.

There is, of course, the problem of deciding how frequently such evaluations must be made. There will be occasions when every pupil will complete a similar individual piece of work that teachers can 'mark' in the traditional sense as part of the evaluation process. Certainly that must be part of the evidence to be collected. Other opportunities can only be provided by observation of individual pupils as they undertake activities and interact with other pupils. It is not, of course, possible to make any hard and fast rule that could be applied across a wide range of situations. It is self-evident, however, that evaluation as a process is only likely to be of value if a sufficient number of aspects of the work in a topic sequence, or a term or a year, are selected for each pupil over the full spread of developmental objectives—in terms of understanding of ideas, intellectual skill and affective progress.

If the points in the work to which evaluation processes are to be applied are spasmodically selected at infrequent intervals then there is as much danger of superficial and unbalanced judgements being made as there is with subjective impressions, since each point in the process of continuous evaluation provides only a small sample of the quality of performance related to a particular area of development. These, together, will eventually provide a more comprehensive and complete picture as they are collected and pieced together, but only if a sufficient number of items in each category has been chosen and acted upon.

This is the crux of good evaluation and is essential if teachers are to know how pupils are progressing and how effectively they are teaching. It needs as much careful consideration as the selection of objectives and the planning of activities to achieve those objectives. At the same time, the task of evaluation must be one that teachers can reasonably undertake in a situation that is already onerous in the demands it makes upon them. If this can be achieved then the data that is recorded allows teachers to make more than an evaluation of the quality of the response at a particular time and in a particular situation—valuable as this may be. Durkin *et al.* (1969) note three other ways in which frequent and quite specific evaluations add up to give a widely comprehensive picture. In the first place each subsequent and similar evaluation will indicate progress or otherwise in an individual skill, understanding or attitude. Secondly, a picture will develop in relation to the total class group and to the range of ability within the group. Thirdly, it becomes possible to use such data as a basis for comparing the quality of the teaching term by term or year by year as a factor in the school's appraisal of what it offers its clients and how that programme might be improved through staff development, resource provision and so on.

We have already suggested that evaluation is not likely to be easy. This is particularly so in the period during which teachers are learning how to establish appropriate criteria and how to use them. Initially it may be more time-consuming and less easy to administer than teachers would wish it to be—if it is then it will need the kind of responsibility, self-discipline and perseverence that teachers claim they wish to foster in their pupils to overcome such problems.

One way of making evaluation easier to administer and less time-consuming is to accept the contention that once an idea is selected as being worthwhile in a given context, then the gradual increase in understanding desired can be procured by getting pupils to think about the idea in a variety of different ways. By this means specific skills are applied at particular points in the learning sequence to produce a limited but definite increase in understanding.

Consider the topic on Whitby outlined on page 35. A main concept shown on the teacher's plan is that of interdependence. This is an important concept for children to acquire since it is basic to part of the understanding of the way society is organised and works. Generally society is organised in groups whose members have special knowledge, skills and functions—doctors, teachers, police officers, farmers, bricklayers, etc. We all depend upon these groups and the people within them for things we need but cannot readily provide for ourselves. What each of these groups is able to do affects what other groups are able to do in very important ways. Some of these effects are direct and straightforward and can be understood by even very young pupils, some are indirect and not readily evident, needing careful teasing out—a task for older, more experienced and more practised pupils. So we have a worthwhile concept—it tells us about an important aspect of society, it can be understood at different levels of sophistication and it can obviously transfer. Learning about interdependence in a topic on police officers will provide for conclusions to be drawn which could be applied to a situation where the importance of farmers or workers in the fishing industry was being considered.

In the context of Whitby, as a result of their visit to the town, the pupils identify a number of important people who have special jobs to do: the harbour officer, people who work in fishing, customs officers, coastguards, harbour pilots, weather forecasters, the lifeboat crew. Here is a wealth of information that can form the basis of a study of the concept of interdependence. Following the ladder for thinking about an idea or concept the first task the pupils might be asked to undertake would be, with perhaps some sharing out of the task:

1. Describing

- Identifying and making a list of all the people who have special jobs to do at the harbour.

- Arranging to interview them about their job or inviting them to come into school to talk about their job.
- Writing descriptions of their daily routine, things they do at special times, kinds of problems they have to deal with, etc.
- Drawing pictures of them working, showing the kind of tools and machinery they use, practising particular skills, etc.

This would be followed by the succeeding steps on the ladder:

2. Classifying

Listing and describing the special knowledge and skills each person has. Reading about their training and how they learn their job. Classifying the various knowledge and skill in terms of criteria such as:

- ensuring people do not break the law
- keeping people safe and out of danger
- interpreting maps and pictures
- understanding difficult ideas like tides, navigation procedures, etc.
- getting on with other people
- helping other people to do their job more efficiently.

3. Reasons for/causes of

Making a recruitment brochure for each job, showing what sort of people are needed, what has to be learned and how important the job is in terms of things like safety, etc., as classified above.

4. Consequences and effects

Writing a story, making a simulation or drawing a comic strip which tells of a ship that has to enter port without a harbour pilot, of a fishing boat crew who cannot receive the weather report because their radio is out of order or of the sailors who are rescued by the skill of the lifeboat crew.

5. Making judgements and giving opinions

- Writing about the job we would most like to do and why.
- Trying to compare jobs and give reasons why one is more important than another.
- Group presentations at assembly to include descriptions of one of the jobs. Justification of its importance in terms of: which other groups depend on them and in what ways; what would happen if their skills, etc., were not available; why it is a job worth doing and gives job satisfaction.

It can be seen that such a sequence of work may take quite a long time to complete—certainly it is likely that pupils will return to it on several occasions. However, each time they are dealing with the same idea but from a different point of view—so going up the ladder of understanding. Simultaneously they are practising different skills—first simple listing and description, then classifying, comparing and contrasting. This is followed by looking for reasons, suggesting causes, then predicting consequences, extrapolating from known to unknown situations and finally making evaluations and judgements and expressing opinions.

Such a wide range of activities over a reasonably long period of time provides:

- for evaluation to be a continuous process with evidence of performance being collected as it occurs
- for performance to be measured clearly and precisely in a small unit of behaviour relating to a specific stage of understanding and/or a specific thinking process
- for fairly rapid comparisons to be made across the group, so that faults in the teaching process affecting the whole group can be quickly identified and remedied.

What are described above are the activities the pupils are involved in as they climb the conceptual/skill ladder. At what points and against what criteria might evaluations be made? Devising appropriate and valid criteria for the purposes of evaluation presents problems in the area of topic work unless the curriculum in this area is based on an adequate set of objectives. In the chapter on Planning it was suggested that objectives are only likely to be of value as a basis for the process of evaluation if they are clear, precise and particular. In the same context we have suggested earlier in this chapter that the points in the learning sequence selected for evaluation must be sharply focused on quite specific situations concerned with knowledge, skill or attitudinal growth. As Hilda Taba (1962, page 325) suggests, 'The evaluation programme is only as good as is the platform of objectives which it serves!'

Teachers need therefore to select sufficient evaluation points to provide information about the full range of skills and the kind of knowledge and understanding the objectives are seeking to foster.

It is not possible to provide a model evaluation programme that can be applied to all topics, but certain principles have now been established and others can be added:

1. Evaluation needs to be continuous and relatively frequent.
2. Evaluation needs to be closely related to the learning objectives.
3. Evaluation must cover the full range of learning that is intended.
4. Aspects of the learning process selected for evaluation should be sharply focused on a specific situation.
5. The criteria for evaluation must reflect recognisable pupil behaviour in terms of the objective being evaluated and its expected outcomes.

What might such criteria be? Again, as with the selection of fundamental ideas, help has been around for some time, but has been largely ignored. Taba (1962) and her colleagues made a number of valuable suggestions that are applicable to a wide range of objectives, and Harlen (1977) and her colleagues have, similarly, provided checklists as a means of measuring progress and achievement. There follows an attempt to use both these systems to provide a procedure which, with practice and a little perseverence, teachers could apply, so that progress in topic work can be both secured and assessed.

The first criterion is *inclusiveness of thought*. The concern here is whether the child has provided a multiple response to the task. In tasks based on the visit to Whitby this criterion can be applied in a precise way to most of the tasks set. If it were applied to task 2—which is concerned with the first stage in understanding the concept of interdependence, i.e., listing, describing and classifying the skills and knowledge people have—then evidence about attainment of this objective is provided by the extent to which they have included in their answer all the skill and knowledge it is reasonable to expect from the information the pupils had about each individual. For example, in the case of the harbour pilot, the child who has referred to

- knowledge about the channel danger areas
- the effects of tides, winds and currents
- the meaning of the various signals and messages
- the rules of the seaway
- the ability to read radar
- the ability to use the radio
- the ability to handle a variety of ships
- the ability to estimate speed and distance in relation to different ships

has made a better response than the pupil who has only mentioned being able to use the radio, read the radar screen and know the rules of the seaway.

The objective demands, and the notion of developing understanding, demands a multiple response in this context. A multiple response is a better quality answer in a listing activity than a single response.

This task also included classifying the various skills and knowledge the people working in the harbour need to have. The same criterion can be applied. The pupil who can think of four ways of classifying the knowledge and skills identified has made a better quality response than the pupil who only classified in two ways. Inclusiveness of thought is a criterion that can be applied to any situation where the objective seeks a multiple response from the pupil in the analysis of the information that was available (see Figure 6).

This listing/describing activity (stage 1) tests the extent to which Lindsay has gathered and retained the important information her visit to the RSPCA shelter provided.

A second criterion is *elaboration of response*, and this can be applied in conjunction with the criterion of inclusiveness of thought or independently of it. Elaboration simply means giving more detail in connection with each item included in a response. Returning again to the consideration of interdependence in the context of Whitby, task 4 is concerned with making judgements and giving opinions.

One reason for selecting a job as being the one we would most like to do might be that it is a responsible job and a lot of people depend upon it being done properly. If pupils included statements of that kind in their response teachers would be reasonably happy. However, they would be much happier, presumably, if the pupils elaborated by indicating the different ways in which different people did depend on that job being done well. The first response of 'Being a harbour pilot is an important job because a lot of ships have to be brought into harbour safely', would develop into 'Being a harbour pilot is an important job because a lot of ships have to be brought into harbour safely. The pilot has to make sure the ship does not hit a sandbank which might damage the ship or even make it sink. This would mean that the harbour might be blocked so that other ships could not get in or out, the cargo would be damaged and the passengers and crew might be killed.' The difference in the quality of response here is not simply that the initial opinion is justified but that the extent of the pupil's understanding of the concept of interdependence is made significantly clearer. Similarly Lindsay, our seven-year-old from Radcliffe Infants, is able not only to indicate changes but to elaborate on the reasons and effects of those changes. She indicates clearly that not only can she identify and provide evidence of change from the pictures she has seen and drawn (see Figure 7) but she can discuss, reason about and justify those changes, so making her greater understanding manifest.

A third criterion is *tentativeness*. This criterion can be applied to all those responses where the teacher recognises possible limitations to the evidence on which conclusions are likely to be drawn. Primary school pupils ought to be encouraged, right from the start, to appreciate these limitations and to accept that their conclusions may not be definitive or absolutely accurate. Encouragement from teachers for pupils to try to see the full range of variables in a situation, to look for qualification of first impressions, to seek 'cons' as well as 'pros', is essential for both cognitive and affective development. The earlier this quality of thought is encouraged the more likely it is that children will become truly analytical and critical thinkers.

Tentativeness could certainly be a criterion applied to the task of comparing jobs, which is one of the activities suggested on page 71. A pupil who suggested that customs officers do not have as dangerous a job as the lifeboat crew but added that, on the other hand, customs officers may have to deal with quite dangerous people who are trying to smuggle drugs and other things into the country, would be showing signs of tentativeness and a willingness to qualify and temper conclusions. Any response by a pupil which suggests that the information they have presently available has possible limitations and therefore the conclusions that can be drawn may not be entirely accurate should be given credit for moving away from the uncritical, assertive stance young people often adopt.

Gunning, Gunning and Wilson (1981, page 133) give a sample of the work of a pupil, Lester, whose general level of presentation was very incompetent but who, in considering the reasons for siting a castle (stage 3), wrote

> 'at the castle we saw was high walls so peple cold see a long way and thick to keep peple out it was on a big hill but i think not too big so peple could get in if attackers.'

Here, despite his problems, Lester makes it quite clear that the siting of a castle has to take into account the ease with which the people in the surrounding settlements could reach safety at a time of attack as well as presenting problems to the enemy.

Similarly pupils at an Armthorpe school near Doncaster were considering whether they would prefer living in Armthorpe today or a hundred years ago. Their immediate choice was for the clean, quiet rural Armthorpe but subsequent discussion suggested that perhaps there were pros as well as cons about modern Armthorpe which could not be ignored and which made the decision harder—hence their tentativeness.

A fourth criterion is *abstractness*. This is a sign of both sophisticated thinking and, probably, appropriate vocabulary matching the thinking.

We will stay with the questions of interdependence and task 3—writing a story intended to get the pupil to consider the effects of people having the kind of skill and knowledge that other people can depend on so that they in their turn can work

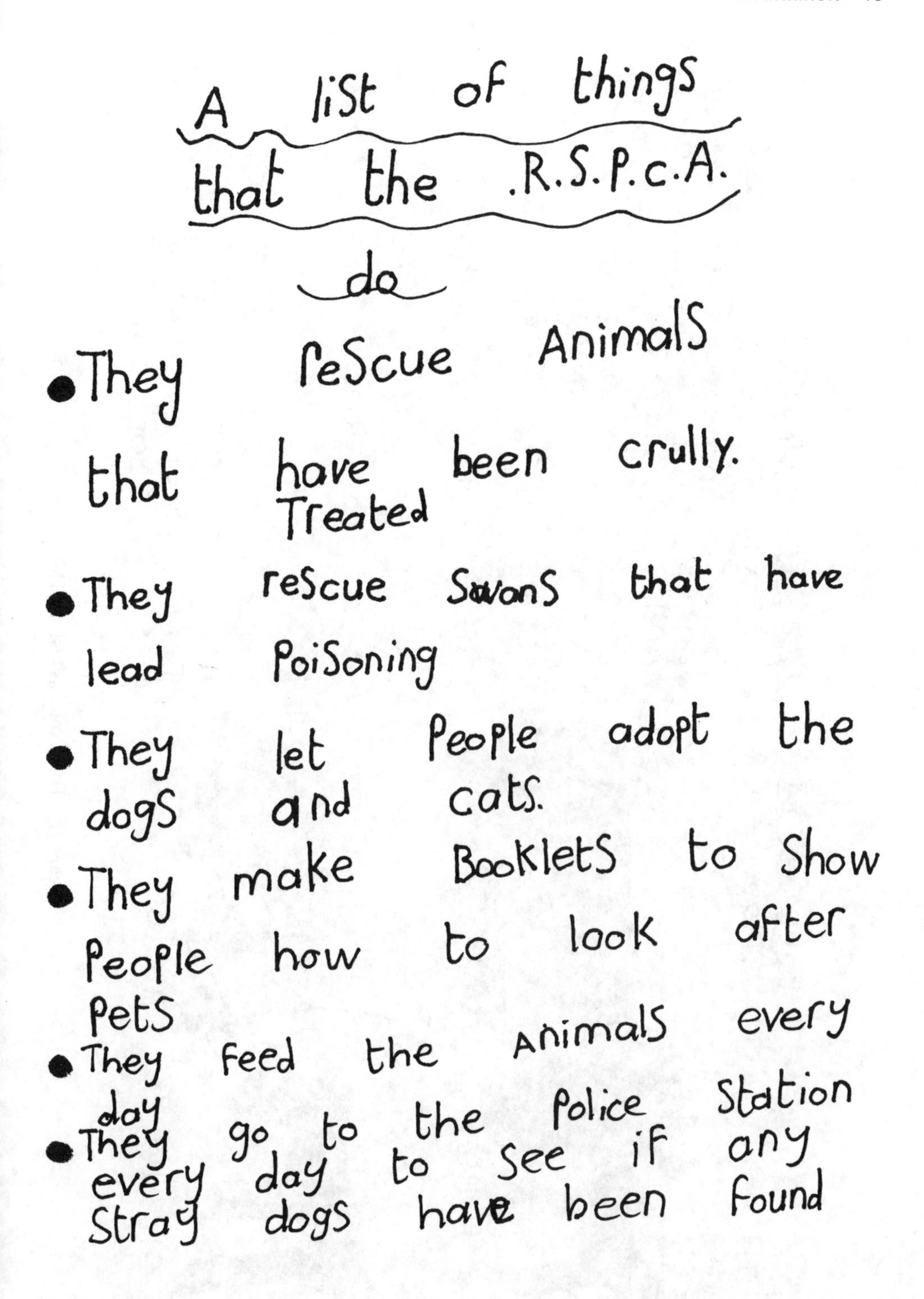

Figure 6. Lindsay, a seven-year-old, lists six aspects of the work of the RSPCA.

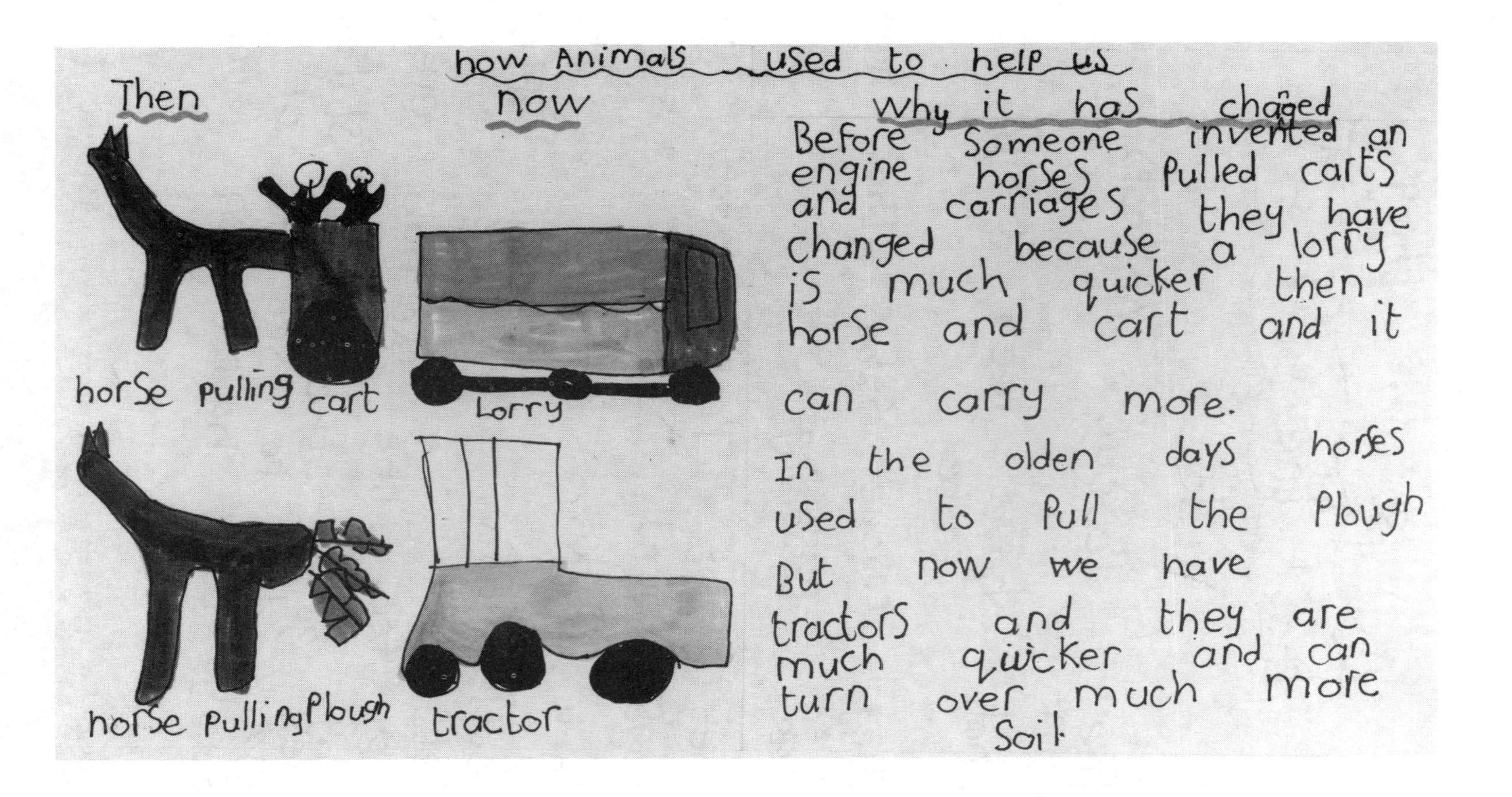

Figure 7. 'How Animals Used to Help Us'.

effectively. Suppose a pupil's answer to this task included a statement which suggested that having a harbour pilot who knew the channel and tides, etc., well was a more *efficient* way of getting a ship into harbour than leaving every ship's captain to do it himself. Suppose also a pupil referred to an echo sounder as helping the fish workers to be more *economic* or to a piece of equipment as being a means of *labour saving*. Such suggestions, of efficiency and economics, even if expressed in different vocabulary, e.g., 'to make more money in a shorter time' instead of 'to be economic', ought not to be ignored. The pupil who is beginning to think in this way needs to be encouraged to use such abstractions since they encompass more meaning than answers expressed in concrete terms. The pupil who suggests that more money can be made with less time and effort can be introduced to the word 'economic' by the teacher so that he or she comes to use that word and other similar abstractions without specific prompts.

There will be other examples of pupils moving away from the immediate and concrete which ought to be encouraged through teachers' questions and prompts. For example, a ten-year-old boy at Armthorpe Junior School was considering the effects of not having a damp course in a house during his topic on Homes, a stage 4 task on the ladder. His immediate conclusion was that the house would be damp and the wallpaper and plaster might come off. With further encouragement he began to consider, include and elaborate such second-order and more abstract notions as the health of the occupants and even the fact that the house would be expensive to live in because of constant redecoration and repair. This is really quite sophisticated thinking. However, such thinking is not confined to pupils as old as ten. Jayne and Leah, six-year-olds at Radcliffe-on-Trent Infants, Nottingham, were considering the effects of living without fire (see Figure 8). They knew it would be cold but moved into such second-order extrapolations as coalmen losing their jobs and it not being possible to manufacture metal. Their inclusiveness encompasses both immediate concrete and more abstract consequences.

There will be no sudden dramatic change towards abstractness, since the majority of pupils will tend to use concrete terms throughout their primary school career. This is not a reason for being unaware of this criterion for evaluation and for not applying it whenever it seems appropriate. Certainly teachers who are not aware are unlikely to develop a teaching strategy that will encourage the use of more abstract words referring to a quality or condition without immediate and tangible elements.

The literature (see Durkin *et al.*, 1969) refers to a range of possible evaluation criteria, and it is certainly possible for teachers to develop their own. However, the four listed above are perhaps the most useful and applicable across a wide range of tasks when looking for signs that the pupil is making progress in terms of developing ideas and thinking processes. They are especially useful in that they can be used by teachers as they look over the pupil's shoulder as the task is undertaken or alternatively when the work is reviewed on completion. In both such situations the ability to use such evaluation criteria as the basis for teaching interventions and feedback to pupils about the quality of their work is clearly an important skill. In addition, the basis for records and profiles and for conveying sensible and understandable information to colleagues and parents is established.

In the context of this book and our general intention to develop an equal opportunities perspective one further criterion needs to be given special attention. It provides both teacher and pupil with the same valuable feedback and information about progress

Good things

- No fires in houses.
- No cigarettes.
- No forest fires.
- No one would catch fire.
- No Volcanoes to burn houses.

Bad things

- it would be cold.
- it would be dark.
- we could not cook.
- we could not have Bonfires.
- no electricety.
- we would not be able to go on holiday. abroad
- we would not be oble to make metal.
- coalmen would loose their Job.
- rockets would not be able to blast off

Figure 8. 'Living without Fire'.

and quality in understanding as the criteria mentioned above but from a slightly different viewpoint. This criterion can be referred to as *decentring*.

Teachers should seek every opportunity to recognise this ability in their pupils and the work they produce and to encourage it. Pupils who are able to decentre are readily able to see another person's point of view and will attempt to express the opinions and feelings of others and include them in reasoning about a problem or situation. Such pupils will see, for example, good things and not such good things in different cultures, including their own. On the other hand, pupils who have not yet developed this ability will tend to be self-centred and ethnocentric. They will see their point of view as being the most appropriate and logical—the way things should be.

It is hoped that decentring will lead to what Bhikhu Parekh (1985) calls sympathetic imagination, and any evaluation needs to consider this area. We agree with Parekh who writes:

> We simply cannot understand other cultures, societies and historical epochs without sympathetic imagination, that is, without rising above our own values, preferences and views of the world and entering into their world with an open mind. We cannot understand others if we refuse to recognise their identity and respect their individuality, but insist on seeing them in our terms. It is only by means of sympathetic imagination that we can cross the space that separates us from other individuals and understand why they view and respond to the world in a certain manner. Without sympathetic imagination we remain prisoners of our own limited worlds and lack the ability to enrich and expand them.

The value of these criteria is in their universal applicability. They can be used as a framework for a wide range of observation—many rather than few—over a significant period in situations that are observed and listened to, as well as in looking at written, drawn or other more tangible outcomes the pupil has produced.

Details of how some of the criteria might be applied are included on pages 82–7 from examples of lesson notes provided by a postgraduate student for an exercise on how an idea might be pursued through activities and how evaluated. The numbers in the third column refer to the stage on the ladder of (1) identifying and describing, (2) classifying, etc., as described earlier. The ideas chosen to be pursued are 'interdependence', 'environmental influence' and 'social and technological change'. This exercise is based on Figure 9, which suggests that progression can be evaluated along two dimensions—a hierarchical progression of understanding which manifests itself by the pupil's ability to provide evidence of reasoning about the particular idea at each stage on the ladder, and a lateral progression where the quality of response at each stage is measured in terms of three of the five criteria mentioned above. This table summarises the principles on which the process of evaluation of understanding and thinking described so far in this chapter is based.

The strategies the student teacher is employing here make up the final stages of a coherent evaluation process and allow statements to be made not simply about the quality of the pupil's work (i.e. that the pupil is including more facts or reasons or consequences, etc., is able to give more relevant details about each and is willing to see different points of view), but also about the pupil's general intellectual development in fairly specific but easily understood terms which are valuable yardsticks for parents, other teachers, employers and so on. We must have in mind the long-term value of this development. Aspects of development which are signs of increased intellectual ability include the ability to handle and control an increasing number of variables simulta-

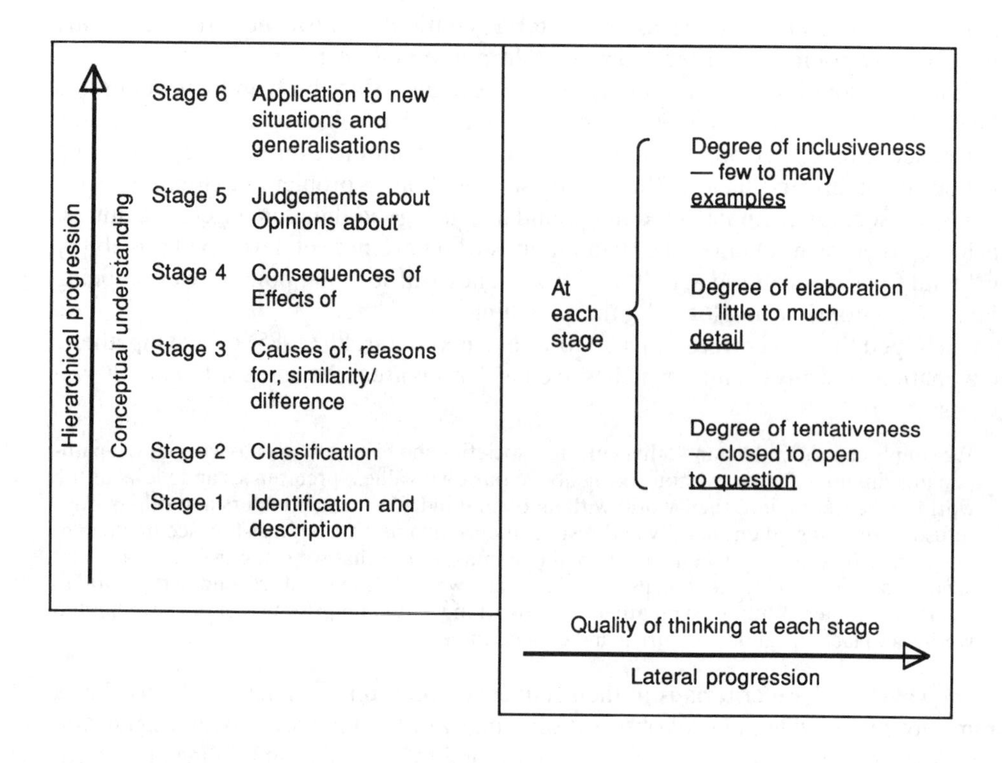

Figure 9. Lateral and vertical progression.

neously and an increased ability to develop and sustain more elaborated logical sequences of explanation, argument, justification, etc. (see Figure 10). Evaluations based on the criteria listed help us to do this.

In order to monitor and evaluate children's progress in Designing and Making one Nottinghamshire school has devised a system for continuous assessment of a child's behaviour/response to problem-solving. The assessment takes the form of a three-stage behavioural checklist and is intended to be used for the whole of the primary age range. The checklist identified the types of behaviour, from low level (1) to high level (3), that may be observed/expected at each stage of the Designing and Making (problem-solving) process. The first part of the checklist deals with the child's ability to identify/ tackle a problem in terms of relevance, to break the problem down into component parts, to tackle the problem without help, and so on. The design aspect of the process is more complex and is split into two parts. The first deals with the child's ability to demonstrate originality and the second deals with the more straightforward matter of skills.

Designing: skills

1. Is unable to understand scale. Sometimes makes two- or three-dimensional pictorial representation.

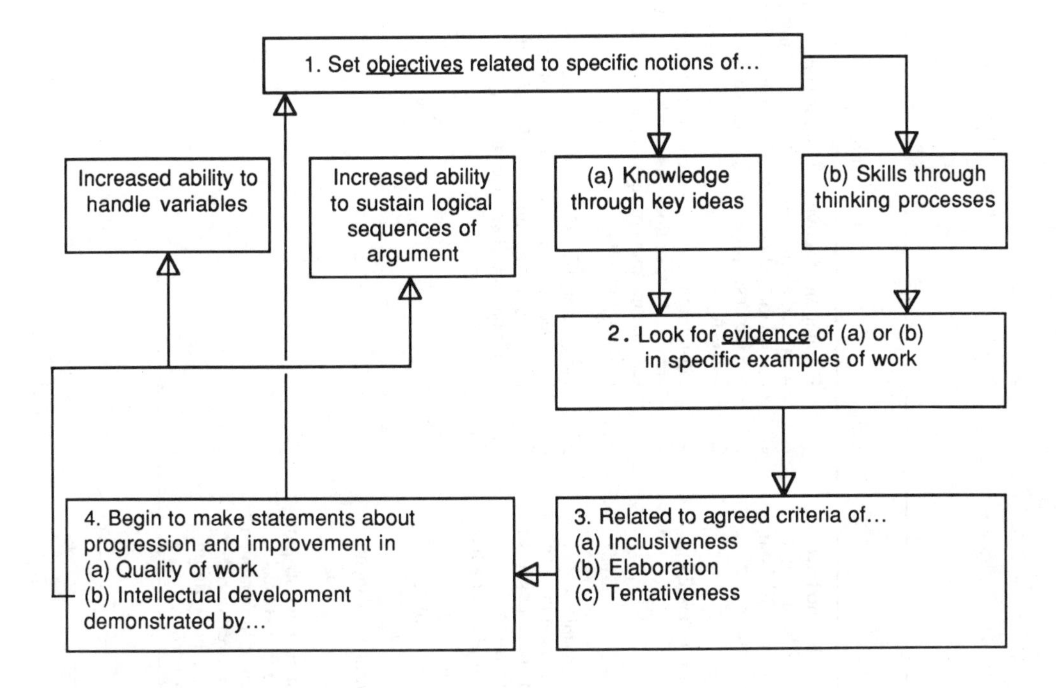

Figure 10. Evaluation strategy.

2. Attempts a two-dimensional representation with more than one view. May attempt an estimate of dimensions. Includes a number of details. Takes into account and records the suitability of certain materials.
3. Draws to scale and includes all relevant details. Draws plans and elevations. Takes into account and records the suitability of certain materials. Communicates ideas clearly in a variety of media.

Modelling and testing are dealt with in a similar way.

Modelling the design

1. Child's solution fails because of inappropriate materials. Frequently needs to seek help. Lacks physical skills necessary. Has difficulty translating the ideas and realising the solution.
2. Generally selects suitable materials and tools and is able to use these to model the design, but sometimes needs help.
3. Models a design with efficiency and minimum help. Shows a willingness to adjust to ideas and makes appropriate modifications as he or she progresses.

Topic title	Idea	Ladder stage	Activities	Criteria	Evaluation
Whitby Any port harbour topic	Interdependence	1	1. Identifying the range of people who have special jobs to do at a port/harbour, e.g., harbour officer, fishing boat crew, lifeboat crew, coastguards, customs officers, weather forecasters, pilots. Describing, listing their jobs. Interviews, drawings of them working.	INCLUSIVENESS	Evaluation of activities 1 and 2. Have they identified all the people whom they have information about? Have they included in the job descriptions their main knowledge and skills? Pilot: knowledge about channel, danger areas, effects of tides and winds. Rules of the seaway, meaning of signals. How to use radar, radio, etc.
People who help us Fishing boat crew Could be adapted to any similar group, e.g., police, fire officers		1/2/3/4 3 4	2. Listing and describing the special knowledge and skills each person has. Reading about training and how they learn their job. Classifying their various knowledge and skill in terms of criteria like: • doing their job efficiently • keeping people safe and out of danger • making sure people obey the law Making a recruitment brochure saying how important their job is. 3. Writing a story, simulation or comic strip of the problems that beset a ship that has to enter port without a pilot or of lifeboatmen who lose certain equipment overboard, etc., or of fishermen whose echo sounding equipment or radio is out of order.	ELABORATION	Do they explain why each skill or area of knowledge is important in relation to the criteria and what might be the effect if they didn't have such knowledge?

Topic title	Idea	Ladder stage	Activities	Criteria	Evaluation
		5	4. The job we would like to do best and why. Group prepare presentation to include descriptions in written, oral, pictorial form of one of the jobs. Justification in terms of criteria like: • why job is worth doing • who depends on them • why it provides job satisfaction, etc.	INCLUSIVENESS	Evaluation of activity 4. Have they included all the main aspects of the job—training, skills, use of technology, how people need them, etc., in presenting the case?
				ELABORATION	Do they go into detail about the different ways in which people would depend on them; the ways in which training/skills, etc., would make them more competent and efficient; what they like about the nature of the job compared with other jobs, e.g., open air, not routine, meeting people, helping people?
				TENTATIVENESS	Do they acknowledge their *interdependence* and how they would rely upon others?

Topic title	Idea	Ladder stage	Activities	Criteria	Evaluation
Farms	Environmental influence	1	1. Listing, describing the farm in terms of physical features—relief, soil, drainage, climate/weather, position in relation to centres of population, etc.	INCLUSIVENESS	Evaluation of activity 1. Have they included all the main features that can reasonably be expected from their observations, or from drawings, maps, diagrams, descriptions in books or by farmer? Hilly areas, low or flat areas, streams, ditches, kind of soil.
Farming in a given area		1	2. Comparing one farm with another in relation to 1 above at descriptive level.		
Farm study in locality		1	3. Drawing plans, maps, pictures to show use of land—crops and animals. Using colour, symbols, keys, scale, contours, as appropriate.	ELABORATION	Do they describe different areas in terms of windswept or sheltered, well drained or wet, stony, sandy or loam, even if in simpler vocabulary? Do they refer to seasonal differences, to length of grass at different heights, etc?
Food		1	4. Making display/frieze of maps, drawings, diagrams, photographs, describing and detailing characteristics of one or several farms.		
People who help us		2	5. Classifying farm(s) according to pupils own criteria—hilly, lowland, upland, dairy, beef, sheep, arable, as appropriate. Labelling pictures, the display, etc.	TENTATIVENESS	Do they include any good *and* bad points, advantages *and* disadvantages? There is a stream which is useful for drinking water for the cows in summer but very often floods in the winter.
Plants		2 2	6. Taking and recording weather readings on different parts of the farm or on the different farms. Making simple analyses of soil samples.	INCLUSIVENESS	Evaluation of activity 7. Do they set up tests for all variables • good loam—cold • good loam—warm • good loam—dry • good loam—wet • clay soil—cold, etc.
		2 3	7. Testing soils in relation to composition when wet/dry. Growing plants in different soils. Comparing rates of germination, growth. Suggesting reasons for differences. Recording in pictorial form, using graphs, written records.		

Topic title	Idea	Ladder stage	Activities	Criteria	Evaluation
		2	8. Observing, reading about animals in terms of feeding habits, ability to withstand weather conditions, soil conditions, etc.	ELABORATION	Do they give reasons for their results which indicate they have considered cause and effect on farmers' productivity? Seeds grown in good loam but cold took a long time to germinate and grew slowly. *This would mean the harvest would be late and possibly the crop would not ripen.*
			9. Observing, reading about farm routine—intensity of care required by different animals.		
		3	10. Suggesting reasons, making inferences about which part of farm or which farm best for growing crops, rearing animals. Comparing inferences with actual records.	TENTATIVENESS	Do they suggest other possibilities—can brighter children see the possibility of choice of breed or variety overcoming problems? 'Even though this farm is in *x* it may be best to have highland cattle because . . .'
		6 2	11. Making generalisations about optimum conditions for different kinds of farming. Summarising and classifying plants/animals—drawing and labelling.		Evaluation of activity 12.
		1 5	12. Looking at or drawing maps of other areas. Identifying and describing main characteristics. Suggesting what sort of farming might be carried out. Using maps on various scales. Case studies. Making judgements about best place to develop a dairy farm—arable farm, etc.	INCLUSIVENESS	Have they identified, listed, described *all* the relevant features it is reasonable to expect: • land height • drainage • soil types if possible • wind direction • liability to flooding Have they linked characteristics to farming activity, soil type to crop/animal, land height to crop/animal, etc.?
		5 6	13. Simulation group activity. 'This is your island'—what kind of farming could you develop there?	TENTATIVENESS ELABORATION	Have they given reasons why a soil/height/drainage characteristic is suited, e.g., sheep like short grass and have thick woollen protection so are most suited to higher, windswept areas where soil is poorer and only supports short grass growth? Do they see more than one possibility? This area is better for cattle than sheep although in a very dry period sheep could be put on it.

Topic title	Idea	Ladder stage	Activities	Criteria	Evaluation
Victorians My family Living in the past Homes	Social and technological change	1	1. Comparison of pupil's home with great-grandma's home or home of specified period, listing and describing differences in relation to such factors as, • how the house is heated • how the cooking/washing is done • storing food • how people entertained themselves, etc. Many other areas possible. Describing in writing, drawing, plans, possibly photographs. Reading books as appropriate. Visits to museums.	ELABORATION INCLUSIVENESS	Evaluation of activity 1 Have they described/listed all the major differences that is reasonable to expect? Are the differences detailed? Not just coal fire as against central heating but coal fires which have to be made in each room, laid and lit each morning and frequently 'mended' as against radiators in each room which are all heated from one boiler—all of which can be turned on or off quickly and simply.
		2	2. Listing and labelling differences under different headings: • keeping the family clean • keeping warm		
			3. Identifying causes for difference in terms of new knowledge, inventions, discovery of new materials, changes in values. Finding out about and writing/drawing about how electricity, plastics, etc., were discovered.		
		1	4. Drawing a time-line for washing day in great grandma's day and today. Noting differences in procedures, amount of work involved, how hard work is, e.g., getting washing boiler started, and using dolly tub, mangle, etc., compared with washing machine.		
		1 2	5. Drawing cartoon strips of other activities—shopping and food preparation/cleaning house, having a wash/bath. Noting, listing and classifying differences against criteria such as time, labour, people involved, convenience, etc.		

Topic title	Idea	Ladder stage	Activities	Criteria	Evaluation
		2/3	6. Testing materials in terms of ease of cleaning, e.g., plastic *v* wood. Recording and displaying differences.	INCLUSIVENESS	Evaluation of activity 6. Have they set up tests for a range of materials? • paint, plastic, tiles, stainless steel • distemper, wood, cement, stone.
		2/3	7. Testing machine operations—hoovering *v* hand brushing.		
		4	8. Writing a story, acting out a time when there were no refrigerators, tinned food, vacuum cleaners, central heating. Emphasising effects in terms of convenience, labour, leisure.	ELABORATION	Do they record detail of time taken, effort required, quality of finish, feelings involved?
			9. Interview Mum—which thing would she miss having in the home and why?	TENTATIVENESS	Have they identified any possible arguments in these situations? Possibly not in activity 6, but if task were above entertainment there might be a lot of reasons why making own entertainment is better in some ways than just watching television.
		4	Listing and labelling things that are in the home that: • save a lot of time • save a lot of hard work		
			10. Making a frieze, display of lists under appropriate headings.		
		5	11. Relating changes to new knowledge and values—especially such things as bathrooms, food storage, diet, foods out of season, etc. Effects on health, etc. Which four things do you want to have in your home, etc? Why I prefer my home to a home in Victorian times.		
			12. Reading about, looking up statistics about reasons why people died, became ill, did not grow so tall, etc., in Victorian or other times.		

Testing the design

1. Is unable to plan a test in a systematic way and tries to test in a random manner related to the original problem and design.
2. Sets up some criteria for testing, relating this to the problem and design. Carries out tests in a fairly efficient manner but may need help.
3. Sets up comprehensive criteria for testing related to problem and design. Carries out testing in a methodical and efficient manner. Shows an ability/willingness to modify ideas according to test results.

Affective development and the measurement of its progress is of no less importance to teachers who seek to evaluate the work they are doing with their pupils. Perhaps the best approach to this is that devised by Harlen *et al.* (1977) in their excellent materials published under the *Match and Mismatch* banner.

The approach to evaluation of the understanding of ideas and development of skills described earlier in this chapter proposes criteria that can be applied to measure progression in both simultaneously. For example, one stage in the understanding of 'efficiency' is that the consequences or effects of being efficient can be predicted—the vertical progression in the chart (Figure 9). At the same time the quality of the reasoning about consequences can be measured by applying criteria like inclusiveness, elaboration and tentativeness. Affective development is of a different character. Here we are looking for signs of quite distinct behaviour which in total add up to a willingness and ability to participate effectively in learning situations but which are nevertheless discrete and separate forms of behaviour. Harlen *et al.* (1977, page 248) list them quite comprehensively—curiosity, originality, co-operation, perseverance, open-mindedness, self-criticism, responsibility and independence. What they stress is that any evaluation of progress in the affective domain is likely to be based on:

(a) an extension of what good teachers do already
(b) a broad interpretation of the practice of observing pupils, i.e., watching, listening and talking to pupils as well as looking at the products of their activities
(c) a range of frequent observations made in specific but varied situations
(d) a recognition that observations can be used immediately as a means of formative evaluation from which an immediate teaching point can develop to reinforce or modify the behaviour observed
(e) a recognition that keeping a record of observations in a systematic way adds to the value of those observations in terms of each individual's profile of overall progress and achievement, and of the teacher's own effectiveness.

In principle the procedures and the rationale for those procedures are the same for the evaluation of both cognitive and affective development. The criteria Harlen *et al.* (1977) suggest are more detailed, and provide for observations to be interpreted in relation to normal behaviours at different stages of development. Each characteristic is described on a three-stage checklist on a similar basis to the approach used for the evaluation of CDT activities described earlier (see page 80). As is pointed out by Harlen *et al.*, level 1 does not represent behaviour that is less good than level 2, but behaviour at an earlier stage of development—similarly between levels 2 and 3. The chapter on

'Making and recording observations about children' in the *Match and Mismatch* book 'Raising questions' suggests how these checklists might be used and how cumulative records might be compiled. (See especially pages 51–8 on 'the value of making and recording observations'.)

It is significant that Harlen *et al.* also stress, as we have done earlier, that evaluation is not an easy process. Providing teachers with criteria or checklists for evaluation will not suddenly make the task of providing systematic, informative and comprehensive details about children free of difficulties in practice. Teachers must accept that they are learners in this situation and need time, perhaps quite a long time, to practice and internalise both the procedures and the criteria against which behaviour and outcomes are to be evaluated. If teachers persevere in this way until they reach the stage when they find themselves using the criteria almost automatically, then they and their colleagues, as well as parents and employers, will have available a profile of each individual child which will indicate:

(a) progress over a wide range of clearly understood and recognisable abilities and knowledge
(b) areas of strength and weakness and therefore what help may be needed
(c) the effectiveness of the curriculum offered in securing agreed aims and objectives
(d) the extent to which the curriculum planning has been dynamic and reflective of the cyclical process where aims and objectives are constantly under evaluative review

FURTHER READING

Durkin, M. C. *et al.* (1969) *The Social Studies Curriculum*. Menlo Park, CA: Addison-Wesley.

Eggleston, S. J. and Kerry, T. (1985) Integrated studies. In Bennett, N. and Desforges, C. (eds), *Recent Advances in Classroom Research*. Edinburgh: Scottish Academic Press.

Gunning, S., Gunning, D. and Wilson, J. (1981) *Topic Teaching in the Primary School*. London: Croom Helm.

Harlen, W. *et al.* (1977) *Schools Council Science 5–13: Match and Mismatch*. Edinburgh: Oliver & Boyd.

Parekh, B. (1985) Exercising the imagination. In Twitchen, J. and Demuth, C. (eds), *Multicultural Education*. London: BBC, 83–90.

Taba, H. (1962) *Curriculum Development, Theory and Practice*. New York: Harcourt, Brace & World.

Part II

The Equal Opportunities Perspective

George Antonouris

Chapter 5

Race and Gender

Part I attempts to offer a series of new dimensions, starting with three fundamental concepts—environmental influences, group behaviour and change (pages 14 and 19)—and progressing to ways of helping pupils identify and describe, classify and categorise, compare and contrast, look for causes and reasons, work out consequences and effects, make judgements, offer opinions and try to generalise (pages 15–17). A 'concept ladder' is proposed, beginning with the simple, concrete, specific tasks of researching, identifying, describing and fact finding, and climbing to the complex, abstract, general skills of seeing patterns and relationships, giving explanations, seeking reasons, making judgements and forming transferable generalisations (pages 27–29). It is suggested that as pupils progress up the ladder they will develop qualities of curiosity, perseverance, independence, open-mindedness and social responsibility (pages 30–31), together with writing competencies, commencing with formational tasks (identifying, listing, describing) and building up to interactional (expressing opinions, reasoning) and imaginative skills (page 50–52). Pupils at the top will attain the ability to make judgements, recognise limitations of evidence, be willing to qualify and temper conclusions, move from concrete to abstract thinking, and be able to see another person's point of view by using what Parekh called 'sympathetic imagination' (page 79).

The second part of the book recognises another area that we feel needs improving, that of equal opportunities in race and gender. It is our view that an insufficient number of schools include this dimension—hence the need for a summary of the Swann Report philosophy with a brief discussion of issues in this chapter, and eight introductory topic examples accompanied by resource material in chapters 6–8. The authors' message is that there exists another major dimension based around the Swann Report philosophy of 'education for all' that teachers should consider *now* as a matter of urgency; many teachers, especially those in predominantly white schools, will not be involved in the new dimension so a summary of issues and resource help is offered. If the material was readily available elsewhere, and if teachers in the majority of schools were involved in the equal opportunities perspective, there would be no need to present such an overview.

We hope readers will understand the importance we place on a perspective that attempts to encompass a variety of insights from the so-called 'anti-sexist' and 'multicultural/anti-racist' movements. We focus on issues and materials while still showing the possibility of applying dimensions in the first part of the book. We start with a topic on British clothes (pages 113–16) and apply the concept ladder approach in greater detail than in other topics. For every topic we include activities and questions that will help develop the ladder skills of classifying, interpreting, extrapolating and evaluating while offering teachers and student-teachers ideas and resources to help them permeate topic work with the kind of equal opportunities issues discussed in the remainder of this chapter.

In no way do we consider these chapters as prescriptive. Rather, we hope they will be used as collections of issues and collators of information for teacher appraisal and adaptation to a specific age-level and class group.

THE RACIAL DIMENSION

The first part of this section offers a summary of the 'education for all' philosophy recommended in chapter 6 of the 1985 Swann Report. The second section focuses on implications for all practising teachers in Britain, irrespective of type and racial intake of school.

Education for a pluralist society

Swann suggests that teachers should stop believing in assimilation 'where the minority group loses all the distinctive characteristics of its identity and is ultimately absorbed and subsumed within the majority group' (note 3, page 4), and should help minority communities to maintain their distinct ethnic identities within a framework of commonly accepted values, like equality of access to education and employment, equal treatment and opportunity to participate fully in social and political life, equal treatment and protection by the law, and equal freedom of cultural and religious expression (note 4, page 5). This pluralist perspective would require combating racism and offering cultural knowledge which should permeate every subject in schools with an 'all-white' population as well as those with a multiracial intake. Such 'good, relevant and up to date education for life in Britain and the world as it is today' (1.2, page 315) would involve 'appreciation of the diversity of lifestyle and cultural, religious and linguistic backgrounds which make up this society and the wider world' (1.4, page 316), 'catering for any particular needs which an ethnic minority pupil may have, arising for example from his or her linguistic or cultural background' (page 317), and 'countering the racism which still persists in Britain today' (2.13, page 319).

Curricular guidelines are offered for a variety of subjects. For example, in geographical studies there is a need to 'move from a perception of other countries, especially those outside Europe, solely in "British" terms. . . . Other nations and cultures have their own validity and should be described in their own terms. Wherever possible they should be allowed to speak for themselves and not be judged exclusively against British or European norms' (3.4, page 329). In historical topics, there needs to be a national dimension concerned with 'the patterns of migration which have created today's multi-racial society', and an international dimension which does not present an ethnocentric view 'exclusively in terms of British interests, experiences and values' (page 318) but a global perspective (page 330). In the Mathematics area, there is support for the Cockcroft Report view that teachers should use Rangoli and Islamic patterns to help develop geometrical concepts, and discuss the contributions to the development of mathematics of different countries and cultures (page 333). The history of Science needs to be developed comparatively and the selection of examples for classroom use should take account of the contribution and participation in scientific endeavours of people from a range of backgrounds and cultures (3.6, page 332). Finally, Music and Dance 'lend themselves to the development of an appreciation and awareness of a range of cultures through the study of art forms drawn not only from a European context', and Drama can help 'youngsters to reflect on the nature of prejudice and racism through role-playing situations, in which the influence of stereotyping and the ways in which misunderstandings can arise from ignorance about communities other than one's own are explored' (page 333).

Education for an anti-racist society

Swann sees the above examples of multicultural awareness training, as applying to *all* schools, *all* pupils and, where possible, *all* levels of education. Similarly, *all* teachers need to be involved in combating prejudice and stereotyping. Black Britons face racial disadvantage in housing, social services, employment and racial violence, abuse, harassment such as 'assaults, jostling in the streets, abusive remarks, broken windows, slogans daubed on walls' and 'more serious racially-motivated offences (murders, serious assaults, systematic attacks by gangs on people's homes at night)' (5.11, page 31). In the face of such racism the school cannot remain neutral and uninvolved because this would be 'a failure in terms of its educational responsibilities' and it would in effect be condoning and 'thereby encouraging the persistence of such occurrences' (5.14, page 35). Teachers should therefore not ignore or dismiss racism in the form of harassment and attacks, but challenge name-calling and 'its frequent companion racist graffiti' because these hit at the individual characteristics of pupils and insult their families and communities (5.15, page 35).

These ideas are supported by an important group of British writers (e.g., Arora and Duncan, Twitchen and Demuth, Houlton) and American academics and practitioners like Banks, Katz and others in the Bibliography at the end of this book.

Implication for practising teachers

It seems to us that Swann is asking *all* teachers to be involved in a variety of actions, some already practised, others new, some quickly implemented and others taking a long time to work. A selection is presented below for discussion and debate.

Similarities approach

A 'global village' perspective would be stressed in a multicultural school. Topics areas such as shelter, food, clothing and family patterns would focus on *similar experiences* and *common themes* first and foremost, and then work would be done on differences. Such a perspective would help reduce the risk of seeing others as quaint, strange, exotic or even inferior. Other useful topic areas could be: health, celebrations, religions, entertainment, law and order, rites of passage, languages, Olympic and Commonwealth Games, work, education, getting on with others, art and craft work, hairstyles, common names in different cultures.

Teachers should see all human groups as sharing needs and meeting these needs in *similar* and diverse ways according to local circumstances. For example, different cultures have created practical clothes for work and decorative ones for celebrations but different adaptations have been made because of economic, religious and cultural reasons.

Regional perspective

Schools should focus first on their own locality, which should include a large town or city. This *regional perspective* would involve links with the multitude of groups, organisations and associations in the area. Local languages and cultures could act as a start to any multicultural teaching, with relevant ethnic minority group members being invited to talk or lead topics or offer help in the form of leaflets, posters, etc. Visits could be made to places maintaining and promoting cultural heritage, traditions or customs.

International perspective

Teachers should try to attain an international perspective and omit a purely Anglocentric and Eurocentric bias. Their culture should not be regarded as the world's greatest culture with others relegated to inferior status.

Positive images

Teachers need to learn the contributions and achievements of local minority groups and present heroes and heroines from these cultures. A positive view is needed of all groups, with stress placed on common experiences and common adaptations to living in Britain. Poetry, music, art, craft, literature, history, geography, extra-curricular societies and clubs—all should include examples from the regional and national minority and majority cultures. The rich contributions found in these cultures could be utilised to benefit all concerned. The knowledge gained could result in awareness and understanding, and a reduction of fear of the unknown and the tendency to stereotype and pre-judge.

Critical attitude

Some common teacher attitudes and statements which need questioning are presented below.

When in Rome do as the Romans do; *they* must be just like *us*.
There are no problems here as we have no black pupils.
We are 'colour-blind' here because we treat all pupils the same.

Teachers should question their beliefs and watch for any actions which stem from the feeling of white superiority, such as labelling black children as (1) troublemakers and (2) less intelligent than white people.

Book analysis

Schools should have a clearly stated policy concerning books, and book purchases should follow policy guidelines. All books would be selected for their world perspective, involving the celebration of achievements from around the world. They would show *positive images of all*, especially of ex-colonial peoples, now citizens of Britain, and they should avoid stereotyping, caricaturing and distortions. Heroines and heroes would reflect the diversity of cultures in Britain.

While teachers try to build up their library corner with books reflecting multicultural aspects in society today, books which do not show common characteristics between peoples should be questioned—differences should be pointed out but not to the exclusion of similarities. Teachers could discuss with children any bias or omissions in story and information books—such books can even be given a *'warning' label* with justification being included with the label (see Figure 11). Questions could be placed inside book covers to focus on omissions, distortions, over-simplifications, caricatures and stereotypes. Perhaps there is only need for a 'beware of bias' label, with children being left to find the bias themselves—this should not be difficult where displays and workcards are deliberately multicultural, and where a whole-school multicultural education policy exists.

Teachers could ask the following questions when analysing books and other material.

1. Are people from other cultures being judged by the measuring-rod of our culture? (If they have what we have, if they believe, feel, act, eat, dress like us, they are 'normal', if not they are in some way abnormal, deviant, inferior, weird, peculiar, exotic.)
2. Are ethnic minorities portrayed in a stereotypical way or as fully-rounded characters?
3. Are ethnic minority characters seen in leadership roles and in professional occupations or are black Britons shown as manual workers?
4. Does the book give the impression that only white Anglo-Saxon people live in this society?

Twinning schemes

Each school and class could be involved in an exchange with a different type of school in a different part of the LEA. Class teachers from two different schools could arrange to

WARNING

THIS BOOK CONTAINS MATERIAL CONSIDERED BIASED

REASONS AND PAGE REFERENCES ARE GIVEN BELOW

WRITTEN PASSAGES

PAGE	REASONS

VISUAL PASSAGES

PAGE	REASONS

Figure 11. The warning label.

do a joint topic. Early in the term, class teachers from two different schools—one in the outer city and one in the inner city—could meet to discuss a joint project.

The two schools would work separately on the topics and come together in exchange visits to finish display material, discuss and work together as a team. Exhibitions, demonstrations and games could be included in a day's working visit. The ethnic minority children who arrive in the 'all-white' school would not feel strange or that they had entered an alien world because the various displays in the school would reflect and celebrate cultural similarities and differences.

Naming practices

Children would be sensitised to the different types of names in British society because these would be prevalent in work-cards produced by teachers and in books and materials selected for use. Examples and problems in all areas of the curriculum would include names like Mark and Mary, Costas and Eleni (Greek Cypriot Britons), Vijay and Meena (Hindu Britons), Amin and Asmat (Muslim Britons), Ajit and Ravinder (Sikh Britons). Stress would be placed on pronouncing names correctly, placing them in their ethnic minority groupings and spelling them.

Display materials

On entering a building, there should be plenty of display material celebrating the diversity of cultures within Britain and the similarities and differences between customs, dress, folk tales, histories, geographies, etc. Wall paintings and children's drawings would involve ethnically diverse patterns, batik design, white and non-white faces, etc. Any child in such an environment would see a daily reflection of a world which is interdependent and open-minded concerning the wealth of cultures and lifestyles. Information and respect for peoples, their achievements and contributions would surround the pupil, teacher, community visitor and helper.

Whole-school policy

The school policy document should state clearly the position of the school within a multiracial and multicultural society. It should stress the desire to eliminate negative images, stereotypes and caricatures from school materials and emphasise cultural diversity and the combating of racism in all its forms.

Standing committee

There should be a standing committee within the school to examine curriculum and organisational matters and develop practices which would ensure that the school became an equal oportunities society.

Support services

Teachers should be able to gain support from the following areas.

1. Their own LEA support service, which would include inspectorate and resource units.
2. Cities may publish their own journals which give practical advice, e.g., Birmingham's *Multicultural Education Review.*
3. National journals disseminate research, ideas and practices, e.g., *Multicultural Teaching.*
4. Other national journals may include certain articles in this area, e.g. *Junior Education, Child Education, Primary Teaching Studies, Greater Manchester Primary Contact, Values.*
5. The local Community Relations Council and the Commission for Racial Equality.
6. Ethnic minority groups have cultural and community centres in the locality and their associations and organisations may offer information and resource material.

THE GENDER DIMENSION

A great deal has been written on this subject in Britain and the USA so readers will be referred to existing literature suggested by Valerie Hannon (1981) and itemised in the

American references at the end of the book. Extensive material and practical advice can be found in Kate Myers' (1987) *Genderwatch!* pack as well as the Hannon publication from the Equal Opportunities Commission. Teachers committed to the equal opportunities perspective will critically examine gender images in story books, which should show females and males involved in the following kinds of behaviour:

- Leadership
- Brave actions
- Heavy physical work or some strenuous activity
- Fighting
- Triumphing over a foe
- Rescuing someone or something
- Exploring alone
- Showing fear
- Outwitting an enemy or competitor
- Caring for animals or people
- Home-making and child-caring roles
- Being referred to or being asked advice.

Lists on pages 19 and 20 of Hannon add factors such as:

- The sexes should be consistently represented in equal balance
- Both should participate equally in intellectual and physical activities
- Both should be seen in a range of occupations and positions, and in authority and power, e.g., women are not all teachers, nurses, secretaries, social workers, librarians
- Both should develop independent lives, searching for their own solutions
- Neither men nor women should be stereotyped, e.g., 'girls are silly', 'boys make the best engineers'
- Language should not exclude women, e.g., firemen, policemen
- Male and female characters should show respect to each other as equals
- Multi-parent families (divorced, remarried, one-parent) need to be portayed and the portrayal should not suggest that such family conditions are automatically damaging to children
- Both sexes should be shown as having a wide range of feelings
- There should be equal number of stories and biographies with girls and boys as central characters
- Girls' accomplishments, not their beauty or clothes, need to be stressed.

In summary, pupil material should show females and males being active and passive, independent and helpless, problem-solving and dependent, child-rearing and in occupations, strong and weak, leader and led, tough and gentle. Focus should be not only on the written word but also on illustrations, especially those that portray males as taller, heavier, stronger or more active than female.

Myers (1987) offers a loose-leaf folder with comprehensive materials for teacher in-service courses and classroom use. Self-assessment schedules are proposed for setting goals, classroom interaction/observation, displays, language, rewards, responsibilities and sanctions, texture and picture books, and curriculum subject areas.

THE SCHOOL AS AN EQUAL OPPORTUNITIES ZONE

Using the previous ideas, we offer a teachers' charter based on the notion of the school as an *equal opportunities zone*, maintaining and reinforcing equal life chances for all. It is our personal act of faith, laying the foundation for action in schools and classroom.

A foundation charter for teachers

Gender

1. Our school reflects a shared world of males and females and when referring to both groups we will no longer use the conventional 'he' but 's/he' or 'she/he'.
2. The word 'man' will not be used to denote both men and women, e.g., chairman, mankind, etc. Instead we will use 'chairperson', 'humankind', etc.
3. The term 'master' will not be used, e.g., masterpiece, mastermind, masterful. A 'master' copy becomes a 'key' copy, etc.
4. We will ensure the visibility of girls and women in all our work-cards, stories, displays, etc.
5. We will combat stereotypes and prejudices, patronising behaviour, and bias against girls and women in books, curriculum and behaviour, e.g., females will not be seen as submissive, passive, playing with dolls, child-rearing and home-making. The parental roles will be shown as a shared endeavour between men and women, as will all types of careers in society.
6. A deliberate effort will be made to help girls fulfil their potential in Science, Mathematics and Technology, career areas in which girls have been under-represented in the past.

Race

1. We will use terms such as Afro-Caribbean Britons, Indian Britons, Pakistani Britons, Bangladeshi Britons, etc., to denote the 'Britishness' of the ethnic minority people living in Britain.
2. We will omit the colonial term 'West Indian', which lumps a number of distinct islands together. Only when this is an official term will we use it, e.g., the 'West Indian cricket team'. We will try not to use the word 'Asian' when referring to a particular group because of the vast difference between those with roots in the Indian sub-continent, let alone the Asian continent.
3. We will not use terms such as 'blacks' and 'whites', but 'black people' and 'white people', because all human beings should be addressed in a respectful way.
4. We will not use the word 'black' to denote something that is negative, e.g., blackmail, blackleg, blacklist, black sheep, black Mass, black mark, black book.
5. We will combat all materials in books which show black Britons or people from African, Asian or Caribbean societies in a negative or demeaning way, e.g., as ignorant, backward, savages, natives, living in mud huts, etc. We will emphasise

positive signs in all groupings and try to show their common strengths and different adaptations.

6. We will object to all jokes which demean any group, whether it be the Irish or Jewish or any other group in the world.
7. We will ensure visibility of all types of Britons in our work-cards, books, materials, displays, stories, etc.
8. We will oppose all prejudices and stereotypes, e.g.,
   'West Indian parents do not take adequate interest in their children, don't encourage them to learn and work hard'
   'West Indian culture values excellence in sports and music rather than educational success, especially in boys'

Social class

1. We will oppose low expectations of working class pupils as 'slow' or 'not very good workers'.
2. We will combat negative images of their families as inadequate or 'culturally deprived', e.g.,
   'Lower-class children lack adequate language and moral training at home'
   'Many working class parents do not really care about the education of their children'
   'Too many pupils come to school dirty and scruffy because parents from the council estate don't look after them properly'
3. We will challenge prejudices and stereotypes, such as, the working class child is 'not very bright' and 'a troublemaker'.
4. We will reject the term 'broken home' and replace it with a more positive view of a loving and caring 'one-parent family'.
5 We will recognise and celebrate the culture, customs, traditions and way of speaking of all social classes and ensure their visibility in our work-cards, displays, materials and stories.

Personal checklist

Following this charter in the everyday teaching situation, each teacher could create her own checklist of items to ensure the establishment of an equal opportunity zone within the classroom. Figure 12 is one proposal for playgroup leaders, incorporating the racial dimension which could be extended to encompass the gender dimension for any age-group and institutional setting.

RESOURCE MATERIAL

The Racial Dimension
Swann Report
Equal Opportunities Perspective

Checklist

Below is a short checklist comprising some items of multicultural practice as I see it. My claim is: the greater the number of statements you feel apply to your situation, the more your playgroup reflects the cultural diversity in contemporary society.

1. My wall displays show illustrations of black Britons as well as white Britons.
2. The home corner includes a range of dolls from Africa and Asia as well as from Europe.
3. I use nursery rhymes from Africa and Asia as well as from Britain.
4. I try to alert my children to the ethnic mix within their immediate region.
5. The materials I use show that there are many kinds of Britons in this country, both white and black Britons.
6. I check books to see that they do not portray ethnic minorities as backward or inferior.
7. I use materials which show black people as British rather than as immigrants or foreigners.
8. The materials I bring to the playground reflect the contribution and achievements of both white and black peoples around the world.
9. Before I use any material I try to ensure that it does not misinform and distort the image of Asian and Afro-Caribbean Britons.
10. My material shows children a positive image of all British citizens, irrespective of colour or culture.

Figure 12. Multicultural checklist.

The Gender Dimension
Genderwatch
Equal Opportunities Commission
Further Reading

The racial dimension

Swann Report

Swann, Lord (1985) *Education for All*. London: HMSO.

This includes:

1. Case studies of all types of schools in chapter 5: infants (pages 251–2, 259–61, 277–9), primary (245–6, 261–3, 288–9, 297–9), middle (299–301).
2. 'Education for All': A New Approach (chapter 6, pages 315–81).
3. Background material on ethnic minority communities, such as the Chinese (pages 653–70), Cypriots (671–93), Italians (695–709), Ukrainians (711–17), Vietnamese (719–32), Liverpool 'Blacks' (733–8), and travellers' children (739–59).
4. Main conclusions and recommendations (pages 767–76).

Multicultural Education Review, Spring 1986.
This comprises a Swann Report special report.

The Runnymede Trust (1985) *'Education for All': A summary of the report on the education of ethnic minority children.*
This summary is reprinted in its entirety in the *Multicultural Education Review* special above.

The equal opportunities perspective

1. Similarities approach

Antonouris, G. (1986) Just checking: how to look objectively at your classroom material and teaching practices to ensure a multicultural approach. *Child Education*, **63**, no. 1, January, 26–7.
Antonouris, G. (1987) Silent minorities? *Junior Education*, **10**, no. 9, September, 17.
Antonouris, G. (1987) Multicultural education at the Danesbury junior school. *Primary Teaching Studies*, **2**, no. 2, February, 122–7.
Phillips-Bell, M. (ed.) (1983) *Issues and Resources: A Handbook for Teachers in a Multicultural Society*. Birmingham: AFFOR (pages 38–47 on Primary school projects: a multicultural approach by Alison Sealey).

2. Regional perspective

Antonouris, G. (1986) Exploring community interests and identities. *Community Education Network*, **6**, no. 6, June, 2.
Antonouris, G. (1986) Developing multi-cultural education in all primary schools: some suggestions. *Primary Contact*, **3**, no. 3, 45–50.
Development Education Centre (1982) *The World in Birmingham*. Gillett Centre, Selly Oak Colleges, Bristol Road, Birmingham B29 6LE.

JOURNAL

Community Education and Network Journal of Community Education. Available from Community Education Development Centre, Briton Road, Coventry CV2 4LT.

3. International perspective

Antonouris, G. (1987) Reflecting cultural differences. *Modus*, **5**, no. 2, March, 75–6.
Crossman, L. *et al.* (1985) Appoaches to Africa at Anglesey junior school. *Multicultural Education Review*, no. 4, Summer, 28–31.
Development Education Centre (1986) *Theme Work—Approaches for Teaching with a Global Perspective.* Manchester: DEC.
Mackay, A. and Najda, R. (eds) (1985) *World Sports and Games Pack*. Lothian Regional Council Department of Education and Moray House College of Education (obtained from Moray House College of Education, Holyrood Road, Edinburgh EH8 8AQ).
Pemberton, E. *et al.* (1987) An anti-racist approach to teaching about African history. *Multicultural Education Review*, Spring/Summer, 24–7.

USEFUL ADDRESSES
CAFOD (Catholic Fund for Overseas Development), 2 Garden Close, Stockwell Road, London SW9 9TY.
DEC (Development Education Centre).
Seven books under the title of *Teaching Development Issues*, comprising work on perceptions, colonialism, food, health, population, changes, work, aid and development.
Address: c/o Manchester Polytechnic, 801 Wilmslow Road, Manchester M20 8RG.
NADEC (National Association of Development Education Centres), 128 Buckingham Palace Road, London SW1W 9SH.
OXFAM Education Department, 274 Banbury Road, Oxford OX2 7DZ.
World Studies 8–13 Project, St Martin's College, Lancaster LA1 3JD (publishers of *World Studies 8–13 Handbook*, 1985).

4. Positive image

Jeffcoate, R. (1979) *Positive Image.* London: Chameleon Books, Writers' and Readers' Publishing Co-operative.
Twitchen, J. and Demuth, C. (1985) *Multicultural Education.* London: BBC, pages 37–40.

FOR PUPILS
ACER (Afro-Caribbean Education Resource Centre) *Ourselves.* This material for 9–13-year-old pupils is based on true-life stories of children from different backgrounds.
Words and Faces. This attempts to develop a positive self-image of all children since it challenges stereotyped images.
Caribbean in the Classroom. Published in 1987, this is a teaching guide and resource list for teachers with sections on history, geography, culture and religion, home economics, language, literature and stories, music, social studies, art.
Resource and Information Guide (third edition). Another useful reference for teachers, giving access to information on books, videos, agencies and people like artists and speakers. Available from the ACER Centre at Wyvil School, Wyvil Road, London SW8 2TJ. Telephone 01-627 2662.
ILEA (1986) *Phototalk.* Photograph booklets for the very young, e.g., *Bathtime with Leandra. Eating with Badre and Nabil. Saiqua and Shan go shopping. Bedtime with Alkan.*
School textbooks which show a positive image of the Caribbean include three written by Lennox Honeychurch entitled *The Caribbean People* and published by Thomas Nelson, London.

5. Critical attitude

Arora, R. and Duncan, C. (1986) *Multicultural Education: Towards Good Practice.* London: Routledge & Kegan Paul (especially chapter 5).
Constanti, A. (1986) Attacking racism. *Junior Education*, October, 20–1.
Hagan, L. (1986) Multicultural/anti-racist education. *Junior Education*, June, 17.
Houlton, D. (1986) *Cultural Diversity in the Primary School.* London: Batsford.

Nixon, J. (1985) *A Teacher's Guide to Multicultural Education*. Oxford: Basil Blackwell.

Twitchen, J. and Demuth, C. (1985) *Multicultural Education*. London: BBC (especially chapter 8 on 'Exercising the imagination' and the last chapter on 'Racism awareness in the school system').

USEFUL ADDRESSES

NAME (National Anti-racist Movement in Education), PO Box 9, Walsall, West Midlands WS1 3SF.

Runnymede Trust, 174 North Gower Street, London NW1.

JOURNALS

Dragon's Teeth, National Committee on Racism in Children's Books, 7 Denbigh Road, London W11 2SJ.

Issues in Race and Education, 11 Carleton Gardens, Brecknock Road, London N19 5AQ.

6. Book analysis

TEACHING ABOUT BIAS IN BOOKS

ILEA (1985) *Everyone Counts: Looking for bias and insensitivity in primary mathematics material*. London: ILEA.

Mcfarlane, C. (1985) Looking at bias with children. *Multicultural Education Review*, no. 4, Summer, 9–11.

Mcfarlane, C. (1986) *Hidden messages?—activities for exploring bias*. Manchester: Development Education Centre.

WARNING LABELS

The journal *Multicultural Teaching* has carried two items: Have you seen the Book Look file? (Summer 1985, page 43), and Letter from Brenda Keyte, librarian at Dick Sheppard School, on her non-racist and non-sexist Book Look file (Spring 1986, page 54).

GENERAL ISSUES

Antonouris, G. (1987) Identifying racism. *Modus*, **5**, no. 7, October, 274–275.

Khalique, R. (1987) Racial bias in children's books. *Curriculum*, **8**, no. 1, Spring, 46–50.

Klein, G. (1984) *Reading into Racism: Bias in Children's Literature and Learning Materials*. London: Routledge & Kegan Paul.

Richardson, R. (1986) The hidden messages in schoolbooks. *Journal of Moral Education*, January, 26–42.

Twitchen, J. and Demuth, C. (1985) *Multicultural Education*. London: BBC (pages 41–4 on 'ten quick ways to analyse children's books for racism').

7. Twinning schemes

BBC TV (1981) *Case Studies in Multicultural Education* (programme 1: 'Anglo-Saxon attitudes').

Carrier, M. (1986) Getting to know you. *Child Education*, March, 37.

Hagedorn, J. (1980) Dear Tracy. *Junior Education*, June, 11.
Houlton, D. (1986) *Cultural Diversity in the Primary School.* London: Batsford (pages 130–9 on Leicester, Nottingham and Bradford/Humberside exchange schemes).

8. Naming practices

Bains, H. S. (1982) *Asians in Derby.* Derbyshire Multicultural Education Support Service.
CRE (1972) *A Guide to Asian Names.* London: CRE.

9. Display material

Centre for Learning Resources, 275 Kennington Lane, London SE11.
Pictorial Charts Educational Trust, 27 Kirchen Road, London W13 0UD (posters on the heritage of Islam, rich world/poor world, African heritage).
Commonwealth Institute, Kensington High Street, London W8 6NQ.

Embassies and travel agents may supply useful material for display purposes.

ILEA. *Welcome posters* (welcome written in 30 languages).
ILEA. *Between future and past* (position of women in society at different times in history).
ILEA. *Whose world is the world?* (historical perspective).
Unity Learning Foundation, for posters in music and worship, dolls, costumes, puppets and musical instruments, 10 Barley Mow Passage, London W4 4PH.

10. Whole-school policy

Each LEA should have a policy document to guide school policies. Some key publications include:

Berkshire Education Committee (1983) *Education for Racial Equality* (reprinted in the Swann Report, pages 366–81).
City of Birmingham District Council (1987) *Education for Our Multicultural Society.*
Derbyshire County Council (1987) *Towards the 1990s: Education for All in Derbyshire.*
ILEA (1983) *Race, Sex and Class.*

PROFESSIONAL ORGANISATIONS

AMMA (1983) *Our Multicultural Society: the Educational Response.*
NUT (1984) *Combating Racism in Schools: a Union Policy Document Statement.*

GUIDANCE FOR TEACHERS

Houlton, D. (1986) *Cultural Diversity in the Primary School.* London: Batsford (chapter 6: towards a school policy).
Twitchen, J. and Demuth, C. (1985) *Multicultural Education.* London: BBC, pages 109–14.

11. Standing committee

Atkin, J. and Richards, J. K. (1983) *A Question of Priorities: an examination of a school-based inservice education programme in Multicultural Education.* University of Nottingham.
Houlton, D. (1986) *Cultural Diversity in the Primary school.* London: Batsford, pages 145–9.
Ruddell, D. (1987) Setting up 'multicultural working parties' in schools. *Multicultural Education Review*, Spring/Summer, 28–9.

12. Support services

A list of all 104 Support Centres, entitled *LEA (UK) Resources Centres and Contacts*, can be purchased from the Multicultural Education Resource Centre at Denbigh Junior School, Denbigh Road, Luton LU3 1NS.

A small selection can be found below:

Multicultural Education Resources Centre, Acacia Road, Bedford MK42 0HU.
Multicultural Support Service, The Bordesley Centre, Stratford Road, Birmingham B11 1AR.
Multicultural Education Centre, Bishop Road, Bishopton, Bristol BS7 8LS.
Minority Group Support Service, Southfields, South Street, Coventry CV1 5EJ.
Multicultural Education Support Service, Dairyhouse Road, Derby DE3 8HN.
Centre for Multicultural Education, Rushey Mead Centre, Harrison Road, Leicester LE4 6RB.

Another major support centre is the Commission for Racial Equality, Elliot House, 10–12 Allington Street, London W8 6NQ.

HANDBOOKS FOR TEACHERS

Craft, A and Klein, G. (1986) *Agenda for Multicultural Teaching*. London: SCDC.
Elkin, J. and Triggs, P. (1985/6) *Books for Keeps: Guides to Children's Literature for a Multicultural Society* (Book 1, 0–7 years; Book 2, 8–12 years). Obtained from 1 Effingham Road, London SE12 8NZ.
Klein, G. (1984) *Resources for Multicultural Education*. Harlow: Longman.
Nottinghamshire Leisure Services/Library (1982) *Many Cultures, Many Faiths*. County Library, Angel Row, Nottingham NG1 6HP.
Oxford Development Education Centre (1986) *Books to Break Barriers: A Review of Multicultural Fiction 4–18*.
Patel, B. and Allen, J. (1985) *A Visible Presence: Black People Living and Working in Britain Today*. National Book League, Book House, 45 East Hill, London SW18 2QZ.
Phillips-Bell, M. (ed.) (1983) *Issues and Resources*. AFFOR (All Faiths For One Race), 173 Lozells Road, Birmingham B19 1RN.

SPECIALIST JOURNALS

Multicultural Educational Review, Bordesley Centre, Stratford Road, Birmingham B11 1AR.
Multicultural Teaching, Trentham Books, 30 Wenger Crescent, Trentham, Stoke-on-Trent ST4 8LE.

The gender dimension

Genderwatch

Readers are recommended to go to the 1987 *Genderwatch!* pack for full resource material, extensive ideas and information. It was devised by Kate Myers and published by the School Curriculum Development Committee, Newcombe House, 45 Notting Hill Gate, London W11 3JB.

Myers (1987) offers a loose-leaf folder with comprehensive materials for teacher in-service courses and classroom use. Self-assessment schedules are proposed for setting goals (pages 9–13), classroom interaction/observation (24–33), displays (40–1), language (58–61), rewards, responsibilities and sanctions (96–100), texture and picture books (110–16) and curriculum subject areas (118 onwards).

Equal Opportunities Commission

Further material can be obtained from the Equal Opportunities Commission, Overseas House, Quay Street, Manchester M3 3HN.

Hannon, V. (1981) *Ending Sex Stereotyping in School: a Sourcebook for School-based Teacher Workshops*, is a key text which offers useful checklists for analysing children's books (reprinted below with permission from the EOC).

List 1: Checklist for analysing children's literature (reprinted from Hannon, 1981, page 19, by permission of the Equal Opportunities Commission).

		Almost Always	Occasionally	Rarely
1. Are girls and boys, men and women consistently represented in equal balance?		___	___	___
2. Do boys and girls participate equally in both physical and intellectual activities?		___	___	___
3. Do girls and boys each receive positive recognition for their endeavours?	Females	___	___	___
	Males	___	___	___
4. Do boys and girls, fathers and mothers participate in a wide variety of domestic chores, not only the ones traditional for their sex?	Females	___	___	___
	Males	___	___	___
5. Do both girls and boys have a variety of choices and are they encouraged to aspire to various goals, including non-traditional ones if they show such inclination?	Females	___	___	___
	Males	___	___	___
6. Are both boys and girls shown developing independent lives, independently meeting challenges and finding their own solutions?	Females	___	___	___
	Males	___	___	___
7. Are women and men shown in a variety of occupations, including non-traditional ones? When women are portrayed as full-time homemakers, are they depicted as competent and decisive?	Females	___	___	___
	Males	___	___	___
8. Do characters deprecate themselves because of their sex? (Example: 'I'm only a girl.') Do others use denigrating language in this regard? ('That's just like a woman.')	Females	___	___	___
	Males	___	___	___
9. Do the illustrations stereotype the characters, either in accordance to the dictates of the text or in contradiction to it?	Females	___	___	___
	Males	___	___	___
10. Is inclusionary language used? (For example: 'police officer' instead of 'policeman,' 'staffed by' instead of 'manned by,' 'all students will submit the assignment' instead of 'each student will submit his assignment,' and so on.)		___	___	___

This list was developed by the International Reading Association: Committee on Sexism and Reading. Reproduced from *Guide for Evaluating Sex Stereotyping in Reading Materials*, *Journal of Reading*, **240**, December 1977.

List 2: Checklist for analysing an elementary reader (reprinted from Hannon, 1981, page 18, by permission of the Equal Opportunities Commission).

Yes	No		
___	___	1.	All members of the family participate regularly and equally in household chores.
___	___	2.	There are favourable presentations of mothers employed outside of the home.
___	___	3.	Women working outside of the home hold administrative and/or technical jobs. They are not all teachers, librarians, social workers, nurses or secretaries.
___	___	4.	Fathers take an active and competent part in housekeeping and child-rearing and are depicted showing feelings of tenderness.
___	___	5.	Girls and boys participate equally in physical activities.
___	___	6.	Girls and boys participate equally in intellectual activities.
___	___	7.	One-parent families are portrayed, and the portrayal does not suggest that children with a single parent automatically suffer from it.
___	___	8.	Male and female characters respect each other as equals.
___	___	9.	Girls and boys are both shown to be self-reliant, clever, and brave—capable of facing their own problems and finding their own solutions.
___	___	10.	Multiple-parent families (divorced, remarried) are portrayed and the portrayal does not suggest that such family conditions are automatically damaging to the children.
___	___	11.	There are no unchallenged derogatory sex stereotyped characterizations, such as 'Boys make the best architects,' or 'Girls are silly.'
___	___	12.	Both girls and boys are shown as having a wide range of sensibilities, feelings, and responses.
___	___	13.	Both girls and boys have a wide variety of career options.
___	___	14.	Adults who have chosen not to marry are portrayed favourably.
___	___	15.	There are equal numbers of stories with girls and boys as central characters.
___	___	16.	The male noun or pronoun (*mankind*, *he*) is not used to refer to all people.
___	___	17.	Girls' accomplishments, not their clothing or features, are emphasized.
___	___	18.	Clothing and appearance are not used to stereotype characters.
___	___	19.	Non-human characters and their relationships are not personified in sex stereotypes (for example, depicting dogs as masculine, cats as feminine).
___	___	20.	(For readers which incorporate biographies . . .) biographies of women in a variety of roles are included.

This material is reprinted from *Self-Study Guide to Sexism in Schools*, prepared by Education Committee of Pennsylvanians for Women's Rights, Pennsylvania Department of Education, Harrisburg, PA, 1975.

FURTHER READING

Antonouris, G. (1987) Images of parenthood. *Modus*, **5**, no. 5, June, 186–7.

Dixon, B. (1977) *Catching Them Young: Sex, Race and Class in Children's Fiction*. London: Pluto Press.

ILEA (1983) *Race, Sex and Class*. London: ILEA.

ILEA (1986) *Anti-sexist Resource Guide* (a 92-page pack). London: ILEA.

Stones, R. (1983) *Pour out the Cocoa, Janet': Sexism in Children's Books*. Harlow: Longman.

Whyte, J. (1983) *Beyond the Wendy House: Sex-role Stereotyping in Primary School*. Harlow: Longman.

Material for pupils

ILEA. *Anti-sexist Photographs*. London: ILEA (shows children involved in a variety of school activities providing positive images of girls and boys in different curriculum areas).

Rednap, C. *et al.* (1987) *Doing Things in and about the Home*. Stoke-on-Trent: Trentham Books (photographs and activities about work, play and equality).

Chapter 6

Traditional Topics

INTRODUCTION

Using the approaches proposed in chapter 5, the second part of the book offers examples of topic work developed on Trent Polytechnic courses between 1985 and 1987. Chapters in this section focus on three key areas incorporating an equal opportunities perspective: this chapter offers selective ideas for traditional topics transformed and extended to encompass the new dimension, chapter 7 stresses the importance of cultural studies as vehicles for developing understanding of neighbourhood or regional communities, and chapter 8 offers three examples of controversial topics which could inspire pupils to question taken-for-granted assumptions, making problematic what had, perhaps, previously remained unquestioned.

Chapter 6: Traditional topics
1. Clothes
2. Food
3. Music

Chapter 7: Cultural studies
1. Diwali
2. Eid

Chapter 8: Controversial issues
1. Mary Seacole and Florence Nightingale
2. Moving home
3. Everybody knows that! A story for young children that attempts to confront prejudice and stereotypes

Each topic is sub-divided into sections elaborating aims, activities and pupil questions, and supplemented by resource materials comprising information sheets, reviews, exercises, further topic suggestions and a select booklist.

In the preface we say that the book presents four new dimensions. The first new dimension proposes three fundamental ideas to help plan the development of pupil understanding, namely influence and control of the environment, social and power relations in group behaviour, environmental and group change. Each topic has aims that reflect these ideas. The second new dimension offers teachers the notion of an activities ladder which suggests that concept-related activities should involve identifying and describing, classifying, comparing, seeking causes, predicting effects, making judgements and generalising. All topics include suggested questions which use this new dimension. The third new dimension presents criteria to help teachers evaluate pupil work by considering the extent to which it indicates inclusiveness of thought, elaboration of response, tentativeness, abstractness and decentring. Topic activities and resources offer material to help bring about these outcomes.

We recommend a critical assessment which could include focus on the following areas.

Questioning

The issue of questioning has been discussed extensively and the sequential stages suggested in chapter 2 have been used throughout this part of the book. A few critical questions about this approach are:

- How acceptable are specific questions?
- Which questions were more successfully answered by your pupils? Why?
- What improvements do you suggest?

Activities

How practical are the proposed activities to your specific class in your particular school placed in its locality and region?

Resource material

How informative, useful, relevant and available are resource materials? In what way are these deficient or sufficient for your purposes?

Planning, teaching and evaluation

While attempting 'new directions' topic work, what were the problems of implementation, learning and teaching? Using the ideas from previous chapters, show how you planned, taught and evaluated the topic and assess the success or otherwise of your endeavours. How have you defined 'success'? With what ideas and practices do you agree or disagree?

Equal opportunities perspective

After this appraisal exercise, we suggest that you stand back from your experiences and evaluate the equal opportunities perspective in the light of your own teaching practices. What new directions do you wish to engage after your personal experiences?

We hope you will find the illustrations interesting and instructive, helpful and thought-provoking, time-saving and practical, as well as essential for educating *all* pupils in schools working *for* an equal opportunity society.

BRITISH CLOTHES

Aims

1. To develop understanding of the idea that British clothes are influenced by a variety of cultural factors.
   (*Influence of environment*)
2. To show that clothes are a means of:
   (a) sharing social identity
   (b) showing power relations
   (c) people controlling their environment.
   (*Group behaviour and change*)
3. To demonstrate that clothes have changed in relation to changes in social values and environmental control.
   (*Change*)

Activities

1. Pupils could explore the influence of environment in the following ways:
   (a) Suitability of clothing to the environment. Clothing in different climates. The relationship between climate, colour, design and materials.
   (b) Clothing that indicates identity—religious, leisure, group, gender, race, ethnic group.
   (c) Clothing for special occasions; similarities and differences in weddings; naming ceremonies, birthday and other festivals.
   (d) Pupils could produce a list of the variety of British clothes they could choose if they were going to a special celebration.
2. Pupils could examine issues concerning control of environment by examining:
   (a) Clothing that indicates authority and/or power—uniforms, ceremonial dress.
   (b) Clothing that provides protection—overalls, reflective clothing, life jackets, space suits, etc.
   (c) Similarity and difference between western and eastern clothing and other articles that are worn, from the point of view of the wearer's gender, social status, religious affiliations and cultural origin.
3. Change could focus on:

(a) Cultural diversity in clothing styles in Britain.
(b) Changes in clothing and articles worn appropriate to gender.
(c) Changes in materials to provide better protection and control.

Development of topic work

1. Language work

(a) Description of clothes of pupils and families worn in class on above occasions.
(b) 'My favourite clothes' writing exercise.
(c) 'Clothes in our region' theme, i.e., examine the different ethnic groups in the region and concentrate on their styles of dress, showing how changes have occurred this century.

2. Mathematics

(a) Measurement of different types of material.
(b) Buying different materials.
(c) Designing clothes (using patterns, symmetry, etc.).

3. Science

(a) Making and processing fabrics.
(b) Properties of materials, e.g., wool. What happens when it gets wet, when it is dyed, when it burns?
(c) Colour and climate, clothes in different climates.

4. Music

Special occasions like official ceremonies, weddings, classical and pop concerts and accompanying music, e.g., Trooping the Colour (marching music, bands, uniforms) compared with other celebrations of black and white Britons.

5. Art and creative work

(a) Design clothes for a special occasion.
(b) Make parts of clothes for this occasion, e.g., head dress, hat.
(c) Print fabrics using batik and other skills.
(d) Make puppets to illustrate stories of multicultural Britain.

6. Fashion show

The end result could be:

(a) A fashion show with the children wearing clothes, displaying them to accompanying music and explanations.
(b) A classroom frieze.
(c) A doll display of appropriate clothing.

Possible questions to raise

Using the sequence of thinking and activity skills discussed in chapter 2 we offer a few suggestions below.

Stages 1 and 2 (see page 80—identification, description, classification)

These questions will help pupils categorise key areas. Here are some general examples using 'which, how and why' questions:

1. Using maps teachers can ask: What places do certain styles of clothes come from?
2. When did Asian Britons, Chinese Britons, etc., settle in your region?
3. Give a list of the variety of British clothes you could choose from if you were going to a special celebration.

Stage 3 (causes, reasons, similarities and differences)

These questions require a further development in thinking in that they expect more elucidation, translation and inference from the pupil. The 'why' questions expect a deeper level of understanding and explanation. Here are some examples:

1. Why do some people laugh at those who wear different clothes?
2. Why do you wear different clothes for different occasions?
3. Why do you like some clothes and dislike others?

Stage 4 (consequences, effects)

These questions invite pupils to extent what they have identified by asking 'what do you think will/would/might happen if . . .'. General examples include:

1. What do you think would happen if every group in this country wore the same clothes for similar occasions?
2. What would happen if you came to school in jeans? Why do you think this would happen?
3. What would make you change your taste in clothes?

Stages 5 and 6 (judgements and opinions, applications to new situations and generalisations)

These questions ask pupils to determine the value of what they have seen, heard, read or experienced. They need to decide between goodness and badness, right and wrong, fairness and unfairness. Some examples are included below.

1. Do you think it is *good* to have a variety of different styles of clothes? Why?
2. Do you think it is *right* to stop people wearing clothes of their choice at any time?
3. Do you think it is *fair* to laugh at people who wear clothes which are different from your own?

On pages 117–18 is a detailed example of planning an equal opportunities topic, as suggested in Part I. Readers will be left to develop this scheme for other topic areas in the book.

BRITISH FOOD

Aims

1. To reinforce the notion that there is diversity in food preparation as there is cultural diversity in Britain.
   (*Group behaviour*)
2. To highlight similarities in the eating habits of different cultural groups.
   (*Group behaviour*)
3. To help children make closer observations of diverse multicultural foods by comparing colour, smell, texture and taste.
   (*Environment and group behaviour*)
4. To attack stereotypes and negative images children hold of different cultural groups.
   (*Group behaviour*)

Activity 1: Food we like and dislike

Children could be offered food dishes which look strange. These dishes could be 'school dinner' foods which have been 'doctored' with colouring to make them look unusual. Then the same foods could be offered in the usual 'school dinner' presentation and children should be asked to taste them and discuss what makes them more acceptable. Afterwards they should be told that the dishes contained the same food: this could lead on to an examination of reasons for choice of the second dish (see the lesson plan in the Resource material, which is based on the work of Pauline Poole, when she was in her fourth year of the Trent Polytechnic BEd course in 1986–7).

Idea	Ladder stage (see page 80)	Activity	Evaluation
ENVIRONMENTAL INFLUENCE	1	Finding and collecting pictures of people dressed in different sorts of clothes.	Has a full range of different reasons for wearing particular clothes been included in the collection?
	2	Making a display that helps pupils classify clothes into different categories, e.g., religious, leisure, group, gender, etc.	Have clothes been categorised in relation to culture (e.g., Kaccha, the pair of shorts worn by Sikh Britons), protection (e.g., overalls) climate (e.g., overcoats), authority (e.g., police officers' uniforms)?
	3	Writing detailed descriptions of clothes which compare the similarities and differences of colour, material and design worn for different occasions like celebrations, work, leisure, etc.	Have similarities between clothes been stressed first and foremost (e.g., all cultures have special clothes for celebration purposes) with differences coming second (e.g., diverse styles of clothes used in celebration)?
	4	Predicting the effects of colour, design and material of clothes originating in different countries. Using library searches and presenting findings with the use of a world map.	Has the interaction of various factors been recognised, e.g., climate, geography, history, political situation?
	5/6	Holding a costume parade of old and new clothes explaining them and giving opinions about the changes that have taken place in colour, design and material. Writing a newspaper report.	Have environmental factors of climate and geography been the most important influences or have clothes changed because of historical, social and political reasons (e.g., the differences between the rich and poor, northerners and southerners, colonised and non-colonised societies)?
GROUP BEHAVIOUR	1	Identifying photographs of ethnic minority and majority Britons wearing a variety of clothes, depending on group interaction.	Has a full range of clothing been included (this should encompass white ethnic minority and majority groups plus African, Caribbean, Asian and Chinese communities in this country)?
	2	Compiling pie charts, bar graphs, etc., helping pupils to classify places of origin of clothes worn by ethnic minority and majority Britons in the region and in the wider society.	Do classifications include all major regional ethnic minority groups (e.g., in the East Midlands this would incorporate Polish, Ukrainian, Afro-Caribbean, Sikh, Hindu, Muslim, Chinese)?
	3	Developing a list of questions for adults and tape recording their replies on the reasons for similarities and differences of clothing worn by them as members of diverse groups in the region.	Have similarities between clothes been stressed first and foremost (e.g., special clothes for key occasions like worship, weddings, naming ceremonies, etc.) with differences coming second (e.g., diverse clothing based on historical and cultural traditions)?
	4	Producing an imaginary newspaper report written by someone who was not allowed to wear certain clothing that was part of his or her culture.	Has the interaction of various group factors been recognised, e.g., history and social/political situations?

Idea	Ladder stage (see page 80)	Activity	Evaluation
CHANGE	5/6	Writing a story about what it feels like to be the victim of prejudice.	Have historical, social and political factors been recognised in the discussion on prejudices against people and their styles of clothes (e.g., British colonialism)?
	1	Describing the changing styles of clothing in Britain over hundreds of years of migration to these shores, using library research skills.	Has a full range of styles been included (e.g., from the Celts, Anglo-Saxons, Vikings, Normans to African, Asian and Caribbean migrations of the post-war period)?
	2	Drawing and labelling a chronological frieze of clothes worn by people over the centuries.	Do classifications include all major groups settled in the region over the centuries as judged by looking at place names (e.g., the Whitby area shows Anglo-Saxon suffixes like *ton* (Sneaton), *borough* (Guisborough), *wick* (Runswick Bay), *ing* (Pickering), plus some Viking suffixes like *by* (Danby), *holme* (Leaholme), *dale* (Glaisdale) and one Norman name signifying a big hill (Grosmont)?
	3	Using pictures to match different clothes to particular historical situations and identifying similarities and changes.	Have similarities between clothes been stressed first and foremost (e.g., distinctive clothes worn by those in power and authority) with changes coming second (e.g., diverse clothing based on history and tradition)?
	4	Making a new clothes catalogue examining the effects of the changes to clothes suitable for different occasions, e.g., work, leisure, etc.	Have the various factors leading to change been recognised, e.g., history, geography, climate, and political situation?
	5/6	Using role play and simulation techniques to give opinions about prejudice concerning people who have migrated to Britain this century and hold special culturally diverse traditions in clothing.	Have historical, social and political factors been recognised in the discussion on prejudices against people who have diverse clothing styles (e.g., feeling of superiority by white people over those from the black community)?

Objectives

1. To consider why people like the foods they eat.
2. To help develop tolerance and understanding towards different types of British foods.
3. To develop knowledge of the variety of British vegetables and fruits sold in supermarkets and shops around the country.
4. To develop positive attitudes towards cultural diversity.

Content

1. Prepare dishes of 'school dinner' food but make them look different using colouring and presentation. Invite children to a tasting.

2. Discuss feelings in a circle using the 'discussion stone' technique, i.e., a stone is passed from hand to hand and only the person holding it can talk. This will stop interruptions and allow for considered discussion.
3. Second tasting of same food but in the usual 'school dinner' presentation. Discuss what makes this more acceptable.
4. Teacher explains that both dishes contain the same food. Discussion questions could include: Why didn't we like the first and prefer the second? What is your favourite food and why? (The notion of prejudice can be introduced at this stage.) What do you know about British fruits and vegetables?

Activity 2: Food diversity in Britain

Objectives

1. To develop positive attitudes towards cultural diversity.
2. To help appreciation of the fact that all groups have food rules and taboos.
3. To explore through role-play activities examples of prejudices about British foods.

Content

1. Discussion of food rules (see Resource material sheet 'What Britons may not eat').
2. Use of drama cards (see examples in Resource material section written by Pauline Poole), e.g.,
   (a) Teachers could create information sheets for children about participants from diverse cultures.
   (b) Pupils could be instructed as follows. Plan short play. Write out main story in note form. Devise two questions to ask the audience after completion of play. Practise and then perform play.
   (c) Using the 'discussion stone' technique again, pupils could explore how they feel. The task of the teacher is to encourage pupils to expand feelings of hurt and anger, e.g., Why did you feel like this? Have you ever felt like this before? Why do people treat others like this? Is it right and fair? If it is bad what can be done?
   (d) Key words could be written on the blackboard.
   (e) Pupils could be asked to write a personal story or a story of one of the drama characters.
3. Diverse cultural rules and taboos will be explained, e.g.,
   (a) Anglo-Saxon Britons don't eat snails.
   (b) Muslim Britons don't eat pork.
   (c) Vegetarian Britons don't eat meat, etc. (see Resource material, 'What Britons may not eat').

Possible questions to raise

Stages 1 and 2 (see page 80)

1. What food did you see, touch, smell, eat?
2. What did you think about the first/second food dish?
3. What new things did you learn from the experiment?

Stage 3

1. Why did you prefer the second dish to the first?
2. What are your favourite vegetable and fruit and why?
3. Why do we like certain foods and dislike others?

Stage 4

1. What do you think would have happened if food at home looked like the first food dish?
2. What would you say if you were given one of these dishes to eat: spaghetti, curry, mousaka, sweet and sour chicken? Explain why you would react in that way.

Stages 5 and 6

1. Do you think it is *good* to say 'I don't like this food and won't eat it'? Why?
2. Do you think it is *right* to stop people eating food of their choice?
3. Do you think it is *fair* to cook the same food for all pupils and expect everyone to eat the meat and vegetables in the dishes?

BRITISH MUSIC

Aims

1. To examine the contribution of different cultures, highlighting similarities and common features.
   (*Influence of environment and group behaviour*)
2. To help children appreciate the role of different cultures in the development of British music.
   (*Change*)
3. To help discussion of prejudice, starting with musical tastes but perhaps extending to prejudices against cultures and races.
   (*Group behaviour and change*)

Activity 1: Similarities approach

1. Show how cultures have music for similar occasions, such as entertainment, ceremonies, dancing, etc. Questions could include: Where do we hear music? What is it used for? (e.g. on the radio, at discos, at ceremonies, festivals, religious events, etc.)
2. Listen to music for various occasions, such as dancing, entertainment, weddings. Questions: What occasion do you think it is for? How do you feel about it?
3. Demonstrate that all cultures use four main methods for making sounds on musical

instruments, i.e., striking (percussion), plucking (strings), bowing (strings), blowing (woodwind or brass).

4. Try making musical sounds by the above methods (this will be dependent on resources and skills). Stress how the same method of sound production results in similar-looking instruments, e.g., the ud (or lute) from Syria; tampura (or lute) from North India; guitar from Europe. Either study pictures or use real examples of various instruments to demonstrate similarity of shape.
5. Examine modern British music as a mixture of styles and influences, e.g.,
   (a) Rock and roll derived from African music via North America (Africans were transported to this continent during the time of the slave trade).
   (b) In the 1960s Indian styles and instruments and Jamaican music influenced British 'pop' music.
6. Listen to a variety of British music and decide where the influences or instruments originate.

Activity 2: Critical approach

Play 'Sun City', which was in the charts between November and January 1986. Time and circumstances permitting, use 'Biko' and 'Redemption Song' (see Resource material section). Teachers could try to explain the content of any one song, e.g., 'Sun City' and 'Biko' on the South African situation, or 'Redemption Song' written by the Rastafarian Bob Marley. There are book references in the Resource material section for those who wish to examine further the South African and Rastafarianism topics.

Naturally, more recent songs concerning racial issues can be supplemented because their topicality might ensure more interest and motivation to learn.

Possible questions to raise

Stages 1 and 2 (see page 80)

1. Where can we hear music? In discos? On the radio? At religious ceremonies? At marriages? During festivals?
2. When did Indian styles of music and instruments begin to influence music in Britain?
3. What are the main methods for making sounds on musical instruments?
4. Listen to this piece of music. What occasion do you think this is for?

Stage 3

1. Why are there different styles of music for different occasions?
2. Why do different ethnic groups have different sounds and sometimes use different instruments?
3. Why did Indian and Jamaican music influence British music in the 1960s?
4. Why do you like a certain kind of music and dislike other kinds of music?

Stage 4

1. What would have happened to British music if there had been no Indian and African influence?
2. What kind of music might you write if you were a British Rastafarian?
3. What kind of music might you sing if you were a black South African?
4. What would you feel like living in a country with an apartheid system?

Stages 5 and 6

1. Do you think this piece of music is *good*? Why? (Play a variety of types.)
2. Do you think it is *right* to stop people making and playing music of their choice, sung in their own language, and performing it on British television?
3. Do you think it is *fair* to treat Rastafarians any differently from those of any other British religion and culture?
4. Do you think it is *right and fair* to have an apartheid system in South Africa?

RESOURCE MATERIAL

Contents

British food

This section includes the following:

1. What Britons may not eat
2. The similarities approach
3. Drama cards
   These aim to raise issues concerning prejudice and were written by Pauline Poole in 1986 during her last year on the BEd course at Trent Polytechnic.
4. Work-card
   One example of the kind of work-card that can be used to stimulate activity work in the cookery area.

What Britons may not eat

Some people are influenced by their religion when choosing what to eat and what not to eat while others feel strongly that killing animals is wrong. Ticks show what is taken and a cross shows what is rejected by those who are strong believers.

	BRITISH							
			Christian					
	Vegetarian	Vegan	Roman Catholic	C of E	Jews	Sikhs	Muslims	Hindus
Eggs	√	×	√	√	√	√	√	√
Milk and yoghurt	√	×	√	√	√	√	√	√
Cheese	√	×	√	√	√	√	√	√
Chicken	×	×	Some prefer to avoid meat on Friday	√	Kosher	√	Halal	×
Mutton	×	×		√	Kosher	√	Halal	×
Beef	×	×		√	Kosher	×	Halal	×
Pork	×	×		√	×	Rarely eaten	×	×
Fish	×	×		√	√	√	√	×
Shellfish	×	×	√	√	×	√	√	√
Animal fat (butter, lard and some margarines)	√	×	√	√	Kosher, no lard	√	Halal, no lard	Butter

Notes: Muslims and Jews have special butchers where Halal and Kosher meat are sold.

Many Jewish people do not eat meat and dairy foods in the same meal, and have separate sets of kitchenware for meat and dairy products.

In every faith there are liberal and strict (orthodox) members.

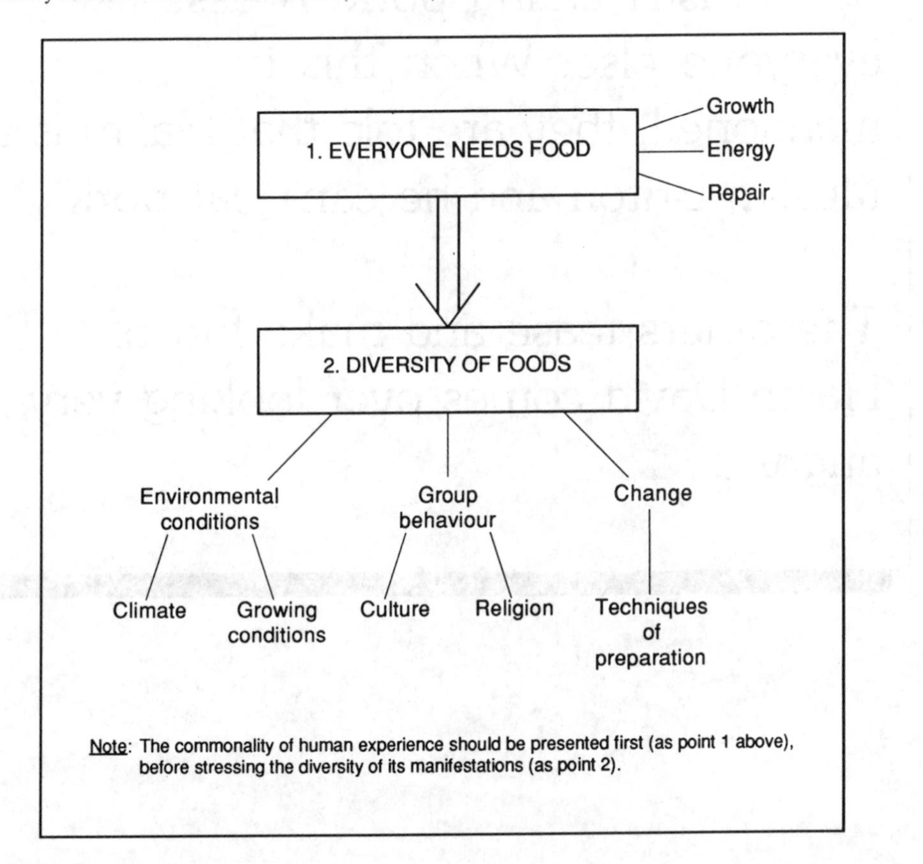

Figure 13. The similarities approach.

Drama Card A

Three children are sitting at a table eating their lunch. They are chatting and laughing.

A fourth person comes and sits down. One of the others notices that this person isn't eating pork fricassé like everyone else. When this is mentioned, they are told that Halim is a Muslim Briton and he can't eat pork

The others tease and make fun of Halim. David comes over looking very angry . . .

Drama Card B

At a birthday party Rachael suddenly bursts into tears as Mrs Parr pours cream sauce on the lamb.

Rachael explains she can't eat the meat because she is a Jewish Briton.

Everyone tells her not to worry: 'God isn't looking!' says Angela.

Rachael runs out of the restaurant in tears. The others talk about it while Alison goes after Rachael . . .

Work-Card

<u>Coconut sweetmeats</u>

Naseem, Aqeel and Neelam are soon going to celebrate 'Holi' which is a Hindu festival. The tricks children play at Holi are very similar to the tricks children play on April Fool's Day. The children in their class think it would be a good idea to have a Holi party so they can all celebrate together and play lots of tricks and games with each other. They have asked Naseem, Aqeel and Neelam to show them how to make coconut sweetmeats for the party.

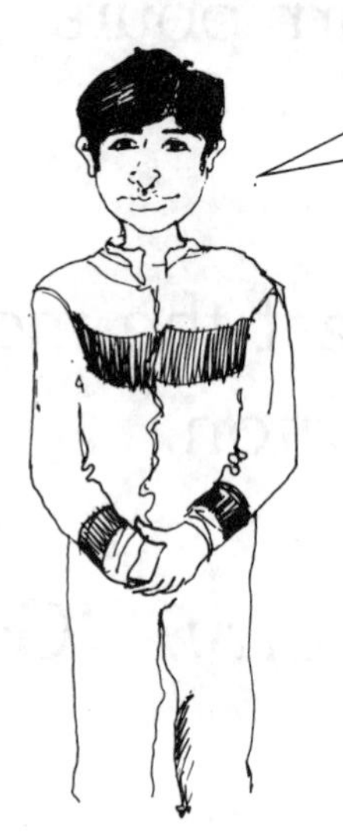

Put on an apron, and then gather together all the ingredients you need.

1. Boil the milk and coconut in a pan until all the milk is soaked up - 'absorbed'.

2. Mix the milk powder and water together.

3. Add this to the coconut mixture in the pan and cook for five minutes.

4. Add the sugar and nutmeg, and cook for another ten minutes until the mixture is quite dry.

5. Leave the mixture until it's cool enough to touch.

Please remember to wash your hands

6. Roll about a teaspoon of the mixture in your hands to make small bite size balls.

Remember to wash and tidy up when you have finished

All the children in Naseem's class really enjoyed these sweetmeats. They enjoyed them so much that they are now making a book of recipes from all over the world. They have asked children, teachers and parents, and have written to people they know in different parts of the country and the world.

Have a go at making your own recipe book - think of all the different people you know and ask them.

British music

Changes in musical tastes will naturally lead to the choice of different examples but it is hoped that the approach will be maintained.

The choices below were made by Geoffrey Lowe when he was a fourth-year student on the Trent Polytechnic BEd course in 1985–6.

Examples of useful music which could be used in multicultural studies

1. 'If It Happens Again' by UB40
   Reggae: Afro-Caribbean influence developed during the 1960s
2. 'Jig of Life' by Kate Bush
   Irish influence and instruments
3. 'Ever so Lonely' by Monsoon
   Indian influence and music
4. 'Afrika' by Manfred Mann's Earthband
   Voices based on South African tribal songs
5. 'Yaman' by Indo-Jazz Ensemble
   Indian and European instruments in jazz
6. 'Portsmouth' by Mike Oldfield
   Traditional English instruments and style

Examples for anti-racist studies

1. 'Sun City' by Artists Against Apartheid
   Comment on the Sun City entertainments complex in South Africa. The artists involved state that they will not be seen to support the system in South Africa by performing in Sun City.
2. 'Biko' by Peter Gabriel
   A comment on the death of Steve Biko while in police custody in South Africa in 1977. See *Apartheid: a Teaching Pack* by M. Kehily and I. Grosvenor (Trade Union Resource Centre publication, 1987; 7 Frederick Street, Birmingham B1 3HE), and *Censoring Reality: an Examination of Books on South Africa*, by B. Naidoo (ILEA Centre for Anti-Racist Education, 1986).
3. 'Redemption Song' by Manfred Mann's Earthband (also by Marley himself)
   Written by Rastafarian Bob Marley in the early 1970s and comments on the situation of those of African descent whose ancestors were originally transported during the slave trade.

Further topics

A variety of traditional topics can be adapted to incorporate the approach of this book. These include the following areas: World Cup; Olympic, World, and Commonwealth Games; the Marathon; Diversity in British Sports; Holidays and Travelling (e.g., what it feels like to be part of a minority group, even for a short time). Historical issues can be modified to incorporate the equal opportunity perspective (e.g., Victorian Britain, focusing on the role of women and the contribution of the Empire to Britain's development and wealth; the two World Wars, stressing the contribution of women and black people from Britain and around the world).

We offer a short selection of ideas for further topic work.

Football topic

Football clubs are microcosms of a culturally plural society with players and other staff coming from different backgrounds, and even speaking different languages. There are, in our view, four approaches that teachers can take. The first involves the local or regional team, preferably one in the higher divisions of the football league. Children could find out the background and mother tongue of the players by reading club programmes, and obtain help from club officials and players. Visits to the club to watch a football match could be arranged and some clubs will even organise a trip around the stadium and a meeting with officials.

The second approach could take a major team in the country and examine its players. For example, Manchester United, the 1985 FA Cup Winners, had a team which reflected the cultural diversity within Britain, starting with its goalkeeper, Gary Bailey, who was born in South Africa but plays for England. Other players include: John Gidman (England player), Kevin Moran (Eire), Paul McGrath (Afro-Caribbean Briton), Gordon Strachan (Scotland), Jesper Olsen (Danish), Norman Whiteside (Northern Ireland), Mark Hughes (Wales), Frank Stapleton (Eire), Arthur Albiston (Scotland) and Bryan Robson (England). The substitute for the game was Mike Duxbury of England; other famous players employed by the club include Remi Moses (Afro-Caribbean Briton), Alan Brazil, Gordon McQueen, Graeme Hogg (Scottish Britons).

So far we have suggested a locality approach (i.e. start with your local team) and a national approach (choose cup final winners). The third approach again focuses on the national game with children picking players from all teams; this will show cultural diversity within Britain, irrespective of team. Research on a wide variety of teams will produce plenty of examples for children to discuss, e.g., Garth Crooks, John Barnes, Brian Stein and others who are Afro-Caribbean Britons; Charlie Nicholas (Scotland), Ian Rush (Wales), Sammy McIlroy (Northern Ireland). These Britons are only a few of many whom the children could find in their researches.

In addition to the exercise which searches for different types of Britons, children can also pick out certain 'guest workers', such as Osvaldo Ardiles from Argentina, who are only here for a relatively short time.

A fourth approach would focus on Europe. If you are fortunate enough to have a team in the region which is or has been in the European Champions Cup, UEFA Cup or European Cup Winners Cup, the club programme could act as a start to a useful project. For example, the Nottingham Forest versus AEK Athens match on 1 November 1978 offers opportunities for such a topic, with all the flags of countries in UEFA and a map of these countries with relevant information. On the first page there is a short greeting written in Greek which could be used to show a different language and to demonstrate linguistic acceptance. The information on the middle page with team names and backgrounds will help familiarise children with Greek names which are found in Britain today, as over 100 000 Cypriot Britons live here.

A fifth approach would be a historical one which would involve the examination of club programmes over a period of time. One example of this exercise would be a study of players from the Nottingham Forest teams between 1980 and 1985. Naturally, the team is dominated by Anglo-Saxon Britons like the famous Peter Shilton, Trevor Francis, Tony Woodcock and Peter Davenport. But these players have been partnered by many other groups of Britons such as Afro-Caribbean (Justin Fashanu, Chris Fairclough, Calvin Plummer, Viv Anderson), Scottish (John Robertson, Kenny Burns, Ian Wallace, Archie Gemmill), Irish (Martin O'Neill), Welsh (Bryn Gunn), Cypriot (Charlie George). In addition, diverse groups of 'guest players' have been included in the team, especially Dutchmen (Hans van Breukelen, Hans Segers, Frans Thijssen, Johnny Metgod), German (Hans Jurgen Roeber), Norwegian (Einer Jan Aas) and an Italian Swiss called Raymondo Ponte.

Commonwealth Games topic

A class of top juniors can be given the task of organising its own version of the Commonwealth Games. Groups can work on charts of different participants with maps of countries and photographs of key athletes. Resources of big and small countries can be compared and contrasted and questions asked about facilities, equipment and coaching. A Commonwealth village for athletes can be designed with general discussions on where the money should go and how the accommodation should be constructed, given the constraints of finance and diversity of cultures, and therefore differences in religion and customs. Should different buildings of worship be constructed? Should athletes be mixed or segregated? Should different catering facilities be arranged? If so, what facilities are needed? Another group can tackle the issue of who is good at what? What are the influences on sport? Can we stereotype by race? Are black people naturally better runners? Why are there so many black runners? Which country is good at what and why?

Once this work has been finished the teacher can try to examine the notion of colonisation by asking why people migrate and colonise, and use can be made of creative writings of the 'I was there' variety, e.g., 'Imagine yourself as . . .'.

Marathon Race topic

Major events such as the London Marathon can be used to show the cultural diversity of participants, whose backgrounds can be studied by the pupils. Teachers can then create an imaginary locality-based marathon run and children can help prepare an appropriate route. In order to counteract the male dominance of major marathon runs, this marathon can be for women. Teachers can furnish a selected list of supposed contestants who are obviously from different cultural origins and who represent the ethnic diversity in the religion. Pupils can prepare background notes for each group of participants to be included in the class newspaper. Interviews can be created and stories recounted, the aim being to help children empathise with those of different cultures.

Details can be given of pre-match food eaten by various groups, clothes worn, customs, languages, entertainments, interests.

Travel Agent topic

Children can imagine that they are travel agents trying to sell package tours to the class group. Teachers can choose the countries of origin of various ethnic groups in the region and delegate each group to produce a document and posters advertising the country to potential tourists. Apart from selecting places of beauty and interest to visit, children can include one or two key words in the language of the country. Local community groups and travel agents can be approached to help in this topic.

Churches and Cathedrals/Kings and Queens

Topics on churches and cathedrals can include the usual architectural features—Norman, Early English, Decorated, Perpendicular, etc.—but stress can be placed on the migration of the Normans, the Angevins, etc., to Britain, as well as explanation of the wonderful architecture built during these periods. Similarly, topics on the Kings and Queens can emphasise their 'multi-culturalism' in origin, from Norman and Angevin to a variety of rulers (e.g. William of Orange, George of Hanover), their spouses (Prince Philip, among many others) and relatives (e.g., the Mountbattens of Battenberg).

Select booklist

British clothes

For pupils
Aggarwal, M. (1984) *I Am a Sikh*. London: Franklin Watts.
Aggarwal, M. (1984) *I Am a Muslim*. London: Franklin Watts.
Aggarwal, M. (1984) *I Am a Hindu*. London: Franklin Watts.
Cooke, J. (1986) *Costumes and Clothes*. Brighton: Wayland.
Lawton, C. (1984) *I Am a Jew*. London: Franklin Watts.
Lloyd, E. (1978) *Nini at Carnival*. London: Bodley Head.
Lyle, S. (1977) *Pavan Is a Sikh*. London: A & C Black.
MacCarty, N. (1979) *Rebecca Is a Cypriot*. London: A & C Black.
Solomon, J. (1978) *Kate's Party*. London: Hamish Hamilton.
Solomon, J. (1981) *A Present for Mum*. London: Hamish Hamilton.
Solomon, J. (1981) *Wedding Day*. London: Hamish Hamilton.

For teachers
Sealey, A. (1983) Primary school projects: a multicultural approach. In Coles, M. (ed.), *Issues and Resources: a Handbook for Teachers in the Multicultural Society*. Birmingham:AFFOR, pages 41–2.

For suppliers in dolls, puppets, costumes, etc., Unity Learning Foundation, 10 Barley Mow Passage, London W4 4PH.

British food

For pupils

Eccleshare, J. (1986) *Fruit Salad: a First Look at Fruit*. London: Hamish Hamilton.
Lawton, C. (1984) *Matza and Bitter Herbs* (Strand series). London: Hamish Hamilton (a Jewish family celebrating Passover).
MacKinnon, K. (1984) *The Phoenix Bird Chinese Take Away* (Strand series). London: A & C Black. (Chinese family in Glasgow: includes wedding, going to school and going shopping).
Mayled, J. (1986) *Feasting and Fasting*. Brighton: Wayland (six groups and their customs and traditions, from the 'Religious Topics' series).
Solomon, J. (1980) *Gifts and Almonds*. London: Hamish Hamilton (Muslim family celebrating Eid).
Turner, D. (1982) *A Day with a Shopkeeper*. Brighton: Wayland (Mr Khan from Brighton).
Child Education, September 1981, contains recipes for pupils, e.g., banana cake, halvas, scone pizza, caramella biscuits, chappatis.
Derbyshire Multicultural Education Centre (1987) *Caribbean Vegetables and Fruit*.

For teachers

Child Education project on bread (1985), no. 43.
Clark, E. P. (1976) *West Indian Cooking*. London: Nelson.
Collymore, Y. (1972) *Cooking Our Way*. Aylesbury: Ginn.
CRE (1976) *Afro Hair, Skin Care and Recipes*. London: CRE.
Deh-Ta, H. (1978) *The Home Book of Chinese Cookery*. London: Faber.
Hutchinson, G. (1985) *Home Economics for You (Books 1 and 2)*. Glasgow: Blackie (probably useful for top juniors).
ILEA (1985) *Food: a Resource for Learning in the Primary School* (book starts from the children's own experiences and offers advice on cooking activities, safety, hygiene, equipment and resources).
Houlton, D. (1986) *Cultural Diversity in the Primary School*. London: Batsford (pages 116–17 on a Harvest Festival topic theme).
Jaffrey, M. (1982) *Indian Cookery*. London: BBC.

Material on world food issues

CAFOD (Catholic Fund for Overseas Development) (1986) *Just Food: School Resource and Education Pack*. 2 Garden Close, Stockwell Road, London SW9 9TY.
Christian Aid (1982) *World Feast Game*. PO Box no. 1, London SW9 8BH. (Designed for 10–12-year-olds and played by 20–35 pupils with the ideal number being 30. You will need 2–3 hours to complete the game.)
OXFAM (1985) *Potato Profile*. 274 Banbury Road, Oxford OX2 7DZ.

British music

For pupils

Burnett, M. (1982) *Jamaican Music*. Oxford: OUP.

Conolly, Y. (1981) *Mango Spice*. London: A & C Black (this book contains Afro-Caribbean songs on food and drink, religion, animals, work, love, games).

Floyd, L. (1980) *Indian Music*. Oxford: OUP.

Sealey, J. and Malm, K. (1982) *Music in the Caribbean*. London: Hodder & Stoughton.

For teachers

Bebey, F. (1975) *African Music: a People's Art*. Westport, CT: Lawrence Hill/London: Harrap.

Clarke, S. (1980) *Shah Music*. London: Heinemann.

Hagan, L. (1984) Keep with the beat. *Junior Education*, April, 27.

Hoyle, S. (1982) Music in the classroom. *Education Journal*, March, 1–6.

Neville, J. (1984) Music in the multicultural curriculum. *Music Teacher*, April, 12.

Neville, J. (1985) Aspects of music in the multicultural curriculum. *Music Teacher*, May, 14.

Shepard, F. (1982) Music and education. *Dragon's Teeth*, no. 13, Spring, 6–7.

Watson, P. (1984) Music teaching. *Multicultural Education Review*, Summer, 8.

Unity Learning Foundation for charts and musical instruments.

The ILEA has published an extensive resource document called *Music in a Multicultural Society*. It can be obtained from the ILEA Music Centre, Sutherland Street, Ebury Bridge, London SW1V 4LH.

Here are some important addresses.

Academy of Indian Classical Dance, 24 Old Gloucester St, London W1. Telephone 01-430 0790. Work in schools. In-service work with teachers.

Africa Centre, 38 King Street, Covent Garden, London WC2. Telephone 01-836 1973. Produces 'Arts Link' concerts/dance/drama. Group membership £30.

African Arts in Education, Cobourg Street, Cobourg School, London SE5. Telephone 01-703 1619. Music, dance, drama, arts courses for teachers. Literature available.

AIMER, Bulmershe College of HE, Earley, Reading RG6 1HY. Telephone 0734 663387. Resources data bank.

Aklowa, Felix Cobson, Takely House, Brewers End, Takely, nr Bishops Stortford, Herts. Telephone 0279 871062. Centre for traditional drumming and dance. Runs courses/workshops/performance.

Centre for Indian Arts, 17 Holdenhurst Ave, London N12. Telephone 01-346 5401. Booklet on music and dance available.

East Midlands Arts, Mountfield House, Forest Road, Loughborough, Leics. LE11 5HU. Telephone 0509 218292. Produce a directory of ethnic arts activities in the East Midlands.

Minority Arts Advisory Service, Beauchamp Lodge, 2 Warwick Crescent, London W2. Telephone 01-286 1854. National information and resource centre.

Background information on Rastafarianism

Barrett, L. (1977) *The Rastafarians*. London: Heinemann.
Davis, S. and Simon, P. (1977) *Reggae Bloodlines: in Search of Music and Culture in Jamaica*. New York: Anchor Press, Doubleday.
Kallyndyr, R. and Dalrymple, H. (1974) *Reggae: a People's Music*. Sudbury: Carib-Arawak Publications.
Nicholas, T. (1979) *Rastafari*. New York: Anchor Press, Doubleday.
Troyna, B. (1978) *Rastafarianism, Reggae and Racism*. Leicester: National Association for Multi-racial Education.

Chapter 7

Cultural Studies

THE COMMUNITY DIMENSION

In our view, topics in Community Studies should involve two essential approaches—the neighbourhood and the regional. Both will be summarised before presentation of two curricular examples.

The neighbourhood approach

Rarely will a school be the centre of a united community involving a common feeling of belonging and group solidarity. Around it can be found a multitude of groupings that are formed by people who wish to share their similar interests. Common housing perspectives may lead to the formation of a residents' association; common ethnic, social class and gender-based perceptions may result in the creation of special organisations for cultural and identity maintenance; similar leisure interests may lead to the development of clubs and societies; certain political views may result in pressure groups for change or conservation. The list is endless.

Interest communities

Both parents and children will belong to a mixture of groups depending on interests, opportunities and financial constraints. Some of these 'interest communities' will have a strong influence on members while other clubs and societies may simply take up time, energy and effort and be 'somewhere to go' and 'something to do'. Whatever the reasons for attendance and participation it is the duty of teachers to learn something about the interest communities which take up some of the time of families with pupils in the school. Knowing the interest and activities of mum, dad and children will help teachers understand the influences surrounding the pupil, and may lead to insights which can then be used to develop pupil learning in the classroom situation.

Locality trail

We would like to propose that schools engage in the production of a locality trail. This would involve a staff study of the local community organisations and amenities followed by discussion on influences and the importance of interest communities on parents and pupils. Perhaps such an exercise could be usefully executed on an in-service training day. Armed with a road map and checklist, teachers could walk around the local area in search of the interest community organisations that influence the daily lives of the families with children in their schools. This day and evening-time activity could involve discussions with local leaders of clubs, societies and associations, and the subsequent creation of an 'Interest community dossier', which can be updated and modified at regular intervals.

Checklist

In order to participate in a locality trail, we suggest that during the search teachers use some of the headings below. We recognise that there is overlap between sections but divisions have been made only for the purpose of study.

1. Cultural activities, e.g., Cubs, Brownies, Scouts, Guides, social and community organisations
2. Sports, e.g., sports stadium, clubs and societies, swimming pool
3. Leisure, e.g., pubs, social and hobby-based clubs, library
4. Entertainment, e.g., discos, cinemas, social clubs, pubs
5. Spiritual welfare, e.g., religious organisations and clubs
6. Social welfare facilities, e.g., senior citizens club, one-parent family group, child minding facilities
7. Training and education centres, e.g., evening institutes, YTS schemes for youth, facilities for unemployed and handicapped, nurseries
8. Employment and unemployment, e.g., job opportunities and social/cultural amenities within the workplace, Job Centre and extent of unemployment
9. General background to locality, e.g., shopping facilities, meeting places in coffee lounges and local cafes, health centre, social services, vandalism, graffiti, private/council house mix

The regional approach

Schools involved in the neighbourhood approach should discover the extent and influence of organisations in the locality. Such knowledge could lead to greater awareness and understanding of attitudes, beliefs and behaviour of pupils in the school and adults in the catchment area. However, this neighbourhood dimension should be

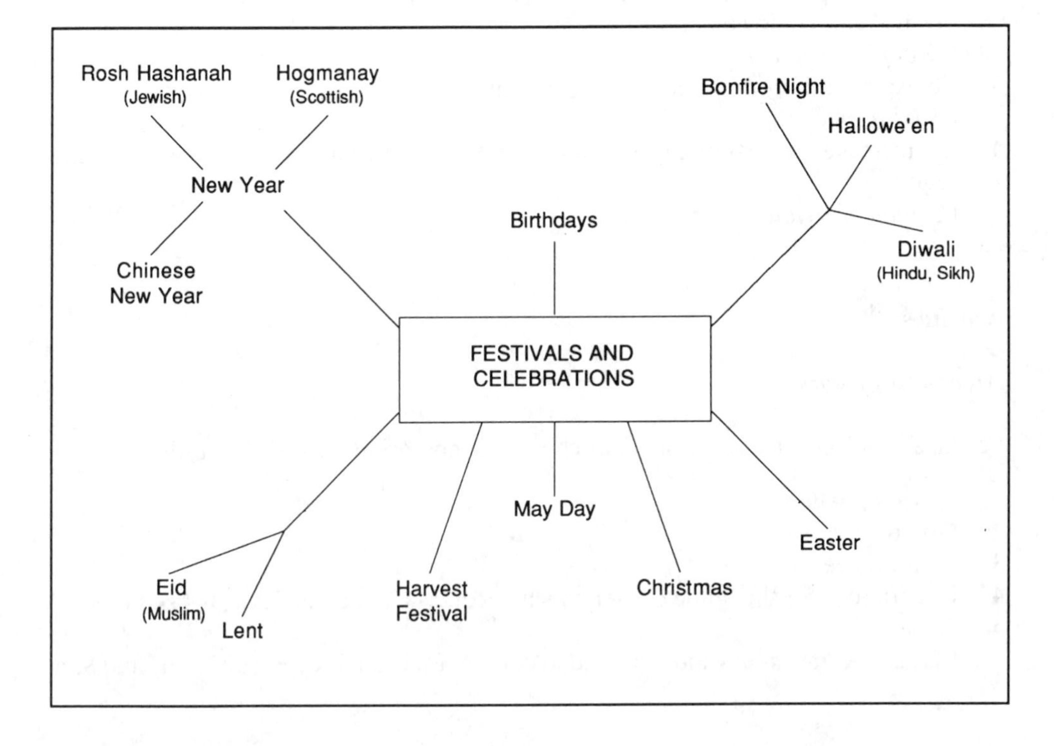

Figure 14. Some British festivals and celebrations.

combined with a regional approach, which widens the school focus to the regional capital and major cities. Any school examining regional community groups will necessarily be involved in ethnic minority and majority cultural studies. As part of a policy of transmitting the richness of cultures around us, a World in our Region theme would develop children's appreciation of diverse cultural groupings in the wider geographical area.

We strongly recommend the inclusion of a variety of celebratory activities at appropriate times throughout the school year, when teachers can present topics on a range of festivals as suggested in Figure 14. Diwali and Eid are examined in the hope that they will act as illustrations for preparing others.

DIWALI

Aims

1. To show similarities between new year celebrations, such as the Scottish and the Chinese.
   (*Group behaviour factors*)

2. To compare celebrations in Britain around this period, e.g., Bonfire Night, Harvest Festival and Hallowe'en.
   (*Group behaviour*)
3. To explain differences and the reasons behind diversity.
   (*All three factors*)
4. To increase understanding of Sikh and Hindu Britons in neighbourhood and region.
   (*Group behaviour and change*)

Activities

Art and Craft work

Produce and decorate classroom and school in preparation for the celebrations, e.g.,

1. Welcoming mats
2. Greetings cards
3. Wall collage
4. Decorations for the home corner which becomes a Hindu or Sikh British home
5. Divas
6. Masks, e.g., monkeys and ten-headed demon, for drama session on Rama and Sita

Language

1. Creative work after the story of Rama and Sita
2. New words associated with Diwali
3. Poetry
4. Work on a variety of festivals and celebrations in Britain
5. Work on moral issues such as good and bad, jealousy and envy, bravery and cowardice

Maths

1. Baking and tasting of relevant foods after measuring and costing ingredients
2. Calculating how many cards, candles, etc., will be needed and costing them
3. Symmetry through Rangoli designs

Music, Drama and Dance

1. Listen to music and learn to dance
2. Dramatise story of Rama and Sita
3. Use Indian musical instruments and learn some Indian folk songs

Possible questions to raise

Stages 1 and 2 (see page 80)

1. At what time of year is Diwali held?
2. What do Sikh and Hindu Britons do to prepare for Diwali?
3. Tell the famous Hindu story which is told at Diwali time.
4. What are the similarities between Diwali and other celebrations held in Britain?

Stage 3

1. Why did Hindu and Sikh Britons settle in this country?
2. Why do people all over the world celebrate New Year's Day?
3. Why do we give cards and presents on special celebrations, dress up and eat special foods?

Stage 4

1. What do you think would happen if your school celebrated Diwali in assembly every year?
2. What would you do if you heard somebody call a Sikh or Hindu Briton 'Paki'?
3. What do you think it would be like to be a Sikh or Hindu British boy or girl in your school?

Stages 5 and 6

1. Do you think it is *good* to celebrate different people's festivals in your school? Why?
2. Do you think it is *right* to stop people working because they wear turbans and look different?
3. Do you think it is *fair* to treat Sikh and Hindu Britons any differently from other people in this country?

EID

Aims

1. To increase awareness and understanding of Muslim Britons. (*Group behaviour and change*)
2. To show similarities between Ramadan and Lent and Eid and other celebrations. (*All three factors*)

Activities

1. Produce materials in preparation for celebrating Eid, e.g., Eid cards, decorations.
2. Discuss similarities between Lent and Ramadan.
3. Read story of Muhammad.
4. Design Mehndi patterns on hand.
5. Point out Islamic patterns on buildings (useful maths activity concerning geometric shapes).
6. Cook sweets and food for the Eid festival such a burfi, samosas, pakaras, halva (show similarities of food between groups, e.g., halvas).
7. Introduce music and dance and appropriate instruments.

Possible questions to raise

Stages 1 and 2 (see page 80)

1. Using maps, teachers can ask: what places in the world believe in the Muslim faith?
2. When did Muslim Britons settle in your region, etc.?
3. What are the main Muslim beliefs?

Stage 3

1. Why did Muslim Britons settle in your region?
2. Why did your own parents/grandparents settle here?
3. Why do Muslims fast for a month? Compare fasting with what should happen at Lent in the Christian calendar.
4. Why do people all over the world have foods they can and do eat and food they cannot eat for religious and other reasons?

Stage 4

1. What do you think would happen if you mocked somebody's religion, the clothes they wear and what they believe?
2. What would you do if you heard somebody saying to Muslim Britons, 'Pakis go home'?
3. What do you think it would be like being a Muslim Briton in your school?

Stages 5 and 6

1. Do you think it is *good* to celebrate Eid in your school? Why?
2. Do you think it is *right* that Muslim Britons are sometimes insulted when they are walking in the street?

3. Do you think it is *fair* to treat Muslim Britons any differently from those whose ancestors have been here for a long time?

RESOURCE MATERIAL

Contents

Diwali

Resources include:

1. Information sheet for pupils
2. Story written for children
3. Useful addresses

A description of work done at Ladypool School in Sparkbrook can be found in *Multicultural Education Review* (see Hamilton, 1985).

3. Useful addresses

Sikh Cultural Society, 88 Mollinson Way, Edgware, London HA8 5OW.
Sikh Missionary Society, 10 Featherstone Road, Southall, Middlesex.
Hindu Centre, 39 Grafton Terrace, London NW5.
Indian Government Tourist Office, 21 New Bond Street, London W1 0DY.

Eid

Resources include:

1. Information sheet for pupils
2. Information for teachers: Islam at a glance
3. Useful addresses for information, books and visual material

2. Information for teachers

This material is reproduced by kind permission of the Islamic Cultural Centre.

1. Information sheet for pupils

1. Diwali, the New Year celebration, is associated with Hindu and Sikh religions.

2. The word 'Diwali' means 'cluster of lights' and is also spelt 'Divali'.

3. It is celebrated during the four days at the end of October/beginning of November and marks the end of the harvest and the start of a new year.

4. Diwali signifies the triumph of good over evil and light over darkness. It coincides with Hallowe'en and they should be compared and contrasted.

5. The story most associated with Diwali is that of Prince Rama and his wife Sita who, after exile, danger and many adventures, returned to their kingdom and were welcomed back by the glow of lamps lit by their subjects. The festival is celebrated by lighting divas or Diwali lamps in homes.

6. New Year's Day is celebrated by visiting relatives and friends, feasting and giving cards and presents. Decorations are put up using patterns of all sorts, especially rangoli patterns.

7. Here is a list of the celebrations that could take place:
   (a) service in the Sikh Gurdwara or Hindu temple
   (b) houses lit up with candles and lamps or divas
   (c) doors, windows and rooms decorated with paper chains, lanterns, flowers and rangoli patterns
   (d) special foods and sweets, e.g., parathas (savoury pancake), pakoras (vegetable fritters), balfi (sweets)
   (e) visit neighbours, friends and relatives
   (f) giving cards and presents

2. The Story of Diwali
(for children)

Diwali is the Hindu festival of lights. The story of Diwali comes from a famous Indian book called the Ramayana and it is a story that is thousands of years old . . .

There was once a king who had three wives and the wives all had sons. One of the sons was called Rama. A few miles away lived a princess called Sita. She had an enormous bow and she would only marry the prince who could string her bow. Many princes came to try their luck, but none of them could even lift the bow. Rama came and he lifted the bow easily and managed to string it. So Rama and Sita were married. They went home to see the king and the king said, 'I'm getting old now and Rama can be king in my place.' Rama's step-mother was jealous. She said to the king, 'You owe me two wishes. I want my own son to become king and I want Rama to go away for fourteen years.' The King had to keep his promise and so he agreed. So Rama and Sita went to the forest and sometimes Rama went hunting. He left Sita in a magic circle to protect her. One day, Ravana the wicked demon came. He tricked Sita into stepping out of the circle. Ravana took Sita to Lanka, his kingdom. Rama searched everywhere for her. While he was searching, he met Hanuman, the monkey god. The monkeys helped Rama to fight Ravana and rescue Sita. Rama took Sita home. Everyone lit lamps and decorated their houses to welcome them back. This is why candles are lit at Diwali. Rama and Sita became king and queen.

1. Information sheet for pupils

1. The followers of Islam are called Muslims and their founder, Muhammad, received the word of God and wrote everything in the Koran (Qur'an) or holy book.

2. Their beliefs revolve around the Five Pillars of Faith, which are:
   (a) belief in God
   (b) prayer five times a day
   (c) giving alms to the poor
   (d) fasting during the lunar month of Ramadan.
   (e) going to the holy city of Mecca at least once in a lifetime

3. The ninth lunar month is Ramadan, when Muslims are expected to fast during daylight. It is regarded as a special month because Muslims believe that it was at this time that Muhammad first began to receive revelations from God. Exceptions to the fast include: children, pregnant women, the sick and travellers.

4. Each day of Ramadan begins with a morning meal (called Sehri) taken as near as possible to dawn. Fasting alerts Muslims to the sufferings and needs of the poor, and they also learn the value of self-discipline. The fast is broken immediately after sunset.

5. Eid-ul-fitr celebrates the end of the fast and occurs on the first day of the new moon. Eid is a family celebration, with feasting, presents and cards.

6. The Muslim calendar is based on the lunar cycle. The months can be 30 or 29 days, according to the appearance of the moon, and this results in a Muslim year 10 days shorter than the western year, which is based on the movements of the sun.

7. The flesh of the pig is forbidden, as is any food which contains lard. Margarine made from vegetable oil is permitted.

8. Muslims should not eat the flesh of animals or birds which have not been slaughtered in the approved ritual fashion (called Halal meat).

9. Muslims are expected to go to the mosque on Fridays.

ISLAM AT A GLANCE

Islam and the Muslim

The Arabic word Islam means submission and resignation, and it is derived from a word meaning Peace. In the religious context it means submission to the Will of God, and a Muslim is someone who recognises and accepts God's absolute Sovereignty and surrenders himself (or herself) totally to his (or her) Lord and Creator. 'Muhammadanism' is a misnomer for the religion of Islam because it suggests that Muslims worship Muhammad, the Messenger of God.

Continuity of the message

Islam does not claim to be a 'new' religion. It is, in essence, the same Truth that God revealed through all His prophets and messengers:

'Say: We believe in Allah and that which was revealed to us, and that which was revealed to Abraham and Ishmael and Isaac and Jacob and the tribes, and that which was given to Moses and Jesus and to (all) the prophets from their Lord; we make no distinction between any of them, and to Him we submit' (Qur'an 3.83).

The message revealed through the Prophet Muhammad was, however, the final and comprehensive revelation, completing all that had come before.

Basic beliefs

A Muslim believes in the unity of the One God. He believes in all His messengers and in the messages—'Books' or 'Scriptures'—which they brought for the guidance of mankind. He believes also in the Angels, in the Day of Judgement, in man's accountability for his actions and in life after death.

Unity of God

The Muslim's faith in the Unity and Sovereignty of God makes him aware that he lives in a meaningful universe and enables him to understand his place in it. This faith must be translated into action, for faith alone is not enough in Islam. Belief in the One God, who is the Creator and Nourisher of all living things, implies that the whole of humanity is a single family. Islam rejects the idea of a 'chosen people'. Faith and good actions are the only criteria by which men and women are to be judged and the direct relationship with God, without any intermediary, is open to all alike.

Man the free agent

Man is the highest creation of God on earth, given potentialities greater than those of any other creature and given the privilege of choosing between good and evil. Through the Qur'an God has shown him the right path to take in his life and, in the person of the Prophet Muhammad, has provided him with a perfect example of how to live. If he still chooses to ignore this guidance, which has been given to him as a mercy so that he may follow the way which leads to happiness in this life and in the Hereafter, then the responsibility is his alone. The only excellence is piety, obedience to God and kindness to our fellow men and women. People occupy different ranks and have different functions in this world, but all this counts for nothing in God's sight. The only true superiority is that of the pious man or woman over those who turn their backs on faith and practice wickedness.

Qur'an and Hadith

The Qur'an is the last revealed Word of God and the basic source of the Muslim's faith and practice. It deals with every subject that concerns us as human beings: wisdom, doctrine, knowledge, worship, history and law, but its basic theme is the relationship between God and His creation. At the same time it provides a basis for the just society and for a system of economic relationships which avoids the pitfalls both of monopoly capitalism and State socialism. Revealed to Muhammad, sometimes called the 'unlettered Prophet' because he was untainted by profane, purely worldly knowledge, the Qur'an was committed to memory and written down by his followers during his lifetime. Not one word of the Book has been changed over the centuries, and the Arabic Qur'an as we know it today is in every detail the Book revealed to him fourteen centuries ago.

The Hadith literature records in minute detail the sayings and actions of the Prophet Muhammad and helps to explain and elaborate the teachings of the Qur'an.

Worship

For the Muslim, to worship God is to know Him so far as is humanly possible, to love Him, to obey His law in every aspect of life, to enjoin goodness and combat evil, to practise charity in justice and to serve Him in accordance with His commands and His guidance.

'It is not righteousness that ye turn your faces to the East or to the West; but righteous is he who believes in Allah and the Last Day and the Angels and the Books and the Prophets; and gives of his wealth, for love of Him, to kinsfolk and to orphans and the needy and the wayfarer, and to those who ask, and to set slaves free; and (who) observes proper worship and pays the poor-due. And those who keep their treaty when they make one, and the patient in tribulation and adversity and time of stress; such as those who are sincere, such are the God-fearing' (Qur'an 2.177).

The Five 'Pillars' of Islam

In Islam everything that is done with the consciousness of fulfilling the divine Will may be considered as an act of worship; but the faithful observance of the religious is said, on the basis of a Prophetic Hadith, to be supported upon five 'Pillars'. These are:

1. The declaration of faith: 'I bear witness that there is no god but Allah, and I bear witness that Muhammad is His servant and His messenger'. The Muslim is expected to put this double declaration into practice in his worship and in every aspect of his life.
2. The five daily prayers which are 'owed' to God, our Lord and our Creator, and which open the human heart to the spiritual blessings which He willingly bestows upon us. The times of prayer are the early morning (between dawn and sunrise), midday, mid-afternoon, the late evening just after sunset, and the earlier part of the night.
3. Fasting during the month of Ramadan. This involves abstaining from food, drink and sexual intercourse from dawn till sunset, but it is no less important to abstain also from all evil and malicious thoughts. Ramadan is in essence a holy month, a time to be devoted quite particularly to prayer and to fellowship with other Muslims.
4. The poor-due, which involves giving away annually two-and-a-half per cent of our net wealth to relieve hardship and bring relief to those less fortunate than ourselves.
5. The Pilgrimage to the Ka'ba in Mecca at least once in a lifetime, provided one has the necessary financial means. Apart from its strictly religious significance, the Pilgrimage brings together men and women from every corner of the Muslim world and reinforces their awareness that the Community of Islam is one community.

The Islamic way of life

Islam provides firm guidelines for men and women in every walk of life and a comprehensive code of behaviour which guarantees the wellbeing of the individual and the security of society. The Qur'an, studied in conjunction with the Prophetic Ahadith, explains to the Muslim the purpose of his life on earth and instructs him in his duties and obligations as they relate to himself, to his family and his community, and to his Creator. He is left in no doubt as to what is required of him, but he is also assured of the rewards due to him provided he fulfils these basically simple requirements.

Historic perspective

Muhammad (after the mention of whose name Muslims usually add, 'May peace be upon him!') was born in the Arabian city of Mecca in the year 570 of the Christian era. Mecca was a major trading centre, and he made his living through trade for a number of years. He received his first revelation from God at the age of forty. As soon as he began to preach the truths which had been revealed to him he and his small community of followers suffered bitter persecution. He therefore migrated to the city of Medinah, which welcomed him and became the nucleus of the first Islamic State. He died at the age of 63, having completed his mission of conveying God's final message to mankind in the relatively brief span of 23 years. By the time he died the greater part of Arabia was Muslim, and within a century of his death Islam had spread as far as Spain in the West and to the borders of China in the East.

Muslim population at a glance

(Approximate figures)

Asia	625 million
Africa	233 million
Europe	24 million
Elsewhere	2 million

So far as can be estimated, therefore, the total figure worldwide is in the region of 884 million.

Aspects of Islam
There are certain apects of Islam which are frequently misrepresented and misunderstood by non-Muslims. These include:

1. **Status of Women.** Cultural practices differ to some extent between one Muslim country and another, but Islamic doctrine allots to women a position of dignity and responsibility often denied them elsewhere, together with certain rights—such as the right of inheritance—which are enshrined in the Qur'an. The basic rules which the religion lays down for human life apply to women just as they do to men. Islam however recognises that there are real differences of temperament as well a physique between men and women and that their spheres of activity, their functions and responsibilities, are therefore different (though complementary to each other).
2. **Marriage.** The lynchpin of Islamic society is the family, together with the network of relationships which links one family with others through intermarriage. The marriage bond is therefore taken very seriously, which is why adultery is punished with great severity. Divorce is permitted, since a truly incompatible couple cannot form the nucleus of a healthy family, and limited polygamy is allowed under certain circumstances (particularly in communities in which women outnumber men).
3. **Warfare.** In permitting fighting in defence of the religion, in self-defence or on the part of those who have been driven forcibly from their homes, Islam lays down strict rules of combat, which include prohibition against harming non-combatants and against destroying crops and livestock. As Muslims see it, injustice would triumph in this world if good men were not prepared to risk their lives in a righteous cause. The Qur'an reminds us: 'Fight in the way of Allah against those who fight against you, but begin not hostilities. Truly Allah loveth not aggressors'.
4. **Food and Drink.** Muslims are forbidden to eat carrion or the flesh of pigs (whether as pork, bacon or ham) or to drink any type of alcoholic beverage (the prohibition of alcohol is associated in the Qur'an with that of gambling, idol worship and divination).

Suggestions for further reading

What Everyone Should Know about Islam and Muslims, Suzanne Haneef (available from the Islamic Cultural Centre, 146 Park Road, London NW8).

The Creed of Islam by Abdul Haleem Mahmud (World of Islam Festival Trust Publishing Co.)

Islam in Focus and *The Family Structure in Islam*, Hammudah Abdalati (American Trust Publications).

(More advanced):

Ideals and Realities of Islam, Seyed Hossein Nasr (George Allen and Unwin Ltd, London).

Understanding Islam, Frithjof Schuon (Allen & Unwin, as above).

Islam, Fazlur Rahman (University of Chicago Press).

The Muslim Mind, Chris Waddy (Longman Ltd).

If you are interested in studying Islam or in knowing in detail about any aspect of Islamic teachings, contact: **Islamic Cultural Centre**, 146 Park Road, London, NW8 7RG, Telephone 01–724 3362.

---

3. *Useful addresses*

As well as the Islamic Centre (146 Park Road, London NW8 7RG), which produced the summary reprinted above, teachers may find the following useful:

Muslim Information Services, 233 Seven Sisters Road, London N4 2AD, for Eid cards, posters, etc.

Soma Books, 38 Kennington Lane, London SE11 4LS.

Islamic Foundation, 233 London Road, Leicester LE2 1ZE.

Muslim Educational Trust, 130 Stroud Green Road, London N4 3RZ.

Further topics

Specific project work could be attempted in the following areas: community folk tales and stories, dances, languages, head gear, hairstyles, naming and wedding ceremonies, growing up in Britain. The large communities in the area could be examined taking the approach suggested in this chapter. Here are some further ideas for topic work.

The World in Our Region

This wide-ranging topic can encompass any cultures found in the locality with any special celebrations that they hold. Different languages, customs and dialects can be included. One part of the project can be involved in finding out the spelling, writing and pronunciation of key words, such as 'good morning', days of the week, months, etc. These 'languages in our region' can be included on the display and referred to every day. The classroom can include a locality map with different cultural groups on it and a world map to show countries of origin. Posters and maps of the Caribbean islands, Asia and Africa can be obtained from the ILEA Learning Materials Service, Kennington Lane, London SE11 5QZ. Unity in the family can be a major area within this topic, with focus on family members celebrating together at important times of the year, especially at New Year. As well as English, Welsh and Scottish New Year celebrations, we suggest sections on the Chinese New Year, the Diwali Indian and Sikh New Year festival and Kwanza, an African holiday celebrated between 26 December and 1 January to give thanks for a good harvest. All show the coming together of families as communities, e.g., the giving of presents, the eating of special foods, dressing-up, decorations, the folk-tales of Rama and Sita and the New Year animals. Pictures of the 12 animals in the Chinese story can be drawn and displayed (cockerel, pig, dog, ox, hare, dragon, monkey, snake, rat, tiger, horse, ram). We are fascinated by a holiday celebration that we know little about—Kwanza—and recommend its inclusion. It seems that Kwanza means 'the first fruits' and has these identifiable symbols, which can be drawn by the pupils: Mshumaa (*m-shoo-mah-ah*) candle, Kinara (*kee-nah-rah*) candle holder, zawadi (*zah-wah-dee*) gifts, mkeka (*m-keh-ka*) straw mat, mahindi (*mah-heen-dee*) corn, kikombe (*kee-kohm-beh*) unity cup. The local Afro-Caribbean association can probably offer further information, material and even a 'helper' to come into school to aid the teacher with this part of the topic.

If teachers are planning to include a section on locality dialects, we suggest that they pin up a sheet of paper on the staff notice board as well as in the classroom, asking for examples of what can be called regional English vernacular (REV) or dialect. Following this, the locality dialect can be compared with black English vernacular (BEV) words used by Afro-Caribbean Britons. However, such an exercise can be extended to include other vernaculars such as the CEV or Cypriot English vernacular and so on. Greek Cypriots, for example, not only speak English and Greek but have a creolised language which mixes English and Greek to describe aspect of their life here in this country. Some examples are: banka (bank), policemanos (policeman), marketa (market), carpeto (carpet), baso (bus). The various cultural groups with which the school has links can give examples to help produce a more comprehensive topic on Dialect.

Select booklist

Celebrations

For pupils

Purton, R. (1981) *Festivals and Celebration.* Oxford: Blackwell.
Ginn series (1985) *Celebrations.* Aylesbury: Ginn.
The Living Festivals series from Religious and Moral Education Press, Arnold Wheaton, Exeter.
Mayled, J. (1986) *Feasting and Fasting.* Brighton: Wayland.

The Commonwealth Institute and Macmillan Education Festival series

This series on *Ramadan and Eid ul-Fitr*, *Carnival*, *Diwali* and *Chinese New Year* is one of the most impressive.

The *Diwali* book for pupils (1986) by Olivia Bennett includes Indian history, Diwali customs, Sikhism and celebrating in Britain. The teacher's notes and pupils' worksheets, written by Rosalind Kerven, include basic facts and guidance for teaching the topic.

Examples are: India and Hinduism, Diwali celebrations, Indian food, religious knowledge, history of India, geography of India, Indian culture.

A term's topic is carefully itemised followed by suggestions for a Diwali Open Day and a Resource list. Finally, a series of workcards are produced for teachers to photocopy: making Diwali lights, making Diwali cards, making rangoli patterns, writing and acting a Ramayana play, closing accounts for Diwali, cooking a Diwali sweet, making a 'Karma' game, time travelling through Indian history, touring India, watching the monsoon, making an Indian mail order catalogue.

Junior Education, October 1987.
This eight-page topic pack gives reasons for celebrating a wide variety of festivals in schools, describes key factors of various British-based festivals, offers suggestions for creative work based on the two themes of 'light' and 'birthdays', and presents a useful list of sources for teachers and pupils.

For display material on different aspects of worship: Unity Learning Foundation.

Diwali

For pupils

Bennett, O. (1986) *Diwali.* London: Macmillan Education.
Candappa, B. (1985) *Celebrating Diwali.* Aylesbury: Ginn.
Curtis, S. (1986) *Diwali.* Derbyshire Multicultural Support Service.
Deshpande, C. (1985) *Diwali.* London: A & C Black.
Kerven, R. (1986) *Diwali.* London: Macmillan (teacher's notes and pupils' worksheets).
Marsh, H. (1982) *Diwali.* Exeter: Arnold Wheaton.
Thompson, B. (1980) *The Story of Prince Rama.* London: Kestrel Books.

Thomson, R. (1986) *My Class at Diwali.* London: Franklin Watts.

For teachers

Bahree, P. (1982) *The Hindu World.* London: Macdonald.
Bains, H. S. (1983) *The Sikhs—a People.* Derbyshire Multicultural Education Centre.
Cole, W. O. (1973) *A Sikh Family in Britain.* Exeter: Religious Education Press.
Cole, W. O. (1980) *Thinking about Sikhism.* Cambridge: Lutterworth Educational.
Ewan, J. (1977) *Understanding your Hindu Neighbour.* Guildford: Lutterworth Educational.
Hamilton, S. (1985) Happy Diwali! *Multicultural Education Review*, no. 4, 35–7.
Sharma, D. (1984) *Hindu Belief and Practice.* London: Edward Arnold.

Eid

For pupils

Blakeley, M. (1977) *Nadha's Family.* London: A & C Black.
McLeish, K. (1985) *Eid-ul-Fitr.* Aylesbury: Ginn.
Minority Group Support Service (1987) *Diwali: Festival of Light* (story book and pupil material). London: MGSS.
Primary RE Materials Project (1987) *Islam.* Centre for the Study of Islam and Christian–Muslim Relations and the Regional RE Centre (Midlands), Westhill College, Weoley Park Road, Birmingham B29 6LL.
Solomon, J. (1980) *Gifts and Almonds.* London: Hamish Hamilton.

Islam and the Muslims

Harrison, S. W. and Shepherd, D. (1979) *A Muslim Family in Britain.* Exeter: Religious Education Press.
Hobley, L. (1979) *Muslims and Islam.* Brighton: Wayland.
Iqbal, M. (1976) *Understanding your Muslim Neighbour.* Guildford: Lutterworth Educational.
James, R. (1982) *The Muslim World.* London: Macdonald.
Kamm, A. (1986) *The Story of Islam.* Cambridge: Cambridge University Press.
Lemu, B. and Heeren, F. (1978) *Women in Islam.* London: Islamic Foundation.
Minai, N. (1981) *Women in Islam.* London: John Murray.
Robson, G. (1987) *Muslims in Manchester.* Sacred Trinity Centre, Chapel Street, Salford, Manchester M3 7AJ.
Tames, R. (1982) *The Muslim World.* London: Macdonald.
Watt, W. M. (1979) *What Is Islam?* Harlow: Longman.

Chapter 8

Controversial Issues

This chapter attempts to take a more direct approach to challenging prejudices and exposing myths and stereotypes.

MARY SEACOLE AND FLORENCE NIGHTINGALE

Aims

1. To show the contribution made to British history by courageous and determined women and so to offer girls positive role models.
   (*Group behaviour and change*)
2. To ask important questions concerning prejudice and discrimination, based on race and gender.
   (*Group behaviour and change*)

Activities

Activity 1: The lives and times of Mary Seacole and Florence Nightingale

1. Mary Seacole and Florence Nightingale were nurses in the Crimean War, 1854–6. Find out something about their lives and times.
   (It is suggested that children be asked to look at encyclopaedias to check the lives of Florence Nightingale and Mary Seacole. They will find that only Nightingale is included and this could start a discussion on bias and omission in history books. Questions which could be asked include: why is Mary Seacole not included in the history of the Crimean War in the encyclopaedias? Is it because she was a black woman or from a poor family? How many female contributions to the history of the nineteenth century can you see in the index? Why are there so few names?

Name ten great men and ten great women of this century. How difficult was it to find ten female names? Why do you think this is the case?)

2. Because there is not much on Mary Seacole, produce a little book called 'Mary Seacole: My life and times'.
   (Give out a summary of their lives on a worksheet; see examples in the Resource material section.)

Activity 2: Creative Work

1. Pretend that Mary Seacole and Florence Nightingale are looking for jobs to help in the Crimean War. Prepare a set of questions to ask them in an interview and carry out these interviews.
2. Divide pupils into groups: two will be asked to play the role of Mary Seacole and Florence Nightingale and a group of four or five will act as an interviewing panel, led by Sidney Herbert, the Secretary of State for War, and including only men.
3. Imagine that you are Mary Seacole and Florence Nightingale living in Britain today. Arrange the same kind of interview to go and help in a war.

Possible questions to raise

Stages 1 and 2 (see page 80)

1. Where did they come from?
2. What kind of upbringing did they have?
3. How were they treated before, during and after the Crimean War?

Stage 3

1. Why did Mary Seacole settle in Britain?
2. Why did your own parents/grandparents settle in this area?
3. Why did both women leave Britain?
4. Why were they treated differently in Britain and in the Crimea?
5. Why is it difficult to find material on Mary Seacole and why is it easier to find work on Florence Nightingale?

Stage 4

1. What do you think would have happened to Mary Seacole's ambition to become a nurse if she had been a white person?
2. What do you think would have happened to the careers of Mary Seacole and Florence Nightingale if they had been from poor families?
3. What do you think would have happened about Florence Nightingale's wish to go

to the Crimea if Sidney Herbert, the Secretary of State for War, had not been a friend of the family?

Stages 5 and 6

1. Do you think each was treated *fairly*?
2. Do you think they were *good* people? Why?
3. Do you think it is *right* to treat Mary Seacole in a different way from Florence Nightingale?
4. Do you think it is *fair* to treat Florence Nightingale in a better way than Mary Seacole?

MOVING HOMES

Aims

1. To develop awareness of the movement of peoples to Britain throughout history. (*Change*)
2. To explore common reasons for movement from place to place. (*Change, environment and group behaviour*)
3. To confront prejudices concerning 'immigrants' and newcomers to the locality. (*Group behaviour*)

Activity 1: Moving house
(Focus on change)

1. Explore the children's experiences of moving house.
2. Examine the background of parents and grandparents. Where were they born? Where did they live? What are their memories of moving? Why did they move? Children (where possible) ask family members and create a dossier on their experiences.
3. Take a large map of Britain and show migration within Britain, e.g., Mary Smith's family came from Liverpool to Nottingham in 1950, etc. Then take a world map and show immigration to Britain. Different coloured ribbons will show movements (see the Resource material).
4. Construct a model concerning why people move. Use the children's notes and develop a typology of movement.

Activity 2: Newcomers
(Focus on environmental and group behaviour factors)

1. Explore children's feelings of being newcomers to a school. Being alone (i.e., not knowing anyone), different (e.g., talking with a different accent), lacking appropri-

ate knowledge (i.e., not knowing the physical environment and school rules and regulations), worried that they are doing the right thing, etc.

2. The following exercise could be attempted:
   (a) The class is divided into two groups—those who have been in the school a long time (the 'oldtimers') and those who have just arrived (the 'newcomers'). The teacher instructs each group separately.
   (b) The 'oldtimers' are not to be 'nice' to the 'newcomers' and they are to organise certain behaviour which the 'newcomers' will not know (e.g., when they first meet they kiss each other on the cheek four times, etc.). The group works out its behaviour patterns away from the other group and must not tell them anything.
   (c) The 'newcomers' have just arrived and do not know anything about the school. They don't know its rules and regulations, where to go, etc. This is their first day. To distinguish them from the others they wear a coloured armband.
3. The whole morning is spent playing this game. Children should play their roles in class and playground.
4. After lunchtime, the teacher asks each group to report back on what happened and how people felt about being treated in this way.
5. A discussion could follow about groups in society today who may also be treated in this way, and why this is the case.

Activity 3: Moving to Britain
(Example of an activity on change)

1. Look at place names in the area because they generally tell us which groups migrated and settled in large numbers.
2. Teachers can then go through place names appropriate to their particular area. (See the Resource material on migrations into and out of Britain in the past 2000 years and the place names that reflect these migrations.)

Possible questions to raise

Stages 1 and 2 (see page 80)

1. Using maps of the area teachers can ask: What places end in 'ton', 'ham', 'wick', etc.?
2. When did Anglo-Saxons, etc., settle in your region, etc.?
3. Have more people settled in Britain in the past ten years than left it to live in other countries?

Stage 3

1. Why did the Saxons (or others) settle in your region?
2. Why did your own parents/grandparents settle here?
3. Why did people leave Britain?

Stage 4

1. What do you think would have happened to migration to Britain if there had been no famine in Ireland in the 1840s?
2. What would have happened to migration in your region if there had been no Second World War?
3. What would make you move from this area?

Stages 5 and 6

1. Do you think it is *good* to move from one area to another? Why?
2. Do you think it is *right* to stop people moving to a country of their choice?
3. Do you think it is *fair* to treat newcomers any differently from those whose ancestors have been here for a long time?

EVERYBODY KNOWS THAT!

A STORY FOR YOUNG CHILDREN THAT ATTEMPTS TO CONFRONT PREJUDICE AND STEREOTYPES

Aims

1. To focus on a young child's journey from reflecting the prejudices he has heard around him to changing them once he becomes aware of their injustice.
   (*Change*)
2. To help children relate to different scenes in the classroom, in home, in school, in the countryside, dining out with the family, eating with friends, buying presents, playing football, working together as a team, being made to cry by hurtful comments from others, apologising when wrong. At the lowest level of development all children should be able to relate to being called names that may hurt; at the highest degrees of awareness pupils may see racial prejudice as morally and socially wrong.
   (*Environment and group behaviour*)
3. To offer pupils atypical scenes which may help them question taken-for-granted assumptions about males and females, black and white, e.g., the class teacher is Afro-Caribbean and referees football matches which involve the participation of girls as well as boys; men cook and serve meals; women put up shelves; streets and shops are filled with people from diverse races and cultures; boys cry; women wear trousers, jeans and sweat-shirts; ethnic minorities are professional people who live effectively within two cultures; similarities between groups are more important than their differences.
   (*Group behaviour and environment*)

Activities

1. Read the story about Ranjit and Stephen called 'Everybody knows that!' (see story in Resource material section).
2. Show the selection of illustrations and add to them yourself, if you wish.
3. Ask the children to write a story imagining they were Ranjit coming into the class for the first time (see example of pupil's work in Resource material section).
4. Ask children about the story using some of the questions below.

Possible questions to raise

Very young children may find difficulty in answering all these questions as they are being asked not only to classify and interpret but also to extrapolate and evaluate. The teacher needs to decide for herself how far she can go.

Stages 1 and 2 (see page 80)

1. What happened when Ranjit slipped and fell while he was helping Stephen build a strong wall?
2. What did Stephen say to Ranjit?
3. What did Stephen learn to say on his uncle's farm?

Stage 3

1. Why did Ranjit cry?
2. Why was Stephen surprised to see Ranjit eating in a Burger Bar?
3. Why did Stephen come home from the park crying?

Stage 4

1. What do you think would have happened if Stephen had knocked down the wall he was building with Ranjit? Would Ranjit have called him names?
2. What would you say if you were called nasty names? Why would you do that?

Stages 5 and 6

1. Do you think it is *good* to say, 'You smell really horrible'? Why not?
2. Do you think it is *right* to call people names? Why not?
3. Do you think it is *fair* to stop playing with people because they look different from you? Why not?

Other stories

A similar approach can be taken with other stories, e.g.,

1. 'The Ndidi story' (see the story by Babatunde and discussion by Dorothy Kuva in the Resource material section).
2. 'The mice next door' (see the review in the Resource material section).

RESOURCE MATERIAL

Contents

MARY SEACOLE:

Information sheet for pupils

1. She was born Mary Jane Grant in 1805 in Kingston, Jamaica, of a Creole family.

2. Her father was a soldier and her mother ran a boarding house in which she also nursed people.

3. From the age of about 12, Mary helped her mother nurse invalid officers and their wives.

4. As a young woman Mary travelled to Panama, Haiti, the Bahamas, Cuba and twice came to Britain.

5. She married Horatio Seacole and they ran a store until he fell ill and died.

6. After this Mary made a living by trading, cooking and nursing people who had diseases like cholera, malaria and yellow fever.

7. In 1854 Britain and France declared war on Russia because of its influence on Turkey. Most of the fighting took place in the Crimea, on the north coast of the Black Sea.

8. After her mother died, Mary came to Britain and applied for a nursing job in the Crimea.

9. She was turned down by the War Office and the nursing service organised by Florence Nightingale.

10. Mary was determined to go and when she discovered the private address of the Secretary of State for War she camped outside his house with a banner asking for work.

11. Although she obtained an interview she was told that no more nurses were needed.

12. She paid for herself to go to the Crimea on the steamer Hollander, which left London for Constantinople (now Istanbul) on 25 January 1855.

13. She set up a `hotel´, which acted as a hospital and convalescent home.

14. Every morning she saw patients at her `hotel´ and every afternoon she visited the official hospital. She worked from daybreak until 8 at night, although she was 50 years old.

15. The war ended in 1856.

16. Mary spent all her money on nursing and when she returned home she was bankrupt.

17. She was honoured by many of the men she saved.

18. She published her autobiography in 1857.

19. She died in 1881.

20. She was courageous, energetic and strong-minded.

MARY SEACOLE: Heroine of the Crimean War

In 1973, when the Lignum Vitae Club and the Jamaican Nurses' Association invited West Indians to attend the reconsecration of the grave of a Jamaican National Heroine named Mary Seacole, 11 people, including the Jamaican High Commissioner of the time took part. Eight years later, when Brent Library Service and Harmony organised a wreath laying ceremony to mark the centenary of Mrs Seacole's death, over 150 people congregated at the graveside.

Part of the reason for this awakened interest in Mary Seacole lies in the fact that her story bears all the hallmarks of the exclusion of Black history-makers in British historiography. White racism is said to be accountable for her failure to become a major actress on history's stage during the Crimean period, and Black invisibility in current British historiography is held responsible for her subsequent relegation to the wings of social history.

To our minds, the resurrection of her name is both symbolic and just, particularly given the modern contribution of Black nurses to our health service. While Florence Nightingale's work is widely acknowledged, Mary Seacole's claim to our attention has only recently been registered; and yet her mixed ancestry and close identification with Britain, makes her an ideal heroine in our racially diverse society.

Born in Kingston, Jamaica in the early part of the nineteenth century, Mary Seacole was the daughter of a Black boarding house owner and a Scottish soldier. Mistress Grant, if that indeed was the family name, was known locally as a competent 'doctress'. Mary Seacole combined the folk medicine which she had learned from her mother, with Western medical practices which she had observed as a result of her close ties with the military surgeons. This commitment to nursing was matched with sufficient business acumen to provide her with the purpose and independent means necessary for a lone woman who loved to travel. By her late forties, she had travelled all over the Caribbean region, notably to Haiti, Cuba and Panama and had made two trips to England, taking with her saleable commodities.

Wherever she went, the medical bag went with her. The first national test of her skills came during the Kingston epidemic of 1850, when she skilfully practised what she termed 'Creole medical art'. By this time, she had lost both her husband and mother, and with no family responsibilities, she was able to resume her travelling. The next four years were chiefly spent in Panama, where her medical reputation was enhanced by the success of her cures in the cholera epidemic which struck in 1851. In 1854, when she returned to Jamaica for a few months, she offered her services when yellow fever raged through the island. Not only did she provide nursing for the sick at her boarding house, but she was asked by the medical authorities to organise the care of patients at the nearby military base.

When news of the Crimean War reached Mary Seacole, she was confident that her experience and expertise in the field of tropical diseases would be vital in Britain's war effort. Deaths from disease were claiming seven times as many lives as deaths from battle wounds. Public protest at the appalling conditions at the Front and the incredible bureaucratic bungling which had affected the distribution of essential supplies, had speeded the departure of Florence Nightingale and a small band of nurses for Scutari. However, when Mary Seacole presented her excellent testimonials to the authorities in the Autumn of 1854, her services were rejected by every conceivable government department. Twenty-one years after the abolition of British slavery, it was still not socially acceptable to appoint a middle-aged Creole woman in the official capacity of army nurse. Florence Nightingale was doing her utmost to change the low status of nursing but the authorities obviously preferred risking the employment of women with a drink problem to hiring an experienced Black medical assistant. Mary Seacole's last hope was to apply to the managers of the Crimean Fund, but she met with equal prejudice here, and she writes about it with feeling, in her autobiography:

> Was it possible that American prejudices against colour had some root over here? Did those ladies shrink from accepting my aid because my blood flowed beneath a somewhat duskier skin than theirs? . . . Tears streamed down my foolish cheeks . . . that anyone should doubt my motives—that heaven should deny me the opportunity that I sought.

However, Mrs Seacole was as persistent in her faith as Victorian society was in its intransigence. She consulted with friends and sought the help of a distant relative, Mr Day, who was going to the Crimea on business. The firm of Seacole and Day was formed, the necessary capital raised, and at the age of 50 years, Mary Seacole made the three thousand mile journey to the Crimea. Once there according to the historian Mrs Tom Kelly:

> Mother Seacole set up her store-dispensary-hospital, and became historic by right of good deeds, which is almost the rarest claim . . . even in an enlightened century Mother Seacole stands out pre-eminent, and cannot be passed over. She had the secret recipe for cholera and dysentery; and liberally dispensed the specific alike to those who could pay and those who could not.

Although overweight and middle-aged, Mrs Seacole seemed to have boundless energy and viewed every new situation as an exciting challenge. She was the first woman to enter Sebastopol after the long siege. In her autobiography she boasts:

> For weeks past I have been offering bets to everyone I would not only be the first woman to enter Sebastopol from the English line but that I would be the first to carry refreshments into the fallen city.

Observers as diverse as the chef, Alexis Soyer, the physician, Sir John Hall, and the Commander-in-Chief, Lord Rokeby, all bore witness to her good deeds. William Russell, War Correspondent of *The Times*, provided eye witness accounts of her escapades:

> I have seen her go down under fire with her little store of creature comforts for our wounded men, and a more tender or skilful hand about a wound or a broken limb could not be found amongst our best surgeons. I saw her at the assaults on the Redan, at the battle of Tchernaya, at the fall of Sebastopol, laden . . . with wine, bandages and food for the wounded or the prisoners.

However, when the war ended abruptly in 1855, England, through the pages of *The Times*, had to be reminded of the recent contribution of her faithful servant. Hundreds of pounds of provisions and stock had to be left to rot in the Crimea and the firm of Seacole and Day was declared bankrupt. Lord Rokeby and other prominent Victorians organised a fund-raising benefit for her and an appeal was launched on her behalf. One letter which appeared in *The Times* called to the Crimeans to rally round Mrs Seacole in her hour of need:

> Have a few months erased from their memories those many acts of comforting kindness which made the name of the old mother venerated throughout the camp? While the benevolent deeds of Florence Nightingale are being handed down to posterity, are the humbler actions of Mrs Seacole to be entirely forgotten, and will none now testify to the worth of those services of the late mistress of Spring-hill?

Monies were raised and with the appearance of her autobiography the following year, Mary Seacole received a modest recompense for her contribution. She died in London in 1881, and in their obituary notices *The Times* and the *Manchester Guardian* paid tribute to a woman whose devotion and sense of vocation, made hers a household name in mid-nineteenth century Britain. A terra-cotta bust of her is now held at the Jamaican Institute, together with two of the medals awarded to her.

Further information about her can be obtained in *Great Men of Colour* by J. A. Rogers and in *Black Settlers in Britain 1555–1958* by Nigel File and Chris Power.

Audrey Dewjee *co-researched the Roots in Britain exhibition and has written articles on the history of Asians in Britain.*
Ziggi Alexander *is a community librarian with Brent Library Service and a researcher of black British history.*

Bibliography

** Great West Indians, by Therese Mills, Longman, 1973.
** Black Makers of History, by Sam Morris, COBS, 1974.
Colonel's Lady and Camp Follower, by Piers Compton, Hale, 1970.
World's Great Men of Colour, Vol. II, by J. A. Rogers, Collier-Macmillan, 1972

** For young readers

This article appeared in *Dragon's Teeth*, no. 15, Autumn/Winter 1982, and is reproduced by kind permission of the Editor.

REVIEW

Wonderful Adventures of Mrs Seacole in Many Lands, edited by Ziggi Alexander and Audrey Dewjee, Falling Wall Press, 1984, £3.95, ISBN 0 905046 23 4

There can be very few school-children or adults who have not heard of Florence Nightingale, the legendary nurse elevated to almost saintly status, who served the British Armed Forces during the Crimean War. Why, then, have so few of us heard of Mary Seacole? A black woman, a nurse of at least equal distinction, famous and feted in her day, she has been forgotten by some of us and is unknown to most of us.

Ziggi Alexander and Audrey Dewjee have provided an immensely important service by reissuing this edition of Mary Seacole's memoirs. It provides us with a rounded and fascinating portrait of a talented, popular and powerful black woman who was best known to the Victorian British public for her humanitarian and medical services to the British army fighting in the Crimea from 1854 to 1856. Indeed, her activities during the war made her a household name!

She was born in Kingston, Jamaica, in 1805 and followed her mother's footsteps by becoming a self-taught 'doctress'. Mary Seacole went to the Crimea without official backing. There she used her unequalled skill in treating cholera and other tropical diseases. She established her famous 'British Hotel' in which treatment, succour and rest were available to all who needed it, including the Russians.

The warm, compassionate, humorous and resourceful figure of Mary Seacole emerges from her memoirs, as does an insight into British racism of the time. While soldiers on the battlefield admired and loved her, she was still subjected to racist abuse on the streets of London.

Her great efforts in the Crimea led to bankrupty. An indication of the esteem in which she was held was the establishment of the 'Seacole Fund' in 1867, to which many thousands of soldiers and members of the public contributed. The fund had the patronage of Queen Victoria, and a Committee of Admirals and Colonels. Helped back to solvency by the fund, and by the original publication of her memoirs, the latter years of her life were divided between Jamaica and England. She died on 14 May 1881. Her grave can still be found and visited in the Roman Catholic cemetery in Kensal Green, London.

This book is essential reading for three reasons: the story it tells, and the insights into the Crimean War and the Britain of that time; for the standing and status it will give to an important black figure; and for the questions it inevitably and sharply raises about the construction of history itself. What processes are at work that can all but erase from popular consciousness a figure of Mary Seacole's stature? Why is it that despite a black presence in Britain since Roman times, there is a resounding dearth of black characters identified in our history books?

How have we all colluded with the manufacture of a British history that would have us believe that it was the history of white heterosexual men? Clearly such an examination ought to be central to any history course that takes multiculturalism and anti-racism seriously. The work of Alexander and Dewjee as part of a move to rediscover the black dimension of British history cannot be praised enough, providing as it does a valuable black hero, and breaching the white male monopoly of history.

Reading Mary Seacole's book reminded this reviewer of the powerful observation, that only by understanding our past, can we begin to take control of the present and future. The *Wonderful Adventures*, along with much more of black, feminist and gay history that has been published over the past few years, shows very powerfully just how much of humanity's experience has been ignored, rewritten, and discarded by those with power. Books such a this, by helping us to recognise and define history and our own identities, can perform a truly liberating function.

Phil Barnett
Education Officer
CRE

This article first appeared in *Education Journal*, September 1984, and is reproduced by kind permission of the CRE.

FLORENCE NIGHTINGALE:

Information sheet for pupils

1. She was born in Florence while her parents were on a visit to Italy in 1820.

2. She was brought up partly at Lea Hurst in Derbyshire and partly at Embley in Hampshire.

3. As was the custom for the wealthy, on her eighteenth birthday she was presented to the monarch, Queen Victoria.

4. She trained as a nurse in convent hospitals on the Rhine and in Paris.

5. In 1853 she became Lady Superintendent of the Institute for Sick Gentlewomen in Harley Street, London.

6. In 1854 Sidney Herbert, the Secretary of State for War, an old friend of the Nightingale family, wrote to her to ask if she would take a group of nurses to Scutari, and his letter crossed with one from her offering to go.

7. She arrived at the hospital in November 1854 with about 30 nurses.

8. The Times newspaper started a campaign to raise money for her hospital needs.

9. In January 1855 there were 12 000 men in Scutari and 42 per cent of them died, but by June only 2 per cent had died of their wounds or of disease.

10. Peace came in September 1855 and Florence Nightingale returned to Britain. She was later thanked by Queen Victoria for her services in the Crimea.

11. Nightingale became adviser in health matters to the British Government in Britain and in India.

12. In 1860 the Nightingale Training School for Nurses was started with £50 000 collected by the public in gratitude for her services in the Crimea. She also opened the Nightingale Home for Convalescents.

13. During the second part of her life statesmen, nurses and viceroys of India came to her house in South Street, Mayfair, to consult her in health and nursing matters.

14. In 1907, the King awarded her the Order of Merit, an honour which only 24 British people can receive at any one time and which had never before been given to a woman.

15. She died on 13 August 1910.

Moving Homes
Movements into Britain
Information sheet for pupils

BC	
350	Celts from central Europe settled.
55	Romans invaded and occupied.
AD	
410	Romans withdrew.
500	Angles and Saxons from what is today called Germany and Jutes from Denmark settled.
600	Anglo-Saxons conquered Celts and formed kingdoms.
850	Danish Viking invasions and settlement.
1066	Normans conquered and settled.
1575	French Huguenots escaped Catholic persecution in France and settled in places like East Anglia.
1700-1800	With the Industrial Revolution, Irish settlers arrived as labourers.
1840s	Irish escaped from social problems in their country.
Late 19th century	Russian and Polish Jews forced to leave. African sailors settled in dockland areas like Cardiff, Bristol and Liverpool.
1920s	Jewish refugees arrived from communist Russia.
1930s	Jewish refugees arrived from Hitler's Germany.
1940-5	Poles and Czechs escaped from the Nazi invasion.
1940-5	Jews fled from countries occupied by Germany. About six million of those who remained were killed in concentration camps.
1945 onwards	Refugees arrived from countries like Poland, Czechoslovakia and Hungary, which became communist after the Second World War.
1945 onwards	Western Ukraine was incorporated into the USSR during the Second World War. Some of those who did not want to be part of the Soviet Union settled in Britain.

1950s	Settlers arrived from the British colonies in the Caribbean because they were offered jobs by London Transport, the National Health Service, etc. Also, some of the thousands who fought in the British forces during the war decided to settle. All members of the British Empire had British citizenship and therefore had the right to settle.
1956	Hungarians opposed to communist government were allowed to settle.
1950s	Cypriots, Maltese, Chinese, Italians and others found employment in booming economic conditions.
1962-8	Migration of Indians and Pakistanis. The old Indian Empire had been divided by the British in 1947 into India and Pakistan. Some Muslims left India for Pakistan as refugees and some Hindus migrated in the opposite direction to India. Some of these people were unable to find work and settle so they emigrated for a second time to Britain.
1960s	The newly independent black states of Africa wanted their countries´ economies to be run by nationals of their countries, so they began to expel British subjects of Asian origin.
1971	General Amin came to power in Uganda and expelled Asians who held British citizenship.
1974	Turkish troops occupied Northern Cyprus and refugees from those areas arrived in Britain.

Movement from Britain:
Information sheet for pupils

1290	Jews expelled from Britain.
1620	The Pilgrims went to America to escape religious persecution and to be able to practise freely their religious beliefs.
Seventeenth century onwards	Settlement in the New World.
Nineteenth century onwards	Settlement in Australia, New Zealand, Africa (e.g., Rhodesia, Kenya, South Africa) - wherever there were British colonies.
Twentieth century	More people leave Britain to live elsewhere than come to settle (see Table 4).

Table 4: *Immigration and emigration figures 1968–77 (Reproduced with permission)*

In 1980–81 more people left Britain (emigrated) than entered to live here. Fewer people immigrated than in any year since records began in 1964.

	1970–71	1980–81
Immigrated	216,000	156,000 (23% less than 1979–80)
Emigrated	255,000	235,000 (12% more than 1979–80)

	In	Out	Net
1968	221,600	277,700	−56,100
1969	205,600	292,700	−87,100
1970	225,600	290,700	−65,100
1971	199,700	240,000	−40,400
1972	221,900	233,200	−11,400
1973	195,700	245,800	−50,100
1974	183,800	269,000	−85,300
1975	197,200	238,300	−41,200
1976	179,800	210,400	−30,600
1977	162,600	208,700	−46,100
Total	1,993,500	2,506,500	−513,400

(Office of Population Censuses and Surveys).
And the population of Britain has fallen in each year since 1974 (OPCS).

COMING AND GOING

Myer Domnitz and Philip Sauvain summarise the movement of people into, out of and within Britain

Since the beginning of our history, we have *never* been a mono-cultural, mono-racial society; and each wave of immigrants brings something new in the way of language, custom, skills and appearance to enrich our varied and complex multi-cultural society.

The first evidence we have of settlers from abroad are the blue glazed beads found in Bronze Age graves which have been traced to the East Mediterranean. Later came the *Celts* from Europe. Their descendants are to be found in Wales, Scotland and Ireland.

Celtic literature is reflected in Irish, Scottish and Welsh literature with cycles of heroic legends. The Celtic language survives in Welsh and Gaelic.

The *Picts* came to East Scotland and the Orkneys over 2000 years ago. They were linked with the Celts of North East Ireland who settled in the North West of Scotland. The Picts and Scots later came south to Roman Britain and Northern England.

The *Romans* were the next immigrants and made their mark on our language (about one in five of our words is of Latin origin), our roads and our towns.

Then came the *Saxons*—from Northern Germany. They were joined by the Picts from Scotland and the *Scotti* from Ireland (who gave Scotland its name).

With the decline and departure of the Romans in 410, the Saxons and their kinsmen the *Angles* and the *Jutes*, settled here.

The next major movement occurred with the arrival of the *Vikings* from Denmark, Norway and Sweden in the 9th century. They settled in Scotland, Northumbria, East Anglia and half the Midlands and in 1016 Cnut, a Dane, became King of England.

1066 saw the arrival of a new wave of immigrants—the *Normans*. They had a profound influence on our language, law and social structure.

In the 14th century, the *Flemish* weavers, fleeing from French attacks on their cities, arrived. They improved the English cloth trade and the products of the Welsh woollen mills. Another influx of Flemish and *Walloons* (from the Lowlands which became Belgium and Holland) occurred in the 16th century. About 30,000 found homes in London.

In 1572, the *Huguenots*, French protestants who were being persecuted in France, started to arrive. They established themselves in Sandwich, Bristol and London. A hundred years later, about 120,000 more Huguenots came to settle here.

It was Oliver Cromwell who first permitted the *Jewish* community to be established in 1656. These Jews were refugees from the Spanish inquisitions. During the 18th century, more Jews arrived from Central Europe. They settled in London, Portsmouth, Plymouth, etc. Further immigrants in the 19th century settled in provincial cities, especially Bradford.

The chief immigration of Jews from Eastern Europe took place between 1880 and 1905—about 100,000 came because of the pogroms, savage attacks on them in Czarist Russia. They settled mostly in the East End of London.

The last large movement of Jews was after 1933 when about 37,000 people settled here after fleeing Nazi persecution.

Black people first came to this country in Elizabethan times as a result of trade contacts, which developed into the slave trade. There were estimated to be about 20,000 black people in London in the 18th century.

At the end of the 19th century there were small settlements of *West Indians*, who had been sailors, in dock areas. Then, during the Second World War, West Indians came to work in the factories in Britain and to fight but the large scale population movement from the Caribbean began after 1945 when West Indians were recruited to work here.

Although *Indian* seamen had settled in dock areas from the end of the 18th century, immigration from the Indian sub-continent occurred chiefly after partition in 1947 when the separate states of India and Pakistan were created. The settlers came chiefly from the Gujerat (Hindus) and the Punjab (Sikhs). Later, Indians arrived from East Africa when, after independence, Kenya and Uganda carried out 'Africanisation' of jobs.

Pakistanis came to this country chiefly from Mirpur, near the Himalayas and speak Punjabi. Settlers from *Bangladesh* (which was East Pakistan before it broke away from West Pakistan) speak Bengali. Most people from East Pakistan and from Bangladesh are Muslims.

Some people came from Cyprus before the Second World War and many *Greek* and *Turkish Cypriots* arrived in the '60s and '70s settling mainly in London but also in Birmingham and Manchester.

Once again *Chinese* settlers were often, previously, seamen. Their numbers increased after the Second World War when they came from Malaysia and Hong Kong. They were established chiefly in London but they are, perhaps, the most widely scattered of all recent settlers.

London has a fairly large community of *Polish* people—chiefly political refugees coming after the Second World War.

Italians came here at the end of the 19th century and settled in the Soho and Clerkenwell areas of London and in seaside towns all over the country. More Italians arrived this century and, lately, employers in Bedford and Peterborough recruited people from Southern Italy to work in the brick industry.

The latest groups to arrive have been from Vietnam and Indochina.

All these people and many others (Russians, Spaniards, Maltese, Hungarians) have come to Britain for centuries. They come because of religious or political persecution in their home countries, to escape hunger and war, to meet our labour shortages and to seek a better life for their families.

This article first appeared in *Junior Education*, December 1980, and is reproduced by kind permission of Scholastic Publications.

Everybody knows that!

A story for young children that attempts to confront prejudice and stereotypes

1. Stephen was sitting quietly at his desk when Mrs Thomas walked in. To his surprise she was not alone.

Following her was a small wiry boy, who had brown skin and wore a turban. Stephen stared in amazement.

There had never been a boy like this in school before, although he had seen boys like him down the Highfield Road. Stephen thought the turban looked very smart.

After doing the register, Mrs Thomas announced that Ranjit's parents had moved to the area and that he would now be coming to Weston Primary, and would be in class 6.

Illustration

A classroom scene:
- **with an Afro-Caribbean teacher**
- **all the children are white.**

2. That afternoon Mrs Thomas told Stephen that he could carry on with his experiment using the blocks. When Stephen had been trying for a while to build the strongest wall possible, he saw Ranjit heading towards him. This made him angry. Perhaps he would knock down the wall that Stephen had so carefully built.

To Stephen's surprise Ranjit just stood around and watched. After some time Stephen decided to ask him to help make the wall better as it was beginning to look unsteady.

Illustration

Ranjit watching Stephen building a wall that looks unsteady.

3. The boys worked together for a while, Stephen couldn't make up his mind whether he liked him or not. Ranjit was good at building but he didn't say much. There was also a smell which Stephen had never come across before.

Illustration

The two boys building a strong wall.

4. When the wall was finished the boys stood back to admire it. While Stephen went to ask Mrs Thomas to come and look, Ranjit slipped and fell.

Stephen heard a noise and saw Ranjit and the blocks crash to the floor. He was very angry and wanted to make Ranjit cry. He remembered what his Dad had said about that lot down the Highfield Road. Dad was right, they did smell.

'You lot are all the same. You smell really horrible,' he shouted.

Ranjit started to cry.

Illustration

The wall collapsed on the floor.

Stephen shouting and Ranjit crying.

5. When Stephen arrived home from school, his Dad told him that they were going to visit Uncle Richard. Stephen liked going to Uncle Richard's because he lived on a farm in the countryside.

Illustration

Dad in the kitchen cooking, Stephen talking to him.

6. At the farm, Uncle Richard was out in the field. Stephen and his Dad went over to him.

'What's that funny smell everywhere?' asked Stephen. 'I don't like it.'

'We've been haymaking,' replied Uncle Richard, 'that's the smell of freshly cut grass, and I love it. It's just different from all the smells you know in town. If you lived on a farm you might like the smell. There are lots of different smells and not everybody likes the same ones. EVERYBODY KNOWS THAT!'

On their way back to the farmhouse they walked past a row of tall pine trees.

'Even those trees smell funny,' said Stephen.

'Yes,' agreed Uncle Richard, 'that's another smell I like, but it is not funny, just different. EVERYBODY KNOWS THAT!'

Stephen thought about what Uncle Richard was saying. Perhaps he was right.

Illustration

Stephen, Uncle Richard and Dad walking past pine trees towards the farmhouse.

7. On Saturday morning, Mum asked Stephen if he would like to go to town with her. Stephen thought there might be a chance that she would take him to the Burger Bar so he decided to go.

On the way into town, Stephen and his mother stopped at the flower shop. Mum was going to visit grandmother the next day, and they were going to buy some flowers for her.

Inside the shop, Stephen and his Mum admired the beautiful flowers and their different scents.

'I think these roses are the best,' said Stephen's Mum. 'They smell so nice.'

'Oh no,' said Stephen, 'I know that Gran doesn't like the smell of roses best. She told me so last summer when I stayed with her. The smell of freesias is her favourite.'

Stephen's Mum looked quite upset. She had been buying roses for Grandmother for many years.

Stephen thought about what his Uncle Richard had said.

'Don't get upset, Mum,' he said, 'we all like different smells. EVERYBODY KNOWS THAT!'

Illustration

The florist's shop:
- **male shop assistant**
- **some black and brown people in the shop**

- **mum in trouser suit.**

8. Once they were in town, Stephen and his Mum looked around lots of shops.

Illustration

Stephen and his Mum walking through town which includes:
- **black/brown female police officers**
- **shoppers include black/brown/white female** and **male Britons**
- **shops/restaurants showing cultural diversity.**

9. In the Chemist's, his Mum decided that she would like to buy some aftershave for Dad's birthday. At the counter of the shop there were lots of different bottles of aftershave. Stephen wondered how his Mum was going to choose which one to buy.

One by one she began to smell them. Eventually she chose one in a rectangular bottle with a fancy red top.

'Do you like the smell of this one?' she asked Stephen, as she passed him the bottle. He didn't like it. It reminded him of the disinfectant they used at school, but he didn't tell his Mum. He simply said, 'There are lots of different smells, Mum, and we don't all like the same one. EVERYBODY KNOWS THAT!'

Stephen's Mum thought about what he had said and decided to buy it.

Illustration

Black or brown shop assistant as well as white assistants.
Stephen and Mum selecting aftershave.
Cultural diversity of customers.

10. When it was lunchtime Stephen hoped that his Mum would take him to the Burger Bar, and she did.

He decided to have a Strawberry Thickshake and a Cheeseburger. While they were eating their lunch, Stephen noticed Ranjit, the new boy in his class, sitting at another table with his Mum and Dad. Stephen was very surprised to see him there.

Illustration

The Burger Bar.
Black, brown and white people working and eating there.

11. After lunch Stephen and his Mum spent more time going around the shops. When they returned home Stephen was feeling a little tired and hungry.

Dinner was waiting for them. Dad had cooked fish pie as he knew it was Stephen's favourite.

After dinner, Stephen's Mum gave his Dad the aftershave. He put some on straight away and said he liked it very much. Stephen wondered whether he was just being kind!

Illustration

Dad serving the good quality meal he has just prepared.

12. Later that evening Stephen went to play in the park with some friends from school. He had not been there long when he ran home crying.

Illustration

Stephen running out of the park, crying. Among his footballing friends are girls. One girl is holding the ball. Another is playing in goal.

13. 'What's the matter?' asked his Mum.

'Those boys in the park, they say I smell . . . of fish.'

'Oh, Stephen, why are you so upset? Perhaps those boys don't like fish pie as much as you do. We all like different smells. It was you who told me that, wasn't it?'

Stephen remembered what his Uncle Richard had told him. He stopped crying, looked at his Mum, smiled, and said, 'Yes Mum, EVERYODY KNOWS THAT!'

Illustrations

Stephen and Mum talking. Mum has changed her clothes: she is now wearing jeans and sweatshirt. She has put down an electric drill she has been using to make holes in the kitchen wall in preparation for a new shelf she is constructing. Dad is washing up the dishes.

14. Back at school on Monday morning, Stephen saw Ranjit in the playground before the bell went. He felt very sad about what he had said. He remembered the nasty things he had said to Ranjit and felt sad.

Inside the classroom Stephen decided to talk to him.

'I'm sorry I said all those awful things to you the other day. It's wrong to call people names. EVERYBODY KNOWS THAT!'

The next day Stephen and Ranjit played football for the school team. Ranjit scored the only goal of the match.

'Well done, Ranjit,' said Stephen. 'You were the best player in the team.'

The others all agreed.

'You all played well today,' added Mrs Thomas, the team's trainer. 'You worked together. You helped each other. You were a good team.'

Stephen smiled at Ranjit, 'And when people work together, they can win anything, can't they?'

'Yes,' laughed Ranjit, 'EVERYBODY KNOWS THAT!'

Illustrations

Mrs Thomas in track suit talking to team members who comprise boys and girls. Mrs Thomas has just refereed this match. She has a whistle and is holding the football.

15. After the match Ranjit invited Stephen back to his house for tea. They ate lots of different food that Stephen had never tried before.

Of course they did!

People are different.

EVERYBODY KNOWS THAT!

Illustration

Stephen at Ranjit's house for tea.
Dress emphasising cultural similarities. (Father in suit, tie, etc. He has just returned from the office. Mother in trouser suit: she has also just returned from her teaching post.)
Mother is sitting marking school exercise books at a table on one side of the room.
Father is bringing food to the table in preparation for the meal. This food recognises cultural differences.
Ranjit, his sister and Stephen are playing a computer game in front of the television on another side of the room.
The house and its furniture show similarities between cultures. However, the differences in religion can be seen by decorations and artefacts around the walls.

The Day who learned something.

I followed Mrs. Thomas, the teacher, into my new classroom. All of the other children were already there and they were all staring at me. After about 10 minutes mrs Thomas Told all the other children who I was. Then a few minutes later The Teacher sent a boy called stephen to play with the blocks because he had worked hard in the morning. About 20 minutes later mrs Thomas sent me to play with the blocks. as well. The boy called stephen was Angry seeing ~~the~~ me ~~boy~~ coming to the blocks. After a few minutes stephen asked me if I would like to help him build a house with him. When ~~they~~ we had Finished building the house we went to play in it. Then Suddenly I slipped and knocked all the house over. The boy called stephen was angry and called me That I smelt horrible I went & I was crying I told the teacher but she did'nt do anything. That night I told my Mum that stephen had called me names that Day. But the next day stephen came up to me & said I am sorry for calling you names. Every-body is ████ different and everybody knows That. That night stephen went to My house for Tea.

Figure 15. Third year junior school pupil's work.

THE NDIDI STORY

Once upon a time there was a little black girl called Ndidi. She had beautiful eyes and a nice wide smile. Her country was Nigeria in Africa, and her town was Onitsha.

Ndidi lived with her parents in England where most of the people are not lucky enough to be black. Their eyes and skins are pale, sometimes grey like the ashes of a dead fire. In the whole school Ndidi was the only black child. The white children thought this was very funny. Often they would stare at Ndidi, then laugh and say rude things. They thought that being black was bad, and that everybody in the world should be like them.

'Get out!' they shouted at Ndidi, 'go away and take your nasty black face with you then we white people will be better off!' Ndidi went home and told her grandmother who was old and very wise. Then her grandmother told her many things.

She told her that black people were the first people to live in the world. She told Ndidi of the first civilizations in the world, which the African peoples had built along the banks of the Nile, and in the great grasslands of the Sudan. The old lady told Ndidi of how the African people had grown food, and mined gold, and worked copper, and tamed animals, and built great cities and written books, and sailed the sea and fought battles and made peace, and grown so mighty that men travelled from everywhere to learn from the black people the secrets of arts and science.

Then eventually, the white people came to Africa; at first few, then many. They took the food and stole the gold, burnt the cities down and destroyed the libraries full of books. They crossed the sea and fought battles but they never made peace. Instead they encouraged people to fight and kill each other, until the arts and sciences were lost. Worst of all, they captured many millions of black people, and took them to the Caribbean, to America, to Brazil, where they forced them to work as slaves, to grow sugar and cotton. They sold black men and women to other white landowners. They sold the sugar and cotton to each other and some white slaveowners and traders became so rich that they now ruled over all their own countries. Then they built great cities in America and Europe, they built machines and factories to make more goods which they sold for more money. They formed great armies to fight other people. They invented strange new weapons to kill people who would not give up their land and wealth. With these armies and weapons they built great Empires, but in doing these things they had to be so cruel that they dare not admit that they could be so terrible to other people.

So they began to tell lies to each other and to themselves: they said that black people were not really human beings. They lied to each other that black people had built no cities. They lied to each that black people had no art, and no culture.

In their hearts they knew that they were telling lies, so they felt more and more guilty, until every time they saw black people, they became more and more angry. Thus they hated and feared black people would destroy them in revenge for what they had done to Africa.

They taught their children to be afraid of black people, so that they might never learn how white people had become rich and black people had become poor.

The grandmother said that the children were not wicked, they were afraid, because they had been taught to be so. They would therefore have to learn a different lesson.

Ndidi's grandmother told her what to do. The next day, when Ndidi went to school the white children shouted at her. 'Take your blackness away from here!' Ndidi said 'You would not be better off if I took the blackness away. In fact you would not be able to live!'

But they did not believe her. So Ndidi began to gather up all the blackness so that she could take it away to Africa with her.

She stretched out her finger and pointed at the blackboard, and all the blackness flowed off the board and through her finger back into her body. The board became completely white, so that no one could see what was written on it.

Then she pointed to the book shelves and all the words flowed off the pages into her body, until there was no writing left. Bit by bit, she pointed to everything in the room until all the black had been taken away. When she had finished, the room was completely white. The walls were white, the floor was white, the clothes on the children and the teacher were white; even their shoes. The children's hair was white, and their skins completely white like the belly of a dead fish.

Then Ndidi went outside. She pointed at the bus and the blackprint flowed off the board at the front which showed where the bus was going. She pointed at the road, and all the black flowed off the road into her body. No one could tell where the pavement was so the cars and lorries had to stop.

Ndidi walked about the town, pointing her finger at everything. Everywhere she went, the blackness flowed back into her body until the whole town had turned white. Everything lay white and still under the terrible glare of the sun reflected by a million white surfaces.

Finally, as night began to fall Ndidi pointed at the sky and all the black flowed out of the sky, and into her body. Now no one could sleep. No one could rest, and all work began to stop.

Then the headmaster said to Ndidi: 'Put back the blackness at once!' Ndidi said 'No!' Then the mayor of the town came in a huge white car and said 'Little girl, put back the blackness!' Ndidi said 'No!' The Queen came in an even larger white car and said, 'My husband and I insist that you put back the blackness!' Ndidi said 'No!'

There was a great fear throughout the land. No one knew what was happening, because the television screens only showed white lines, for there was no blackness to make it work.

Committees met committees, councils met in council. But nothing could be done without blackness. Then people began to fall ill and no one could find the right medicines because the black writing had disappeared from the labels on the bottles.

Then Ndidi's grandmother explained to her that taking away the blackness was killing the country. Apart from being a very serious thing in itself, she would become no better than the greedy and foolish white people who had committed such terrible crimes. So Ndidi called all the people together. She told them all the things her grandmother had taught her. She showed them why white people were rich and black people were poor.

Then the people became angry with the leaders who had got them into this unhappy position. They dismissed all the Queens and Kings and took away all the power and money from the very rich people.

They decided to run things themselves from that day on, so that they might never be misled or fooled again.

Then Ndidi stretched out her finger and began to put the blackness back into the world. She pointed at the blackboard and it became black again. She pointed at the books and the words flowed back. She pointed at the buses and the words came back so they knew where to go. She went through the town and put the blackness back wherever she went.

Finally, she pointed her finger at the sky, and the blackness flowed back into the sky making it soft and quiet and warm.

The people were very happy to see the blackness. A great sigh went up all over the town.

'How beautiful blackness is!' they said to each other.

Babatunde

Reprinted from *Dragon's Teeth*, February 1979, by kind permission of the Editor.

REVIEW

Ndidi's Story, by Babatunde, The Pan African Institute, Manchester.

I am delighted to see that Ndidi's Story is now published in book form. The NCRCB printed the story in the first edition of DT (volume 1.1, February 1979) because we felt it was a good example of an anti-racist children's story and therefore deserved wide publicity.

Black parents welcomed the story warmly. Some teachers were delighted and used it as a focus for discussions and projects in the classroom. A painting produced by a child on a project was printed in DT, volume 2.1, March 1980. A few teachers thought the story racist or too political; but we've heard of black children asking for the story again and again, and white children being very moved by Ndidi's dilemma and supporting her. A piece of research has been done around the use of the story in the classroom (Dragons Teeth will publish this soon). The story appeared in the international journal of the World Council of Churches, 'One World'. It is regrettable that Collins, in its multi-racial book competition in 1978, found it unacceptable.

Why do I think it is a good anti-racist book, and relevant to Britain? The reasons are as follows:

- The central character is a black girl, Ndidi, 'with beautiful eyes and a nice wide smile'. She plays a positive, constructive and leading role.
- Although she came from Nigeria, she lives in Britain.
- There are positive and supportive black adults in the story to whom she relates.
- These adults enable her to cope with the racial abuse which she encounters by supporting her when she is distressed and by giving her information which enables her to deal with this abuse.
- Ndidi, with the help of the grandmother, deals with the racism by teaching a lesson which will have sufficient impact without long term damage. Through the strength of her African ancestry, she is able to take certain steps. Here is the realisation that action has its own power. To be passive is to be powerless.
- Ndidi, a black girl, begins to realise what power she has and rejoices in it. However her grandmother, in all her wisdom, points out that she will be no better than those she sets out to punish if she continues with her actions.
- Ndidi shares the wisdom of her culture with those white people who originally abused her, and this leads to a change; she used her power to restore things to what they were. But nothing will ever be the same again, even if on the surface they look the same. All is changed.
- There is an opportunity for both black and white people to learn a little of the history of black people. Enough to stimulate interest, to show the contribution made to the world by black people and sufficient to show the nature of colonialisation and imperialism; more than adequate in showing how distortions, lies and fear grew out of such a history.

It is as much an adult's as a children's story. It poses many questions and provokes much discussion. It has to be read again and again in order to understand its many meanings.

The author, Babatunde (a pseudonym), whose ancestors were forcibly removed from Africa to Guyana and then, through further imperial exploitation of their new home, forced to flee to the land of their oppressors, Britain, has brought to this story all the wisdom and understanding of his cultural and historical experience. It is only from such a wealth of experience and understanding can we create a literature that is relevant to children growing up in a multi-ethnic society. A literature which entertains, excites, develops creativity and understanding and enriches all our lives.

Dorothy Kuya

This article first appeared in *Dragon's Teeth*, March 1981, and is reproduced by kind permission of the Editor.

REVIEW

The Mice Next Door, by Anthony Knowles, illustrated by Susan Edwards, Hodder & Stoughton, 1986, ISBN 0 340 36436 X

Teachers who try to promote greater multicultural awareness and combat racism expect children's reading books to reinforce values such as cultural diversity and equality for all, irrespective of race, colour or ethnic group. In the past few years publishers have increased their output of books offering information and appreciation of cultural and religious diversity in black and white British homes and communities. However, there appears to be a feeling that infants are too young to be affected by racism so should only be offered knowledge about lifestyles, religions, festivals, clothing, customs, food, etc., to cushion and protect them from the disease of racism they will find later in the junior and secondary part of their school career.

Anthony Knowles does not agree. He feels that very young pupils can be prepared for an anti-racist society by facing up to the prejudices and stereotypes prevalent in their present family-oriented world. So he has created a family-based story as seen through the eyes of a child. It starts when new neighbours build a house next door and move in. Nothing remarkable about this! But the neighbours are totally different from the writer's family—they are mice rather than human beings! The scene is set: an un-named white nuclear family of human beings living next door to the Hardys, a family of brown-coloured mice.

The child's father is prejudiced against all mice and does not want them living next door: 'That night I heard Dad say it was outrageous and that it shouldn't be allowed. . . . Dad said he would ring the Council in the morning and have the little pests taken away.'

He does not like the neighbour's house because 'it was not in keeping with the neighbourhood' and his stereotypical images of mice lead him to believe they are going to be noisy: 'Dad told Mum that we could always expect a lot of noise from the Hardys in the future. Mice were known for the din they made—they were only interested in having a good time.'

The father also complains about 'the smell of cooking from next door' which makes an 'unpleasant nuisance' and he attacks the mice for 'lowering the tone of the village' because they own a motorbike and sidecar rather than a car 'like ordinary folk'.

'Dad' has plenty of pre-conceived notions which he uses to attack all mice as 'smelly, stupid, greedy, noisy, a nuisance, only interested in having a good time.'

He does not think they are very honest: 'About a month after they moved in the Hardys built a shed and erected a fence around their garden. Dad said they probably did not have planning permission and he wasn't going to stand for it.' Or caring: 'it was most unusual for mice to care about their gardens'. Or well brought-up: 'they just don't have decent manners . . . the parents never teach their youngsters how to behave'.

In one incident the father wrongly accuses baby mouse of being 'a wretched little thief' and finally decides that it is time to sell the house and 'move to a more respectable neighbourhood' after the mice paint their front door in colours that are not acceptable to him. These different and 'inferior' creatures can no longer be tolerated!

The mice are shown as hard-working, happy, friendly, generous and caring of property, garden and people. Mrs Hardy comes round with a cheese pie and Mr Hardy unblocks his neighbours' drain-pipe. This final neighbourly act changes the father's perceptions and the two families become very friendly, culminating in Mr Hardy bringing round 'three dozen bottles of home-brewed cheese wine that he'd mentioned to Dad the evening before. Mr Hardy drank three bottles and Dad finished the rest. They fell asleep in our living room, and were both late for work on Monday morning.'

And they lived side-by-side happily ever after!

I have deliberately itemised issues representing the 'them and us' view of some white people towards Afro-Caribbean and Asian Britons on which anti-racist teachers can focus. Perhaps practising teachers can offer us the benefit of their experiences. For example, will the use of mice help children relate to real situations or will it distance their world from that portrayed in the book? How do teachers tackle issues of racial bias, prejudice and stereotyping with very young children? How can they use this highly recommended, well-written and illustrated moral tale to promote anti-racism?

George Antonouris

Further topics

Other topic areas could include: black and female achievements throughout history; black and female contributions to British history, e.g.: World Wars; freedom movements fighting for the abolition of slavery; achievements of African and Asian states since independence from British rule; colonialism; slavery; image of race and gender in the media; racism and sexism in contemporary Britain; apartheid in South Africa. A selection of ideas and exercises is offered below.

Place names

As part of a Moving Home topic the teacher could add to the theme of migration by examining local place names.

Using the historical work already discussed, we could start with ancient British/Celtic words like *pen* (meaning hill), *ceto* (wood), *ecles* (church), *dun* (fortified hill), *ben* (a mountain); the Romans gave us *chester*, *caster*, *cester* (a fortified camp); the Anglo-Saxon and early English suffixes include *ham*, *ton*, *worth*, *wick*, *borough*, *bury*, all signifying a homestead or village; *ing* also signifies a settlement with the name of the chief coming first, e.g., Reading (people of Reada) and Hastings (people of Haesta). Settlements along the old Roman roads were called *straet*, which came from the Latin *strata* or paved way, so we get name such as Street, Stratton, Streatham, Stratford, Stratfield, Streatley. The Vikings left *by* and *thorpe* (settlement), *thwaite* (clearing), *holme* (island), *fell* (hill), *dale* (valley), *toft* (settlement). The Normans bequeathed words like *beau* and *bel*, meaning beautiful; so we have *beaumont* (beautiful hill), *beamish* (beautiful mansion) and the famous *Belvoir* castle, meaning beautiful view.

Such a list would offer pupils a chance to examine their region for its migratory history, and help reinforce another key teaching theme, that of cultural diversity as a historical process and not as a post-1945 phenomenon.

Prejudice-awareness exercises

Once teachers have become more confident and experienced in multicultural education, they may wish to try some prejudice-awareness exercises. These will be difficult to handle but they are important if racial awareness is to grow and develop. There is the 'letter from a parent' exercise which involves a letter from an irate parent claiming racial name-calling. Pupils can discuss this and decide on their reactions and even write a letter in response. Role play activities could be included. Similarly, an incident involving prejudice outside school could be the basis of debate and discussion. Teachers may prefer this exercise because it distances the child from the incident if adults only become involved. Thus, children would not be threatened and would examine the incident and its implications in a more detached way. Examples could include prejudice at work or in housing.

The 'friendship' exercise would involve giving children photographs of a diverse group of children and asking them who they would like to play with, or sit with, and why. A variation would be the 'nuclear survival' exercise, which would see the world destroyed by a nuclear war and only one spaceship left with a number of people of different cultural backgrounds. The children would be asked to organise their flight to a new planet where they should arrange housing, food and general living and working conditions. This complex activity may be too difficult for primary children but it has been tried at top junior school level with some success.

Other difficult activities would be the 'orange squash', 'brown eyes/blue eyes' and 'purple armband' exercises. The first would entail children arriving at their places and finding orange squash selectively spread over the room. After observing the pupil reaction, a discussion can ensue on the discriminatory activity of advantaging some with orange and disadvantaging others. Criteria could be, 'I like brown-eyed people so I decided to give them orange'. An interesting discussion would no doubt follow such a remark! The 'blue eyes/brown eyes' experiment need not be confined to orange squash but the courageous teacher may wish to make a more detailed list of advantages and disadvantages and watch for the reaction. For example, brown eyes cannot dine first, they must clear up, they leave the room last . . . the list of possible disadvantages is endless. This activity was attempted over a period of several days in the United States and proved very painful for most pupils; I am suggesting a more limited activity of perhaps half a day, with follow-up discussion after lunch, but it should only be tried by the most confident teachers! The most difficult experiment is the 'purple armband' experiment which most will find totally inappropriate for the primary school sector. Purple is the chosen colour because it has no party political connotations and the idea is to use the whole class for this experiment. A selection of pupils wear an armband for a few days which signifies their distinctiveness from others. All are sworn to secrecy and no explanation must be given to pupils and teachers. Naturally, permission must be obtained from the headteacher and parents, but nobody else should be told about the armband. Children just wear it and their other colleagues record reactions. All pupils say is, 'I am sorry but I cannot tell you why I am wearing this armband'. The idea is: how are distinctive groups treated by those who do not understand their 'culture' (which, in this case, involves wearing a purple armband). Later discussion could involve the feeling Sikhs have about wearing a turban and the possible reaction of those who do not understand. A detailed study of Sikhism could follow with material supplied by the regional Sikh community or the 'twin' school.

Select booklist

Mary Seacole

Alexander, Z. and Dewjee, A. (1982) *Mary Seacole: Jamaican National Heroine and 'Doctress' in the Crimean War.* Brent Library Service, 2–12 Grange Road, London NW10 2QY (excellent 12-page booklet which can be used by pupils).

Alexander, Z. and Dewjee, A. (1982) Mary Seacole: Heroine of the Crimean War. *Dragon's Teeth*, no. 15, Autumn/Winter, 8–9 (useful summary of events and issues found on pages 159–60).

Alexander, Z. and Dewjee, A. (eds) (1984) *Wonderful Adventures of Mrs Seacole in Many Lands.* Bristol: Falling Wall Press. (Autobiography plus good illustrations.)

Barnett, P. (1984) Review of Alexander/Dewjee book. *Education Journal*, September (summary which children can be given. See page 161).
Mills, T. (1973) *Great West Indians*. Harlow: Longman.
Minority Group Support Service (1987) *Mary Seacole: Nursing Heroine*. Coventry: MGSS (brief note and eight transparencies, including a map of the Caribbean and a portrait of Mary Seacole).

Teachers who wish to make a comparison between the treatment of Mary Seacole in nineteenth century Britain and someone living in the twentieth century can use the following autobiography for this purpose:

Marke, E. (1986) *In Troubled Waters: Memoirs of Seventy Years in England!* London: Karia Press (from B.C.M. Karia, London WC1N 3XX).

If young people's personal experiences are required, then the ACER centre has published annually since 1980 the best essays written by black youngsters from its competition on growing up in Britain's inner cities.

Readers who wish to include other famous black women in their syllabus could choose Harriet Tubman. The Harriet Tubman pack published by the Minority Group Support Service, Coventry, comprises material for assembly and lessons, but also includes transparencies, pupils' books and posters. Books for teachers include: A. McGovern's *Wanted—Dead or Alive—a True Story of Harriet Tubman* (Leamington Spa: Scholastic Press) and *A Woman Called Moses*, by M. Heidesh (New York: Bantam).

Moving home

Junior Education, Moving and Settling topic, December 1980, 13–20. (Excellent ideas and resources. It includes a summary of the movement of people into, out of and within Britain by Myer Domnitz. In 'We're all "strangers"', Bob Catterall describes the work that one school did on this theme.)
Houlton, D. (1986) *Cultural Diversity in the Primary School*. London: Batsford (description of two teachers and their attempts to develop a topic on migration on pages 122–5).

Background information on migration and settlement

FOR TEACHERS

Channel 4 (1986) *Passage to Britain* (programmes on Asians, Chinese, Irish, Jews, Poles and Hungarians, and Afro-Caribbeans).
Channel 4 booklet (1986) *Passage to Britain*. (This includes migrations of Asians, Chinese, Irish, Jews, Poles and Hungarians, and Afro-Caribbeans. There is also an excellent resource section comprising addresses of key organisations which could help the teachers.)
Walvin, J. (1984) *Passage to Britain*. Harmondsworth: Penguin (an extended version of the Channel 4 booklet).

Walvin, J. (1971) *The Black Presence: a Documentary History of the Negro in England.* London: Orbach & Chambers.
Walvin, J. (1973) *Black and White: The Negro and English Society 1555–1945.* London: Allen Lane.

FOR TOP JUNIORS

File, N. and Power, C. (1981) *Black Settlers in Britain 1555–1958.* London: Heinemann.

Everybody Knows That!

Adams, C. (1984) Ndidi's Story. *Junior Education*, February, 14–15.
Akhar, S. and Stronach, I. (1986) 'They call me blacky': a story of everyday racism in primary schools. *Times Educational Supplement*, 19 September.
Antonouris, G. (1986) Just checking: how to look objectively at your classroom material and teaching practices to ensure a multicultural approach. *Child Education*, **63**, no. 1, January, 26–7.
Antonouris, G. (1987) The multicultural playgroup. *Contact*, July/August, 20–1.
Babatunde (1979) The Ndidi Story. *Dragon's Teeth*, **1**, no. 1, February, 11–12.
Babatunde (1980) *Ndidi's Story.* London: A & C Black.
Constanti, A. (1986) Attacking racism. *Junior Education*, October, 20–1.
Counsel, J. (1986) *But Martin!* London: Corgi Books.
Knowles, A. (1986) *The Mice Next Door.* London: Hodder & Stoughton.
McKee, D. (1978) *Tusk Tusk.* London: Arrow Books.
Milner, D. (1975) *Children and Race.* Harmondsworth: Penguin.
Seuss, Dr (1961) *The Sneetches.* London: Collins.
For further details on suitable books for infants see Judith Elkin and Pat Triggs, *Books for Keeps: Guides to Children's Literature for a Multicultural Society.* Address: 1 Effingham Road, London SE12 8NZ.

Chapter 9

Conclusion

POLICY AND PRACTICE

Throughout the book we have assumed that teachers are not working in isolation but are supported by a whole-school policy on race and gender issues. We offer a personal selection of problems faced by schools and some solutions that have been included in actual policy documents. Racism and sexism are combated with anti-racist/anti-sexist actions, ignorance is countered with knowledge, negative images are transposed into positive ones, indifference is discarded for concern, and a male-dominated/Eurocentric curriculum is changed to include cross-cultural and female achievements from around the world. In their opposition to racism and sexism, these schools show a strong commitment to the equal opportunities perspective. It is hoped that teachers engaged in the type of topic work presented in this book find support from colleagues who have reviewed their existing school organisation and curriculum provision and negotiated a policy that guides the actions of teaching and non-teaching staff.

SCHOOL ORGANISATION

Problems

1. Staff lack information in equal opportunities educational developments around the country.
2. The school is relatively isolated in its locality.
3. Staff lack knowledge of regional communities.
4. The topic policy is seen as separate from an equal opportunities policy so does not include a racial and gender dimension.
5. No committee is working to review and identify areas of need.
6. No teacher is responsible for equal opportunities initiatives.
7. School-based in-service training ignores the equal opportunities dimensions.

Solutions

1. An equal opportunities notice board informs staff of the latest training courses and materials currently available in the staff resource library.
2. There is an organised exchange or twinning scheme with schools comprising a different racial intake.
3. Staff obtain information of equal opportunities through the use of a community notice board and news-sheet. This includes learning to pronounce and spell the names of members of different ethnic minority groups.
4. Equal opportunities issues are tackled in the topic policy, e.g., questioning of terms based on racial prejudices and stereotypes.
5. A permanent working party is formed to examine relevant issues, propose changes and develop resources.
6. Appointment of a co-ordinator for equal opportunities education to take the lead in identifying areas of change, designing new programmes, implementing innovations and systematically evaluating success or failure.
7. In-service training for teaching and non-teaching staff examines racial and gender issues.

BEHAVIOUR

Problems

8. There are incidents of intimidation and name-calling based on racial and gender motives.
9. There is a refusal to join groups or work with others because of racial and gender prejudices.
10. There are examples of exclusion of people or groups on grounds of race and gender.

Solutions to 8, 9 and 10

(a) Report incident to senior staff.
(b) Write offence in equal opportunities incidents book.
(c) Discuss the incident with offender and victim.
(d) Send the offender to a senior member of staff to signify gravity.
(e) Explain the incident to the offender's parents and the steps to be taken to eliminate future offences.
(f) Offer the victim some support.
(g) Tackle the issue on a school and tutor group level, i.e., use classroom discussion and school assembly, meeting with parents, community news-sheet and letters to parents.
(h) Discuss incident with the governors.

CURRICULUM

Problems

11. How to combat misinformation, misrepresentation, misunderstandings, prejudices and myths.
12. How to challenge negative images.
13. How to ensure historical as well as cross-cultural understanding of Britain's past and present.

Solutions

11. (a) Encourage discussion of racism, sexism, discrimination and prejudice.
    (b) Enhance equal opportunities understanding through awareness activities which help pupils question their taken-for-granted assumptions and actions.
    (c) Train pupils to recognise bias in written and visual material so that they can evaluate the validity of a particular perspective.
    (d) Offer factually accurate knowledge of diverse ethnic religious beliefs, naming systems, languages spoken, dress styles, dietary habits, rules of behaviour and family relationships.
    (e) Permeate topic work, stories, art, craft, poetry, mathematics, science and CDT with an equal opportunities perspective.
12. (a) Promote a positive image of black and white people, men and women throughout the world focusing upon their achievements and contribution to global knowledge.
    (b) Analyse the contribution of ordinary men and women in shaping British life, history and culture.
13. Teach pupils about migration to and from Britain over the past 2000 years to show that migration and settlement is not a post-1945 black phenomenon.

THE EQUAL OPPORTUNITY PERSPECTIVE AND THE POLITICAL EDUCATION APPROACH

The Swann Report (1985) suggested that 'school pupils can in no sense be considered immune to the general political climate' and that it is the school's 'clear responsibility to provide accurate factual information and opportunities for balanced and sensitive consideration of political issues in order to enable pupils to reflect upon and sometimes reconsider their political opinions within a broader context' (3.10, page 337). We see the equal opportunity perspective and the political education approach combining together to develop abilities in assessing situations on the basis of knowledge, and encouraging reasoned and rational judgements, rather than the acceptance of mistaken impressions and hearsay evidence acquired from family, peer group, local community and media. We support a philosophy which sees every educational institution as equipping students with a questioning attitude and the knowledge and skill to fight sexual and racial injustice and inequality. This book has tried to show how topic work can contribute to this vital educational endeavour of opening pupils' minds to 'a full appreciation of the role they as adults can and should play in shaping their futures' (Swann Report, 3.7, page 334).

Glossary of Terms

Afro-Caribbean Britons People whose origins are in Africa or the Caribbean.

Anti-racist teachers Those who practise the '4 Cs' of combating, confronting, counteracting, criticising racism.

Asian Britons Those whose origins are in the Asian continent.

Assimilation Those who believe in the doctrine 'when in Rome do as the Romans do', i.e., those who endeavour to help others to 'fit into the system' and lose their distinctive language and culture. The Swann Report claims that full assimilation is 'where the minority group loses all the distinctive characteristics of its identity and is ultimately absorbed and subsumed within the majority group' (note 3, page 4).

Culture According to Peter Worsley (*Introducing Sociology*, Penguin, 1970) culture is:

> everything acquired by human beings that is not physically inherited. From this point of view sewers are as much culture as symphonies. 'Culture', as traditionally defined, consists of certain forms of the conventionally approved arts: paintings, sculpture, creative literature, music: these are indeed 'culture' in the sociological sense too, but so are hybrid wheat, brake-linings and strontium 90. . . . Neither machine guns, breakfast foods, brassieres, existentialism, or the Goon Show are outcomes of biological dispositions or inborn behaviour. They are 'artefacts' or 'ideofacts', produced, communicated, handed down, stored up (in books, on tape, on film, etc., and in men's brains), internalised and taught, transmitted from man to man, and from group to group (page 24).

Although we would change the male emphasis (e.g., 'men's brains', 'brassieres' and 'from man to man') and delete dated references to the Goon Show, etc., we would accept this definition of culture, which supports the existence of many different cultures based on race, gender, social class, age, region, ethnic group.

Discrimination Negative discrimination is unfavourable *treatment* on the basis of some sort of criterion, whether it be race, gender, social class, nationality.

Ethnic group A body of people marked off by common descent, language and culture, but not necessarily possessing the same colour of skin.

Ethnic minority group A body of people forming a numerical minority with ancestors, language and historical traditions derived from other parts of the world. These groups with common descent outside Britain now relate to this country, which is their home. We therefore feel that they should be called Cypriot Britons, Polish Britons, Afro-Caribbean Britons, etc., because they are Polish, Cypriot, etc., by descent and British through settlement and allegience. Subdivisions occur within them such as: white ethnic minority groups (e.g., Polish Britons, Ukrainian Britons) and black Britons (e.g., Jamaican Britons and other African and Caribbean groups). Some people would include Britons whose ancestors originate from Asia as brown

Britons, others would see them as black Britons because they face common experiences of racism with Afro-Caribbean Britons.

Ethnocentric The glorification of one's own ethnic group to the exclusion of others.

Multiculturalist teachers Those who practise the '4 Cs' of transmitting diverse cultures, costumes, communities and styles of clothing.

Pluralism Swann suggests that teachers should stop believing in *assimilation* and start supporting the notion of *pluralism*, which allows and, where necessary, assists ethnic minority communities to maintain their distinct ethnic identities within a framework of commonly accepted values, such as equality of access to education and employment, equal treatment and opportunity to participate fully in social and political life, equal treatment and protection by the law, equal freedom of cultural and religious expression (4, page 5).

Prejudice Judgement in advance of evidence and information.

Race A group of people who have common inherited characteristics deriving from common ancestors, such as a similar colour of skin.

Racism *Belief* and *treatment* of one group as inferior to another on the basis of inherited physical characteristics such as colour of skin.

Swann claims that black Britons face negative treatment in housing, social services, employment and racial violence, abuse, harassment such as 'assaults, jostling in the streets, abusive remarks, broken windows, slogans daubed on walls' and 'more serious racially-motivated offences (murders, serious assaults, systematic attacks by gangs on people's homes at night)' (note 5.11, page 31).

Sexism *Belief* and *treatment* of one group as inferior to another on the basis of inherited physical characteristics of gender.

Stereotype Caricatures based on putting together over-generalisations and over-simplifications in what is considered a typical case, e.g.,

West Indians are good at sport but are not academic.

Chinese children are reserved and well behaved and are likely to be under pressure at home to help in the family business.

Asian children are hard-working and well-motivated but likely to have unrealistic aspirations.

To challenge stereotypes, teachers need to throw out their 'colour blind' view which says 'we treat all pupils the same' and recognise *distinctiveness of cultures* in contemporary Britain (Swann Report, pages 26–7).

Bibliography

A

ACER (1987) *Resources and Information Guide*, 3rd Edition. London: ACER.

Adams, C. (1984) Ndidi's Story. *Junior Education*, February, 14–15.

Aggarwal, M. (1984) *I Am a Sikh*. London: Franklin Watts.

Aggarwal, M. (1984) *I Am a Muslim*. London: Franklin Watts.

Aggarwal, M. (1984) *I Am a Hindu*. London: Franklin Watts.

Akhar, S. and Stronach, I. (1986) 'They call me blacky': a story of everyday racism in primary schools. *Times Educational Supplement*, 19 September.

Alexander, R. (1984) *Primary Education*. New York: Holt, Rinehart & Winston.

Alexander, Z. and Dewjee, A. (1982) *Mary Seacole: Jamaican National Heroine and 'Doctress' in the Crimean War*. London: Brent Library Service.

Alexander, Z. and Dewjee, A. (1982) Mary Seacole: heroine of the Crimean War. *Dragon's Teeth*, no. 15, Autumn/Winter, 8–9.

Alexander, Z. and Dewjee, A. (eds) (1984) *Wonderful Adventures of Mrs Seacole in Many Lands*. Bristol: Falling Wall Press.

AMMA (1983) *Our Multicultural Society: the Educational Response*. London: AMMA.

Antonouris, G. (1986) Developing multi-cultural education in all primary schools: some suggestions. *Primary Contact*, **3**, no. 3, 45–50.

Antonouris, G. (1986) Exploring community interests and identities. *Community Education Network*, **6**, no. 6, June, 2.

Antonouris, G. (1986) Just checking: how to look objectively at your classroom material and teaching practices to ensure a multicultural approach. *Child Education*, **63**, no. 1, January, 26–7.

Antonouris, G. (1987) Identifying racism, *Modus*, **5**, no. 7, October, 274–5.

Antonouris, G. (1987) Images of parenthood. *Modus*, **5**, no. 5, June, 186–7.

Antonouris, G. (1987) Multicultural education at the Danesbury junior school. *Primary Teaching Studies*, **2**, no. 2, February, 122–7.

Antonouris, G. (1987) Reflecting cultural differences. *Modus*, **5**, no. 2, March, 75–6.

Antonouris, G. (1987) Silent minorities? *Junior Education*, **10**, no. 9, September, 17.

Antonouris, G. (1987) The multicultural playgroup. *Contact*, July/August, 20–1.

Antonouris, G. (1988) Multicultural/anti-racist CDT. *Studies in Design Education, Craft & Technology*, **20**, no. 2, Spring, 110–12.

Antonouris, G. (1988) Multicultural science. *School Science Review* (in the press).

Antonouris, G. and Wilson, J. B. (1989) *Racial and Multicultural Issues: a Training Pack for Teachers and Other Professionals*. Nottingham: Trent Polytechnic. (In the press.)

Arora, R. and Duncan, C. (1986) *Multicultural Education: Towards Good Practice*. London: Routledge & Kegan Paul.
Atkin, J. and Richards, J. K. (1983) *A Question of Priorities: an Examination of a School-based In-service Education Programme in Multicultural Education*. University of Nottingham.

B
Babatunde (1979) The Ndidi Story. *Dragon's Teeth*, **1**, no. 1, February, 11–12.
Babatunde (1980) *Ndidi's Story*. London: A & C Black.
Bahree, P. (1982) *The Hindu World*. London: Macdonald.
Bains, H. S. (1982) *Asians in Derby*. Derbyshire Multicultural Education Support Service.
Bains, H. S. (1983) *The Sikhs—a People*. Derbyshire Multicultural Education Centre.
Barnett, P. (1984) Review of Alexander/Dewjee book. *Education Journal*, September.
Barrett, L. (1977) *The Rastafarians*. London: Heinemann.
Barsley, M. (1970) *Right Handed Man in a Left Handed World*. London: Pitman.
Bebey, F. (1975) *African Music: a People's Art*. Westport, CT: Lawrence Hill/London: Harrap.
Bennett, O. (1986) *Diwali*. London: Macmillan.
Berkshire Education Committee (1983) *Education for Racial Equality* (reprinted in the Swann Report, pages 366–81).
Blakeley, M. (1977) *Nadha's Family*. London: A & C Black.
Bloom, B. S. (ed.) (1956) *Taxonomy of Educational Objectives*, Book 1. Harlow: Longman.
Blyth, A. *et al.* (1976) *Place, Time and Society 8–13: Curriculum Planning in History, Geography and Social Science*. London: Collins-ESL, for the Schools Council.
Bradman, T. and Browne, E. (1986) *Through my Window*. London: Methuen.
Bruner, J. (1966) *Towards a Theory of Instruction*. Cambridge, MA: Harvard University Press.
Burnett, M. (1982) *Jamaican Music*. Oxford: Oxford University Press.
Burton, L. (ed.) (1986) *Girls into Maths Can Go*. New York: Holt, Rinehart & Winston.

C
CAFOD (1986) *Just Food: School Resource and Education Pack*. London: Catholic Fund for Overseas Development.
Candappa, B. (1985) *Celebrating Diwali*. Aylesbury: Ginn.
Carrier, M. (1986) Getting to know you. *Child Education*, March, 37.
Catton, J. (1985) *Ways and Means: the CDT Education of Girls*. Harlow: Longman.
Channel 4 (1986) *Passage to Britain*. London: Channel 4 Books.
Christian Aid (1982) *World Feast Game*. London: Christian Aid.
City of Birmingham District Council (1987) *Education for Our Multicultural Society*.
Clark, E. P. (1976) *West Indian Cooking*. London: Nelson.
Clark, M. (1974) *Teaching Left Handed Children*. London: ULP.
Clarke, S. (1980) *Shah Music*. London: Heinemann.
Cole, W. O. (1973) *A Sikh Family in Britain*. Exeter: Religious Education Press.
Cole, W. O. (1980) *Thinking about Sikhism*. Cambridge: Lutterworth Educational.
Collymore, Y. (1972) *Cooking Our Way*. Aylesbury: Ginn.
Conolly, Y. (1981) *Mango Spice*. London: A & C Black.
Constanti, A. (1986) Attacking racism. *Junior Education*, October, 21–2.
Counsel, J. (1986) *But Martin!*. London: Corgi.
Craft, A. and Klein, G. (1986) *Agenda for Multicultural Teaching*. London: SCDC.
CRE (1976) *Afro Hair, Skin Care and Recipes*. London: CRE.
Crossman, L. *et al.* (1985) Approaches to Africa at Anglesey junior school. *Multicultural Education Review*, no. 4, Summer, 28–31.
Curtis, S. (1986) *Diwali*. Derbyshire Multicultural Support Service.

D
Davis, S. and Simon, P. (1977) *Reggae Bloodlines: In Search of Music and Culture in Jamaica*. New York: Anchor Press, Doubleday.
Deh-Ta, H. (1978) *The Home Book of Chinese Cookery*. London: Faber.
Derbyshire County Council (1987) *Towards the 1990s: Education for All in Derbyshire*.

Derbyshire Multicultural Education Centre (1987) *Caribbean Vegetables and Fruit.*
DES (1987) *The National Curriculum: Consultative Document*. London: HMSO.
Deshpande, C. (1985) *Diwali*. London: A & C Black.
Development Education Centre (1986) *Theme Work—Approaches for Teaching with a Global Perspective*. Manchester: DEC.
Dixon, B. (1977) *Catching Them Young: Sex, Race and Class in Children's Fiction*. London: Pluto Press.
Durkin, M. C. *et al.* (1969) *The Social Studies Curriculum*. Menlo Park, CA: Addison-Wesley.

E

Eggleston, S. J. and Kerry, T. (1985) Integrated studies. In Bennett, N. and Desforges, C. (eds), *Recent Advances in Classroom Research*. Edinburgh: Scottish Academic Press.
Elkin, J. and Triggs, P. (1985) *Books for Keeps: Guides to Children's Literature for a Multicultural Society, Book 2: 8–12 years*. London: Books for Keeps.
Elkin, J. and Triggs, P. (1986) *Books for Keeps: Guides to Children's Literature for a Multicultural Society, Book 1: 0–7 years*. London: Books for Keeps.
Equal Opportunities Commission (1983) *Equal Opportunities in CDT*. Manchester: EOC.
Ewan, J. (1977) *Understanding Your Hindu Neighbour*. Guildford: Lutterworth Educational.

F

File, N. and Power, C. (1981) *Black Settlers in Britain 1555–1958*. London: Heinemann.
Floyd, L. (1980) *Indian Music*. Oxford: Oxford University Press.

G

Gilbert, D. (1984) Multicultural mathematics. In Straker-Welds, M. (ed.), *Education for a Multicultural Society: Case Studies in ILEA Schools*. London: Bell & Hyman, chapter 11.
Graham, L. (ed.) (1986) *Girls into Mathematics*. Cambridge: Cambridge University Press.
Grant, M. (1982) Starting points. *Studies in Design Education, Craft & Technology*, **15**, no. 1, Winter, 6–9.
Grant, M. and Givens, N. (1984) A sense of purpose: approaching CDT through social issues. *Studies in Design Education, Craft & Technology*, **16**, no. 2.
Guilford, J. P. (1971). Creativity. In Williams, P. *et al.* (eds), *Personalities, Growth and Learning*. Harlow: Longman.
Gunning, S., Gunning, D. and Wilson, J. (1981) *Topic Teaching in the Primary School*. London: Croom Helm.

H

Hagan, L. (1984) Keep with the Beat. *Junior Education*, April, 27.
Hagan, L. (1986) Multicultural/anti-racist education. *Junior Education*, June, 17.
Hagedorn, J. (1980) Dear Tracy. *Junior Education*, June, 11.
Halliday, M. A. K. (1969) Relevant models of language. *Educational Review*, **22**, no. 1, November.
Hamilton, S. (1985) Happy Diwali! *Multicultural Education Review*, no. 4, Summer, 35–7.
Hannon, V. (1981) *Ending Sex Stereotyping in School: a Sourcebook for School-based Teacher Workshops*. Manchester: Equal Opportunities Commission.
Harding, J. (1983) *Switched Off: The Science Education of Girls*. The Schools Council Programme 3. Harlow: Longman.
Harlen, W. *et al.* (1977) *Schools Council Science 5–13: Match and Mismatch*. Edinburgh: Oliver & Boyd.
Harrison, S. W. and Shepherd, D. (1979) *A Muslim Family in Britain*. Exeter: Religious Education Press.
Hobley, L. (1979) *Muslims and Islam*. Brighton: Wayland.
Houlton, D. (1986) *Cultural Diversity in the Primary School*. London: Batsford.
Hoyle, S. (1982) Music in the classroom. *Education Journal*, March, 1–6.
Hutchinson, G. (1985) *Home Economics for You, Books 1 and 2*. Glasgow: Blackie.

I

ILEA (1979) *Social Studies in the Primary School*. London: ILEA.
ILEA (1983) *Race, Sex and Class*. London: ILEA.
ILEA (1985) *Everyone Counts: Looking for Bias and Insensitivity in Primary Mathematics Materials*. London: ILEA.
ILEA (1985) *Food: a Resource for Learning in the Primary School*. London: ILEA.
ILEA (1986) *Anti-sexist Resource Guide*. London: ILEA.
Iqbal, M. (1976) *Understanding Your Muslim Neighbour*. Guildford: Lutterworth Educational.

J

Jaffrey, M. (1982) *Indian Cookery*. London: BBC.
James, R. (1982) *The Muslim World*. London: Macdonald.
Jeffcoate, R. (1979) *Positive Image*. London: Chameleon Books, Writers' and Readers' Publishing Co-operative.

K

Kallyndyr, R. and Dalrymple, H. (1974) *Reggae: A People's Music*. Sudbury: Carib-Arawak Publications.
Keene, M. (1986) *Steps in Religious Education*, vol. 1. London: Hutchinson.
Kehily, M. and Grosvenor, I. (1987) *Apartheid: a Teaching Pack*. Birmingham: Trade Union Resource Centre.
Kelly, A. (1981) *The Missing Half: Girls and Science Education*. Manchester: Manchester University Press.
Kelly, A. (1985) The construction of masculine science. *British Journal of Sociology of Education*, **6**, 133–54.
Kerry, T. (ed.) (1982) *Teacher Education Project*. London: Macmillan.
Kerven, R. (1986) *Diwali*. London: Macmillan.
Khalique, R. (1987) Racial bias in children's books. *Curriculum*, **8**, no. 1, Spring, 46–50.
Klein, G. (1984) *Reading into Racism: Bias in Children's Literature and Learning Materials*. London: Routledge & Kegan Paul.
Klein, G. (1984) *Resources for Multicultural Education*. Harlow: Longman.
Knowles, A. (1986) *The Mice Next Door*. London: Hodder & Stoughton.

L

Lawton, C. (1984) *I Am a Jew*. London: Franklin Watts.
Lawton, C. (1984) *Matza and Bitter Herbs*. London: Hamish Hamilton.
Lloyd, E. (1978) *Nini at Carnival*. London: Bodley Head.
Lothian Regional Council Department of Education (1985) *World Sports and Games Pack*.
Lyle, S. (1977) *Pavan Is a Sikh*. London: A & C Black.

M

MacCarty, N. (1979) *Rebecca Is a Cypriot*. London: A & C Black.
MacKinnon, K. (1984) *The Phoenix Bird Chinese Take Away*. London: A & C Black.
Marsh, H. (1982) *Diwali*. Exeter: Arnold Wheaton.
Mayled, J. (1986) *Costumes and Clothes*. Brighton: Wayland.
Mayled, J. (1986) *Feasting and Fasting*. Brighton: Wayland.
Mays, S. (1985) *The Planet of the Monsters*. London: André Deutsch.
Mcfarlane, C. (1985) Looking at bias with children. *Multicultural Educational Review*, no. 4, Summer, 9–11.
Mcfarlane, C. (1986) *Hidden Messages?—Activities for Exploring Bias*. Manchester: Development Education Centre.
McKee, D. (1978) *Tusk Tusk*. London: Arrow Books.
McLeish, K. (1985) *Eid-ul-Fitr*. Aylesbury: Ginn.
Mills, T. (1973) *Great West Indians*. Harlow: Longman.
Minority Group Support Service (1987) *Diwali: Festival of Light*. London: MGSS.
Minority Group Support Service (1987) *Mary Seacole: Nursing Heroine*. Coventry: MGSS.

Murphy, P. (1986) Differences between girls and boys in the APU science results. *Primary Science*, no. 2, Autumn, 18–19.
Myers, K. (1987) *Genderwatch! Self-assessment Schedules for Use in Schools*. Manchester: EOC/SCDC.

N

Naidoo, B. (1978) *Censoring Reality: an Examination of Books on South Africa*. London: ILEA.
Neville, J. (1984) Music in the multicultural curriculum. *Music Teacher*, April, 12.
Neville, J. (1985) Aspects of music in the multicultural curriculum. *Music Teacher*, May, 14.
Nicholas, T. (1979) *Rastafari*. New York: Anchor Press, Doubleday.
Nixon, J. (1985) *A Teacher's Guide to Multicultural Education*. Oxford: Basil Blackwell.
Nottinghamshire Leisure Services/Library (1982) *Many Cultures, Many Faiths*.
NUT (1984) *Combating Racism in Schools: a Union Policy Document Statement*. London: NUT.

O

OXFAM (1985) *Potato Profile*. Oxford: OXFAM.
Oxford Development Education Centre (1986) *Books to Break Barriers: a Review of Multicultural Fiction 4–18*.

P

Patel, B. and Allen, J. (1985) *A Visible Presence: Black People Living and Working in Britain Today*. London: National Book League.
Pemberton, E. *et al.* (1987) An anti-racist approach to teaching about African history. *Multicultural Education Review*, Spring/summer, 24–7.
Phillips-Bell, M. (ed.) (1983) *Issues and Resources: a Handbook for Teachers in a Multicultural Society*. Birmingham: AFFOR.
Pitt-Ballin, V. and Johnson, D. (1987) *Netta's Story*. Derby: Black River Books.
Primary RE Materials Project (1987) *Islam*. Birmingham: Centre for the Study of Islam and Christian–Muslim Relations and the Regional RE Centre (Midlands).
Purton, R. (1981) *Festivals and Celebration*. Oxford: Blackwell.

R

Richardson, R. (1983) A new look at the educational visit. *Education 3–13*, December, 18–21.
Richardson, R. (1986) The hidden messages in schoolbooks. *Journal of Moral Education*, January, 26–42.
Ruddell, D. (1987) Setting up 'multicultural working parties' in schools. *Multicultural Education Review*, no. 7, Spring/summer, 28–9.
Runnymede Trust (1985) *'Education for All': a Summary of the Report on the Education of Ethnic Minority Children*. London: Runnymede Trust.

S

Sealey, A. (1983) Primary school projects: a multicultural approach. In Coles, M. (ed.), *Issues and Resources: a Handbook for Teachers in the Multicultural Society*. Birmingham: AFFOR, 41–2.
Sealey, J. and Malm, K. (1982) *Music in the Caribbean*. London: Hodder & Stoughton.
Seuss, Dr (1961) *The Sneetches*. London: Collins.
Sharma, D. (1984) *Hindu Belief and Practice*. London: Edward Arnold.
Shepard, F. (1982) Music and education. *Dragon's Teeth*, no. 13, Spring, 6–7.
Smail, B. (1984) *Girl-friendly Science: Avoiding Sex Bias in the Curriculum*. Harlow: Longman.
Solomon, J. (1978) *Kate's Party*. London: Hamish Hamilton.
Solomon, J. (1980) *Gifts and Almonds*. London: Hamish Hamilton.
Solomon, J. (1981) *A Present for Mum*. London: Hamish Hamilton.
Solomon, J. (1981) *Wedding Day*. London: Hamish Hamilton.
Stones, R. (1983) *'Pour out the Cocoa, Janet': Sexism in Children's Books*. Harlow: Longman.
Swann, Lord (1985) *Education for All*. London: HMSO.

T

Taba, H. (1962) *Curriculum Development, Theory and Practice*. New York: Harcourt, Brace & World.

Tames, R. (1982) *The Muslim World*. London: Macdonald.

Thompson, B. (1980) *The Story of Prince Rama*. London: Kestrel Books.

Troyna, B. (1978) *Rastafarianism, Reggae and Racism*. Leicester: National Association for Multi-racial Education.

Turner, D. (1982) *A Day with a Shopkeeper*. Brighton: Wayland.

Twitchen, J. and Demuth, C. (eds) (1985) *Multicultural Education*. London: BBC.

W

Walvin, J. (1971) *The Black Presence: a Documentary History of the Negro in England*. London: Orbach & Chambers.

Walvin, J. (1973) *Black and White: the Negro and English Society 1555–1945*. London: Allen Lane.

Walvin, J. (1984) *Passage to Britain*. Harmondsworth: Penguin.

Whyte, J. (1983) *Beyond the Wendy House: Sex-role Stereotyping in Primary School*. Harlow: Longman.

Whyte, J. (1986) *Girls into Science and Technology*. London: Routledge & Kegan Paul.

Wilson, J. (1983) An approach to topic work. *Primary Contact*, **2**, no. 1, Spring, 60–6.

Selected American References

GENERAL ISSUES IN TOPIC WORK

Banks, J. and Clegg, A., Jr (1977) *Teaching Strategies for the Social Studies: Inquiry, Valuing and Decision-making*. New York: Longman.

Beck, C. (1971) *Moral Education: Interdisciplinary Approaches*. Toronto: Toronto University Press.

Bloom, B. *et al.* (1956) *Taxonomy of Educational Objectives*. New York: David McKay.

Bruner, J. (1962) *The Process of Education*. Cambridge, MA: Harvard University Press.

Bruner, J. (1966) *Towards a Theory of Instruction*. Cambridge, MA: Harvard University Press.

Durkin, M. C. (1969) *Communities Around Us* (Taba Social Studies Curriculum). Menlo Park, CA: Addison-Wesley.

Durkin, M. C. (1969) *The Family* (Taba Social Studies Curriculum). Menlo Park, CA: Addison-Wesley.

Durkin, M. C. (1969) *Four Communities Around the World* (Taba Social Studies Curriculum). Menlo Park, CA: Addison-Wesley.

Easton, D. and Dennis, J. (1969) *Children in the Political System*. New York: McGraw-Hill.

Fenton, E. (1966) *Teaching the New Social Studies in Secondary Schools: an Inductive Approach*. New York: Holt, Rinehart & Winston.

Hunkins, F. (1972) *Questioning Strategies and Techniques*. Boston, MA: Allyn & Bacon.

Morrissett, I. and Stevens, W. (eds) (1971) *Social Science in the Schools: a Search for a Rationale*. New York: Holt, Rinehart & Winston.

Taba, H. *et al.* (1969) *Social Studies Curriculum Teachers Guides*. Menlo Park, CA: Addison-Wesley.

Taba, H. *et al.* (1971) *A Teacher's Handbook to Elementary Social Studies*. Menlo Park, CA: Addison-Wesley.

Wann, K., Dorn, M. and Liddle, B. (1962) *Fostering Intellectual Development in Young Children*. New York: Teachers College Press.

THE EQUAL OPPORTUNITIES PERSPECTIVE

Racial dimension

Appleton, N. (1983) *Cultural Pluralism in Education: Theoretical Foundations*. New York: Longman.

Banks, J. (1981) *Multiethnic Education: Theory and Practice*. Boston, MA: Allyn & Bacon.
Banks, J. (ed.) (1984) *Teaching Strategies for Ethnic Studies*. Boston, MA: Allyn & Bacon.
Cross, D., Baker, G. and Stiles, L. (eds) (1977) *Teaching in a Multicultural Society: Perspectives and Professional Strategies*. New York: The Free Press.
Garcia, R. (1982) *Teaching in a Pluralist Society: Concepts, Models and Strategies*. New York: Harper & Row.
Glazer, N. (1983) *Ethnic Dilemmas 1964–1982*. Cambridge, MA: Harvard University Press.
Gordon, M. (1964) *Assimilation in American Life*. New York: Oxford University Press.
Katz, J. (1978) *White Awareness: Handbook for Antiracism Training*. Norman, OK: University of Oklahoma.
Katz, P. (ed.) (1976) *Towards the Elimination of Racism*. New York: Pergamon.
Kehoe, J. (1984) *A Handbook of Selected Activities for Enhancing the Multicultural Climate of the School*. Vancouver: University of British Columbia.
Kirp, D. (1982) *Just Schools: The Idea of Racial Equality in American Education*. Berkeley: University of California Press.
Moodley, K. (ed.) (1985) *Multicultural Education and Race Relations*. Vancouver: University of British Columbia.
Samuda, R. *et al.* (eds) (1984) *Multiculturalism in Canada: Social and Educational Perspectives*. Toronto: Allyn & Bacon.
Tumin, M. and Plotch, P. (1978) *Race and Racism: a Comparative Perspective*. New York: John Wiley & Sons.
Werner, W. *et al.* (1980) *Whose Culture? Whose Heritage? Ethnicity within Canadian Social Studies Curricula*. Vancouver: University of British Columbia.

Gender dimension

Amsler, D. *et al.* (1976) *Undoing Sex Stereotypes: Research and Resources for Educators*. New York: McGraw-Hill.
Anderson, S. (ed.) (1972) *Sex Differences and Discrimination in Education*. Worthington, OH: Charles A. Jones.
Feldman, J. (1974) *Escape from the Doll's House*. New York: McGraw-Hill.
Fishell, A. and Pottker, J. (1971) *Sex Bias in Schools: the Research Evidence*. New York: Fairleigh Dickinson University Press.
Frazier, N. and Sadker, M. (1973) *Sexism in School and Society*. New York: Harper & Row.
Levy, B. *et al.* (1973) *Sex Role Stereotyping in the Schools*. Washington, DC: National Educational Association.
Nemerowicz, G. (1979) *Children's Perceptions of Gender and Work Roles*. New York: Praeger.
Sadker, P. and Sadker, D. (1978) *Sex Equity Handbook for Schools*. New York: Longman.
Sprung, B. (ed.) (1978) *Perspectives on Non-sexist Early Childhood Education*. New York: Teachers College Press.
Stacey, J., Bereaud, S. and Daniels, J. (eds) (1974) *And Jill Came Tumbling After: Sexism in American Education*. New York: Dell.
Weitz, S. (1977) *Sex Roles*. New York: Oxford University Press.

Name Index

Subject Index